P9-EEU-048

To Dad.

Happy Birthday

Love   Ken
        Sladjana
            and
        Miranda

        XO

Dec '98

WORTH REPEATING

A Literary Resurrection

1948–1994

WORTH

PIERRE BERTON

REPEATING

A Literary Resurrection
1948–1994

Foreword by Geoff Pevere

Doubleday Canada Limited

Copyright © 1998 by Pierre Berton Enterprises Ltd.
All rights reserved. The use of any part of this publication
reproduced, transmitted in any form or by any means, electronic,
mechanical, photocopying, recording, or otherwise, or stored in
a retrieval system, without the prior consent of the publisher—
or, in case of photocopying or other reprographic copying,
a licence from the Canadian Reprography Collective—
is an infringement of the copyright law.

Canadian Cataloguing in Publication Data

Berton, Pierre, 1920–
    Worth repeating : a literary resurrection 1948-1994

ISBN 0-385-25721-X

I. Title

PS8503.E79W67 1998   081   C98-930069-2
PR9199.3.B47W67 1998

Jacket and text design by Gordon Robertson
Jacket photograph courtesy *Maclean's*
Printed and bound in the USA

Published in Canada by
Doubleday Canada Limited
105 Bond Street
Toronto, Ontario
M5B 1Y3

To Elsa Franklin

Books by Pierre Berton

The Royal Family
The Mysterious North
Klondike
Just Add Water and Stir
Adventures of a Columnist
Fast Fast Fast Relief
The Big Sell
The Comfortable Pew
The Cool, Crazy,
   Committed World of the Sixties
The Smug Minority
The National Dream
The Last Spike
Drifting Home
Hollywood's Canada
My Country
The Dionne Years
The Wild Frontier
The Invasion of Canada
Flames Across the Border
Why We Act Like Canadians
The Promised Land
Vimy
Starting Out
The Arctic Grail
The Great Depression
Niagara, A History of the Falls
My Times: Living with History
1967, The Last Good Year

Picture Books
The New City
   (with Henri Rossier)
Remember Yesterday
The Great Railway
The Klondike Quest
Pierre Berton's Picture Book
   of Niagara Falls
Winter
The Great Lakes

Anthologies
Great Canadians
Pierre and Janet Berton's
   Canadian Food Guide
Historic Headlines
Farewell to the
   Twentieth Century
Worth Repeating

Fiction
Masquerade
   (pseudonym Lisa Kroniuk)

Books for Young Readers
The Golden Trail
The Secret World of Og
Adventures in Canadian
   History (22 volumes)

Contents

WORTH REPEATING

Foreword

F OR THE SEVERAL MILLION of us who grew up Canadian during the fifties, sixties and seventies, Pierre Berton was like the weather: a force to be reckoned with, alternately benign and blustery, but impossible to ignore.

If he wasn't holding forth with bullish erudition on the unstoppable public broadcasting ritual that was *Front Page Challenge*—the ultimate Canadian game show because it equated current affairs with fun and journalists with celebrities—he was filling miles of column inches with the plainspoken passion that is the hallmark of his newspaper journalism. As I recall, it was a rare bookshelf or coffee table that didn't bear the weight of one of his volumes of—here's a concept—genuinely *popular* Canadian history. His long-running, one-on-one interview program, *The Pierre Berton Show*, was, in my household anyway, in the running with buttered mashed potatoes as a suppertime staple. Indeed, if there were any Canadians to rival Berton for sheer coast-to-coast visibility in those days, they could only be people like Pierre Trudeau or Bobby Hull. But those guys we watched because we had to: they were doing stuff that, as a nation, we couldn't afford to miss. Or so we thought.

Berton, on the other hand, made us pay attention to him. With every media means possible, he held this country by the strings of its parka hood and said, "Listen. I've got something to say which, if you care about this place, you should pay attention to." Which we did, and have, for damned near half a century.

Caught as we were in the identity-warping crossfire of Canadian and American media, it was difficult not to be impressed by

Berton's Dominion-issue distinctiveness. In his multimedia ubiquity, there simply wasn't any equivalent to him beamed in from the United States. There was no single U.S. figure who appeared as author, game-show panellist, in-depth interviewer and op-ed opinion-mongerer in a single week. And week upon week.

There is a peculiarly Canadian media species called The Generalist—a form of maple-leaf hyphenate whose membership would include Thomas P. Kelley, Marshall McLuhan, Robert Fulford, Norman Jewison, Alan Thicke, John Ralston Saul, Don Harron, Rick Salutin and Clyde Gilmour. Pierre Berton is not just a charter member of that species, but possibly the most robust example it ever produced. What Howe was to hockey, BTO to power chords and Madame Benoit to the microwaveable casserole, Berton has been to the underappreciated Canadian public tradition of generalism. (As Berton well knows, it's a Canadian tradition to underappreciate Canadian traditions.)

Timing can certainly take some credit for Berton's sweeping, pan-provincial presence. He arrived, with talent, tirelessness and opinions, at a time when it was possible to marshal all three in a successful multimedia blitz. In those days it was a far different matter to straddle newspapers, magazines, radio and the upstart medium of television than it is now. (Today you have to *own* them to do so.) Our country's geographical eccentricities must also get their due: oversized and underpopulated, Canada not only had a limited number of media organs to conquer, most of them were—and, alas, remain—firmly bolted to the well-swept streets of Toronto. In other words, if a man had mind to make his presence felt everywhere in Canada in the decade after the Second World War, he could do a lot worse than be Pierre Berton in Toronto.

Naturally, it helped if you *were* Pierre Berton. For it is the uses to which Berton put his practice of generalism that compel us to consider him one of our country's most important voices. As you are about to discover, those uses were almost always intimately engaged with a larger sense of the nation itself. Specifically, with what was right or—as often—wrong with our peculiar experiment in nationhood. Generalism in this country, as a creative and journalistic practice, has tended to serve some of the finest thinking in our conspicuously tenacious tradition of liberalism. If anything, Berton's generalism—like Fulford's, Jewison's, Saul's and Salutin's—was the most fuel-efficient vehicle for the expression of a finely tuned sense of libertarian justice. In these pages you will find many stories drawn from the half-century of walking the beat called Canada, but you will also find one: the story of Pierre Berton's belief in Canada as a just and tolerant society, and of his conviction in his own practice as a way to police breaches of that fragile but honourable contract.

For if there is a political idea implicitly endorsed by journalistic generalism, it is that, in a just and tolerant society, everyone has a right to express an opinion on anything they want, especially if it relates to the preservation of that just and tolerant society. (I call it the Tavern Principle: everybody, no matter how obnoxious, gets to belch an opinion.) In other words, journalism has a mission and a purpose, which have to do with making sure we're being the best we can be under the circumstances. You will therefore find Berton sticking a bow-tied neck out to defend or attack a number of unpopular but worrisome issues—such as racism, development, environmentalism, religion, sex, TV—at a time when few were risking their neckwear to do so.

Or should I say "times"? For the material gathered here represents nothing less than a half-century of intense and fruitful engagement with a country still in the process of deciding what it wanted to be when—and if—it grew up. And this is where Berton's prose style—clear, simple and immediate—works its cumulative magic in this retrospective volume. As he always wrote for his time and never with any apparent pretensions to posterity, his collected journalism possesses the raw power to take you back to the moment that created it. To read him on Toronto's Union Station during the fifties, on the *Star* newsroom during the twenties, or on returning with his family to his boyhood home of Dawson City, is to breathe the very aroma of a past moment in our country's history. It is an experience that can only enrich one's awareness, if not appreciation, of the amnesiac self-absorption of the present.

I suppose that's why, in pondering the most apt tribute to Pierre Berton's fifty years of publicly arguing, worrying, celebrating and complaining about this jerrybuilt confederation, I find myself returning to a single thought. For a great many of us not even born when he wrote what follows, he made it impossible to think about Canada without thinking of him.

Geoff Pevere

Geoff Pevere is a broadcaster and columnist. He is also the co-author, with Greig Dymond, of *Mondo Canuck: A Canadian Pop Culture Odyssey.*

Introduction

A S THE SUBTITLE SUGGESTS, this book is more than an anthology: it is a resurrection. The various pieces that follow were written over a period of half a century. All have long since been interred in the graveyard of dead manuscripts; gone, yes, but not all forgotten—at least by me.

Some have been out of print for fifty years. Most were created long before the members of Generation X were born—back in the dear, dead days of the Eaton's catalogue, when television had not yet arrived but was eagerly awaited, when pulp magazines dominated the newsstands, and the *Toronto Star* sold for three cents.

The Korean War is here—it seems almost prehistoric now—and so is the Berlin Wall. I have also chronicled the scandalous (at the time) behaviour of one of our former "Royals" (the adjective had not yet been turned into a noun back in the 1950s). What passed for a king's peccadilloes were played down in the Edwardian gutter press, but could Edward VII and the Jersey Lily have survived today's tabloid onslaught?

Many of the characters who romp through these pages are dead. Thomas P. Kelley has gone to his reward. He phoned me periodically almost to the month of his death, outlining more and more outlandish pulp tales, including *The Gorilla's Daughter*, so farfetched I didn't believe he would ever sell it. But sell it he did. I saw the actual cover that he had outlined to me (blond child, naked mother, slavering anthropoid) when I passed a newsstand about six months later.

The great editor Harry Hindmarsh, who was feared and admired but rarely loved, is gone, too. He had an obsessive fear of death and

I

would not allow his editors to prepare an obituary in the event of his passing. They tried again after my story appeared in *Maclean's,* and he grudgingly agreed. "Let Berton write it," he rumbled. "He's found out more about me than anybody." Sometime later, while attending a play at Toronto's Royal Alexandra Theatre, I was buttonholed during the intermission by a *Star* reporter. HCH had died, and they wanted my permission to publish the obit I had written. Since they'd paid for it handsomely, I had no objection; I just didn't want them to edit it or rewrite it. The *Star* made only one minor change, breaking its own style rules by referring to the deceased throughout as *Mr.* Hindmarsh, a social title it extended to no one else.

In this collection I have included a few personal crusades. Shortly after I wrote about torture in the prisons, the paddle and the lash were banned. We no longer hang children or anybody else; there's progress for you. Stephen Truscott, the subject of the "Requiem" included in these pages, now lives anonymously in Ontario. At this writing he is hoping that DNA testing may prove his innocence. At the time it was published, that piece of rhyming verse caused a firestorm of controversy, most of it directed at me. The mayor of Goderich was close to tears when he phoned me to protest. Caryl Chessman finally went to his death for rape and murder, but it took nearly a decade of legal footwork before he paid the ultimate price. It was an expensive cat-and-mouse game that did nothing to serve the cause of justice. Life imprisonment would have been cheaper, in my view, and more humane.

After I joined the *Toronto Star* in 1958 I wrote one thousand columns—a million and a quarter words—before I moved on to other ventures. I have included a handful of these columns in this book. My assistant at that time was Marilyn Douglas, whom I referred to as Operative 67, thus giving the impression that I had a small army of investigative reporters at my call. Ms. Douglas, who laboured under the useful conviction that everybody in the world was slightly bent, was always able to don the guise of innocent housewife. I have recorded one of her exploits here.

There have been some changes over the past half-century. Consumers have had more protection since Ms. Douglas infiltrated the ranks of the hustlers. The Christian Church has pretty well gone the way of the Eaton's catalogue, although Hogtown is still Hogtown to anyone who lives west of Saskatoon. But we care more about our history today. I'm proud that two of the pieces included here, about Victoria's Crystal Gardens and Toronto's Union Station, played a small part in preserving these links with the past. Each first appeared in a book designed to change public attitudes toward heritage preservation. Both the station and the garden have been preserved as a result of the public outcry.

Since I am known today as a writer of popular history, I have included some earlier stabs at historical reportage: social history, mainly, about the dawn of the automobile age, the temperance movement of the last century, and Hollywood's earlier attempts to exploit the Mounties (a piece that has a certain resonance today, when Disney has been put in control of their image). The story of Van Horne's role in the Saskatchewan Rebellion was written in 1966, well before *The Last Spike*; it certainly served to confirm my growing interest in that subject matter.

I make no pretensions to writing deathless prose. I am a journalist rather than an "author." Yet there are a few pieces that I would like to see survive a bit longer—little essays such as "*La Chasse*," or "Seasonal Reflections," or "Shopping for a Coffin." For them I harbour a lingering affection. I reprint them here not because they are significant or earth shattering but simply because I enjoyed writing them and have not forgotten the magic moment when I first saw them in print.

If this collection seems to recall bygone eras—those of John Kennedy, Jack Kent Cooke, and Cecil B. De Mille—I console myself with the fancy that one or two pieces may have something to say to the present. I have placed them in chronological order, beginning in 1948, with one exception. It seemed proper to start off with an attempt to answer the old question, why did you write all this stuff? The shallow answer is because I got paid for it. But the true answer goes deeper. Back in 1970, when I had just completed *The National Dream*, I tried to explain why I write obsessively. I have published twenty-eight books since then, but the reasons I gave at the time are just as relevant today. Here they are:

The Joy of Writing
From *Maclean's*, September 1970

WRITING IS AN OBSESSION with me, as drugs or alcohol or sex are for others. I do not take drugs, and when I am writing intensively I do not need or even want alcohol or sex. This is not true of all writers, but it is true of a surprising number. Writing provides its own intoxications, its own addictions and hangovers.

Samuel Johnson once remarked that a man who did not write for money was a blockhead, but the truth is that I would write whether I was paid or not. I have done just that, many times in the past. I was hooked early. I was telling stories aloud to my parents at the age of four and writing them down on paper as soon as I learned to spell. From the age of eleven until I became a professional, at nineteen, I regularly published small newspapers of my own in order to have a medium to write in and a public to read me. The first of those little papers was hand-lettered in pencil or ink; later ones were pecked out on a typewriter. I rented them to my schoolmates at two cents a copy.

I once worked a sixty-three-hour week in a mining camp and, though I was bone weary at day's end, still could not come to terms with my obsession. I published a camp newspaper, which I typed myself and tacked to the mess-hall wall. It almost got me fired.

As a private in the army I suffered the terrible frustration of a writer without an outlet. Soldiers were not allowed to write, and this cold-turkey treatment almost destroyed me. I tried vainly to get into army public relations or war corresponding. No one would have me. I wrote skits for camp shows, but this was a poor substitute. At nights, while others snored, I tapped out twenty-page letters to my friends on a Hermes Baby portable, which I kept in my large haversack. I started two camp newspapers (one of which was quickly suppressed) and wrote constantly for a third. Later, as an officer, I was placed in charge of a transcontinental troop train and given the luxury of a private compartment. I retired to it, locked the door, left the troops to their own devices and wrote a book. The manuscript was lost, but the therapy was invaluable. It is one of three books that I have written but never published.

I love the act of writing and I cheerfully admit it. Most writers, of course, pretend that they hate it. They describe it as the worst torture in the world. I have read long accounts from these people and heard longer ones about the terror of the typewriter, the frightening loneliness of the writer and the ghastly pangs of composition. Since all of these writers continue to write prolifically, I take their comments with considerable salt.

It is true, of course, that there *is* torture involved, but it is the same exquisite torture that cause masochists to plead for more. It is also true that writing is a lonely business and that the creation of a long and complicated book, be it novel or history, is a solitary task. This, for me as for most writers, is also its great appeal. The writer is totally alone at such times, but he is also totally in charge of his own work. Films, plays, television programs and most magazine articles are, in effect, the products of committee decisions. The writer becomes a prisoner of deadlines, arbitrary lengths and the complexities and limitations of the various media.

A man and his book are subject to none of these frustrations. The subject can be his own, and unless he is crazy enough to submit to a publisher's deadline, he can proceed at his own pace. The terrible strictures of space do not concern him. A book can be as short as 30,000 words, as *The Golden Trail* was, or as long as 200,000, as *Klondike* was. When I started work on the story of the building of the Canadian Pacific Railway, I thought the book would be about the same length as *Klondike*. It has since become twice as long; I merely expanded it into two volumes. In no other medium does the writer have such total control over his own work.

In that case, people ask, why don't you spend all your time writing books? Why fool around with other media? The answer is partly one of temperament but mainly one of capacity. Words are like blood; every writer has so many in him, and when they are gone he dries up. Capacities vary; mine runs around 200,000 publishable words a year. Ten years ago, when I was writing a daily column, I wrote at about that rate. Last year when I was working on *The National Dream*—the first volume of the railway story—I produced almost exactly the same amount. During this bloodletting, a writer must take time out to refuel. Some do it by travelling, some by going on prolonged drunks, some by building things in the basement; I do it by working in other media where my mind is stimulated by contact with interesting people and where, incidentally, I am paid well enough to support a large family and indulge my sybaritic tastes.

It is not generally understood that most writing takes place away from the typewriter. When you finally approach the machine, it is really the beginning of the end. Nine-tenths of your work has been done; it remains to put on paper what you have already created. It is this creative process that takes most of the time.

Although I am known as a fast writer, it takes me an unconscionable time to tool up for a major book. The process is a subtle one. The decision to write a book about the building of the railway actually came to me in the summer of 1958. I had started writing a daily column at the time and did not have any more words left in me. That is one of the reasons why, four years later, I quit the column; as long as it dominated my life I would produce nothing else.

After the column ended I wrote five short books, partly to get myself back into a book-writing frame of mind and partly because the subjects challenged and intrigued me. But all the time I was really working on the book about the CPR, thinking about the railway and its significance and reading about the period. I was still not ready to plunge fully into the task. I knew from my experience with *Klondike* that it takes considerable time before a writer can be hopelessly seduced by his subject. This courtship period occupied several years until I was able to find and hire a research assistant, Norman Kelly, to dig into the archives and provide me with some raw material. I approached the growing mound of Xeroxes and tapes diffidently at first, but within a few months I was ready to devour everything available on the subject.

It is at this point in any creative process that economic considerations go out the window. I was editorial director of a publishing company at the time. I quit. I was host of a successful new television program, *Under Attack*. I quit that, too. My annual income was reduced to half at a time when I was spending large sums on the book for personal travel and in research and secretarial help.

I think I now understand why men must steal to support a drug habit. There are single sentences in *The National Dream* that cost me as much as one hundred dollars. The book would be perfectly acceptable without them.

To write a book as complicated as this one is rather like putting a jigsaw puzzle together. The pieces arrive in no particular order; you sort them out as best you can. Certain pieces elude you; some are key pieces and some peripheral. But you cannot sleep peacefully until you find them all.

And you *must* find them because, until you do, you do not know how valuable the pieces are. When working on the story of the railway, I became intrigued by the mystery of George W. McMullen, the pivotal figure in the Pacific Scandal of 1873. McMullen was a Chicago promoter who tried to blackmail Sir John A. Macdonald and helped to bring the Conservative government crashing to the ground. No book about the politics of that period fails to mention him, yet he remains a shadowy figure. What did he look like? How old was he? What were his interests? What became of him? History does not tell us. He is a name—nothing more.

I tried for a long time to find something about McMullen, but everywhere—even in Chicago—I met with failure. The manuscript had gone to my publisher when I decided to have another try, with the assistance this time of my wife and our eldest daughter, Penny. We had two clues: McMullen had been born in Picton, Ontario, and his father had been a Methodist minister. It took two weeks of detective work. Then a picture of a fascinating man emerged. Snatching the manuscript from the printers, I added two more pages to the book.

This search for elusive facts can bring to any writer moments of great drama and excitement. The most rewarding of these came to me when I was working on *Klondike*. My wife and I were in Seattle, interviewing old-timers, when somebody hinted that Belinda Mulroney might still be living in Seattle.

The hair rose on my nape. Belinda Mulroney was one of the great names of the gold rush. She had known every Klondike King, made herself a fortune and married a champagne salesman, the "Count" de Carbonneau (he was really a barber from Montreal). Then she had vanished. Could she actually be alive?

We had few clues. There was no phone listing, but in the city directory we found a Mrs. C. Carbonneau on the outskirts of Seattle. It was our last day and it was getting late. I had not yet eaten and I was tired. My wife urged me to take the chance, and so, after a seven-dollar taxi ride, I found myself knocking on the door of a little house in the suburbs. A small, wizened woman opened it.

"I'm writing a book about the gold rush," I said. "Are you Belinda Mulroney Carbonneau?"

"Come on in, m'friend," she said. "We've got a lot to talk about."

Only another writer can understand that for me there could be no sweeter triumph: a Governor General's medal, a book club selection, a handsome royalty cheque, a series of rave reviews—all these pale in the brilliance of that moment.

It is during such a period, when the pieces are being fitted together, that a writer becomes difficult to live with or even to know. He is lost to the world. He stands glassy-eyed at parties, replying to conversation with vague monosyllables. He drives his car erratically. He scarcely speaks to his wife or children.

All this antisocial activity is necessary because what the writer is doing in these moments is *writing*. He is thinking about people and events and scenes, struggling to put them into some kind of order and perspective. He can no more cut off this flow of thought than he can cut off the flow of his own blood. It goes on, day and night, asleep or awake, at mealtimes and even during the act of love. It is a miracle that the divorce rate among writers is not higher.

My novelist friends tell me that at this stage of the creative process their characters become more real to them than living people. I had somewhat the same experience writing *The National Dream,* but because it is a history, my people had actually *been* alive. Now they became, for me, alive once more, and this produced a phenomenon that I can only

9

describe as eerie. Here I was, totally immersed in the past, reading all the newspapers and magazines of the 1870s, reading the actual letters, diaries and documents in the handwriting of the surveyors, politicians, businessmen and builders. It was as if I had been carried back a century by a time machine; these people—Walter Moberly, the passionate surveyor, Marcus Smith, his bristly colleague, George Stephen, the brilliant financier, Jim Hill, the one-eyed railroad builder, and scores of others—all became my contemporaries *except that I knew what was going to happen to them*. If I did not know, I could look forward into time, like a Cassandra, and find out. The sensation was uncanny.

The birth pangs at the typewriter cannot begin until this gestation period is finished. Various writers approach this climactic moment in different ways. Some discipline themselves to produce a certain number of finished words per day. I cannot do that. I prefer to write at top speed, day after day from early morning until late at night, until I have a manuscript of sorts on paper.

That, really, is part of my obsession. In the case of *The National Dream*, I had been waiting for that moment for eleven years. I had been thinking about the book almost constantly for three years and each month with greater intensity. The actual words and phrases were, in many cases, running through my head. Whole scenes had taken shape, right down to the verbs and adjectives. I had wound myself into a state of suppressed excitement and literally could not wait to get to the typewriter.

I began to write the first draft of *The National Dream* on the last day of June, 1969. I wrote every day, usually beginning at 8 a.m. and working right through until late evening, sometimes indeed until three in the morning. I did nothing else. I even had some of my meals beside the typewriter. I told my friends that I had gone to Mexico for a month and swore my family to secrecy. I told the phone company to take the telephone out. It was not an easy time for my wife. I do not suffer interruptions, except those of very small children, when I am writing. I was short-tempered, uncommunicative, jealous of time and totally enveloped in a work I refused to discuss with anybody. I enjoyed every minute of it.

When I emerged, finally, from the cocoon of the mind, I knew that I had a book. It needed a great deal of work. Over the next three months I rewrote it completely. Only then did I show it to anyone. After that I rewrote it again, and then again. One four-page section was rewritten fourteen times. And I enjoyed every minute of that process, too.

The tendency of every writer who loves his craft, I think, is to cling as long as possible to this child, caressing it and spoiling it, knowing that the day is fast approaching when it will be his no longer. I remember when *Klondike* was finally completed I had to fight back the compulsion to rewrite it entirely in a totally different style. Parting is not easy, and when the manuscript finally escapes from the writer's unwilling hands there is likely to be a terrible reaction.

I remember very well Ralph Allen's reaction after he finished *Ordeal by Fire*, a brilliant history of the first half of the century in Canada. He told me that something frightening was happening to him: he could not eat, he could not sleep, he could not relax. The book kept whirling round in his head to the point, he said, where he was actually considering suicide. I was able to tell him that I had had exactly the same experience and to reassure him that it would pass.

One might expect that the completion of such a work would bring a feeling of relief, but what the writer actually experiences is a dreadful letdown. The great days of creation are over. You wander disconsolately about, trying, not very successfully, to read or to look at television. Galley proofs arrive and you attack them joyfully; the publisher has to restrain you from rewriting every paragraph. You look back nostalgically on the long period during which the book possessed you, and you long to relive those days. You know they will return eventually, when you begin a new book, but you cannot yet bring yourself to enter into a new love affair with an unknown subject.

This is the most frustrating period of any writer's existence, this limbo between books. Several months pass and nothing happens. Slowly, however, the writer is turning ideas over in his head. Little tinglings of anticipation ripple up and down his spine. Finally, a little gingerly and then with more confidence, he seizes upon a subject and begins to concentrate upon it. At parties you may see that glassy look return briefly to mask his eyes. By now he has all but forgotten his previous creation. And then, at this very moment, it returns to haunt him.

The publishing process is painfully protracted. Many publishers need a full year between the acceptance of a manuscript and its publication. This poses a dilemma for the professional. He has kissed his book goodbye and is in the process of being seduced by a new one. Suddenly the old book appears in print. Critics review it. Interviewers ask him about it. Friends slap him on the back and ask for free copies. Publishers hold cocktail parties in his honour. His is interviewed and asked to make speeches. He may get an award.

This, really, is what he has been working for, if he is honest with himself—the applause of a grateful audience. Yet now that applause, to him, is strangely hollow and irrelevant. He accepts it and is vaguely warmed. He nods pleasantly and smiles at the appropriate moments. Somebody mentions a scene or a character in his book, and he struggles to recall it. Gaze carefully into his eyes and you are likely to detect mild irritation. Everybody wants to talk about his last book; he wants to talk about his next one. He is already becoming obsessed by it, and the burden that he must bear is that nobody will understand that obsession except himself.

He Was a Love Slave

From *Maclean's*, December 1, 1948

Naked pretty 18-year-old Ann Kempton stood before the bureau mirror in her bedroom, as the flickering rays of a nearby candle cast golden beams on the shapely curves of her body. . . What she did not see was a sinister figure . . . drawing ever closer . . . a man with lust in his mind and murder in his heart. . . .

AT THE MAGAZINE RACK of the nearest cigar store, all hell is breaking loose. Hideous plant men from Venus have attacked the earth and are swarming right off the cover of *Gripping Tales*. Wide-eyed, buxom blondes, clad only in solitaire rhinestones and wisps of surgical gauze, are in the clutches of brutal, pig-eyed monsters. Private Eyes, hats low over brow, roscoes clutched firmly in right hands, are pointing the finger of guilt right at *you!* And, on the uppermost rack, a full-lipped, heavy-lidded brunette in a nightgown and rolled silk stockings is waiting to Confess.

Beneath the gaudy covers of pulp magazines (which get their name from the fact that the paper appears to have been chewed by wasps) there can be found the modern equivalent of the fairy story, the penny dreadfuls of the Atomic Age. What reader, dipping for the first time into this literary witch's brew, has not asked, goggle-eyed: "Who, in the name of the Sacred Moon of Jupiter, writes all this stuff?"

Part of the answer (if not all of it) can be found in one of the back rooms of the Delta Kappa Epsilon fraternity house on the campus of the University of Toronto in the person of its temporary steward, Thomas Patrick Kelley, a man of prolific output, violent imagination and thirty pseudonyms.

Jesse James leaped through the doorway into the open and was before the surprised men, his gun blazing. And then six shots rang out in the midnight air with such rapidity as to be almost simultaneous. And then the six men crumpled and fell dead upon the snow—a bullet between the eyes of each of them!

Kelley, an ex-prizefighter, has been writing for the pulps since 1937. His name—or names—have appeared on stories in *Weird Tales, Fantastic Adventures, Short Stories, Argosy, Adventure,* and *True Police* and run the gamut from *Whispered Confessions* ("He Loved Every Dollar I Had") to *The People's Magazine,* a religious quarterly ("Peter Cartwright, the Pioneer Parson").

In the last decade, Kelley has, by his own count, churned out between two and a half and three million words in the form of some four hundred short stories, fourteen full-length novels and three novel-length poems for children. He has been paid as little as a third of a cent a word, as much as ten cents a word. In peak times he has made as much as $300 a week and $10,000 a year. In bad times he has scraped by on precious little.

This is a bad time. In the steaming jungles of popular literature, pulp magazines spring up and die as swiftly as mushrooms. High production costs and a paper shortage have murdered a host of magazines as ruthlessly as Manuel Da Costa, Wolf of the Desert, murdered a swarm of Arabs in one of Kelley's stories. This and the fact that "I can write good stories but I can't pick good horses" explains why he is cooking French fries for fraternity men. But it is the only time Kelley has had to supplement his writing with other work since he started. (He had a war job for a while, but that was patriotism—not penury.) By midwinter, when old magazines begin to reappear under new names, Kelley expects to be on his own once more.

It is doubtful whether the pipe-smoking young men of good old Delta Kappa Epsilon realize that their steward, under the pseudonym of T.P. Monohan, is the author of such stirring historical novels as *Outlaws Ride the Range.* Inside the paper jacket of this book are advertisements for other novels: *Fast on the Draw,* by Tex Elton, *Western-Gun Justice,* by Zed Kelly, and *Deadshot Riders,* by Rex Hays. All of these authors are Thomas P. Kelley in disguise.

Kelley has written entire issues of *Uncanny Tales, Eerie Stories* and *Recent Detective*. Every one of the first-person accounts of the tortured course of true love that appeared in a recent issue of *Whispered Confessions* ("Actual Confessions by Real People"), all the way from "My Bride of Disillusionment" to "I Married a Gambler," were turned out in about a week by Kelley. Once a reader of *Uncanny Tales* wrote in to say that although Kelley was getting a lot of praise he thought one Gene Bannerman, another author, was being badly neglected. He thought Bannerman every bit as good as Kelley. So he was. Bannerman *was* Kelley.

On one occasion a Toronto pulp editor was horrified to find that his magazine was about to go to press one thousand words short of being full. It was midnight, but Kelley was on hand. He promptly scribbled a short story called "I'll Meet You in the Beyond" on the backs of three envelopes. It was exactly one thousand words long.

Another time, a harassed editor, his hungry presses screaming for fodder and the deadline fast approaching, asked Kelley to sit down and write a story on the spot.

"What shall I write?" asked Kelley.

"Write 'I Was a Love Slave,'" said the editor. Kelley wrote while copy boys tore the manuscript from his typewriter and rushed it into print. Pretty soon the editor shouted that that was enough. Kelley stopped writing, picked up his cheque and left.

I was a very pretty girl, in all truth I can say that. Some five feet four inches in height, with wavy auburn hair and long-lashed brown eyes. I had an unusually shapely figure and the crisp freshness of youth. And I must admit that there was something about the laughing, handsome and reckless Drake Mallory that fascinated me. . .

Kelley looks as Irish as his name, in all truth one can say that. At thirty-nine, he has black brows, a bullet head and a boxer's nose. When Kelley describes the plot of one of his stories his eyes light up, his brow furrows and his face takes on a demoniacal look. As the plot progresses, Kelley becomes more and more excited, waving his

15

arms, slamming his fist on the table, crouching and whirling, acting out each of his characters as he talks. This is not surprising when you consider that, in his youth, Kelley played every male part in *Uncle Tom's Cabin*, from Topsy to Simon Legree, while travelling with his father's medicine show.

Kelley's father, from Newboro, Ontario, was known as "Old Doc Kelley" the length and breadth of the continent. His medicine show was advertised as "The Majestic Tour of the Inimitable Exponent of Irish Mirth and Melody." It included Kelley's Dixie Cotton Pickers and Kelley's Big American Lady Minstrels and was used to promote the sale of cure-alls of the order of The Banyan, Tiger Salve, and Healing Oil. Young Kelley, besides playing Uncle Tom, also doubled on violin and piano and was straight man for the comedians.

Despite all this, Kelley managed to get in his schooling (at the age of ten he sold an essay about a huge bear to a rich schoolmate for a nickel) and take two years at the University of Notre Dame. He toured the southern United States for seven years as a prizefighter, winning no titles but taking part in 107 fights and scoring, according to his own claims, forty-five knockouts. Then he quit the ring and came back to Canada. The Depression and his imagination goaded him into becoming a writer.

My name is Na-Ela. It was in the sunken city of Lothar some two thousand years ago that I first opened my eyes to that weird and watery world ruled by my father Na-Harus the Just—beloved and last king of the Tarkamites. . .

Kelley, hungry and out of work, was walking past a millinery shop on Toronto's Yonge Street when something about the hats, stuck on little model heads, made him pause.

"'Heads,' I thought. 'No bodies!'" said Kelley, describing the incident later. "Heads without bodies! That was 'The Last Pharaoh,' my first story—he was 3,400 years without a body. They kept his head alive on the Bowl of Life Eternal. His body had turned to dust eons ago. It was supposed to be strangely anointed by the old

Egyptian physician, Sarksas—he was going to fix the head back on the body after so the Pharaoh'd be able to live forever—but just then the Hyksos attacked and sent an arrow through old Sarksas's heart. The Pharaoh—he and his wicked paramour Atma (she's the only one of the lot I let live, incidentally, I don't know why)—they lived on through the centuries, just a couple of heads seeking the right bodies—ones with the blood of royal Egypt flowing through their veins. Weird? Sure. But I made it plausible."

Kelley had a hard time figuring out how to kill off the Pharaoh and end the story. "I was living in a filthy little hotel at the time. I was plastering the kitchen when I noticed the place was swarming with rats. So—I got it! I had the Pharaoh hung head downward in a rat pit. They ate him up."

He wrote the story in longhand and sent it in to *Weird Tales*, which promptly bought it for five hundred dollars. (It was 67,000 words long.)

"I tell you I never got a sock in the ring like I got when that letter of acceptance came," Kelley says. "I was hit so hard I went down on one knee."

From that moment, Thomas P. Kelley was a professional writer.

"The champagne is chilled, the supper snack ready, sir." Hendricks, the butler, personified one in manner, looks, dress and speech.

Allen Bedford Marshall III turned. In his early thirties, with wealth and a good social background, Allen Bedford Marshall III was looked upon by the mothers of "the four hundred" who had marriageable daughters themselves as "a good catch"—a term now given added emphasis by his recent inheriting of some six million dollars.

"Very good, Hendricks," he answered. "Miss La Verne will arrive presently."

At first, Kelley stuck to weird, fantastic tales, usually with Egyptian backgrounds. "I guess I know more about Cleopatra than any living man," he says. "I've read Emil Ludwig's book *The Nile* four times."

Often he started a story without any idea how it would end.

"Take in Chapter Six of *I Found Cleopatra*, just after Manuel Da Costa, the Wolf of the Desert, had attacked the oasis with his thousands of villainous Arabs to carry off the Midnight Lady, who's really Cleopatra in disguise. I have him leave Brian O'Hara, the hero, for dead. Then I write: 'Slowly, I got to my feet, hardly knowing where I was or what I'd do next.' Well, you know, I didn't actually know what he *would* do next. Had no idea at all."

When Kelley exhausted the past, he decided to move his locales into the future, on the theory that everybody knew all about the present. "I decided as long as I was jumping into the future I might as well take a good jump, so I wrote 'A Million Years in the Future.' It was only the pleadings of my wife stopped me from making it a *billion* years."

Kelley's wife, Ethel, takes a lively and personal interest in his stories. "Ethel helps a lot," Kelley says. "In that Million Years story I had them on this planet riding strange beasts. I couldn't figure out what to call the beasts. 'Call them kangs,' Ethel says. 'By gad,' I says, 'I will.' Kangs. The name fitted exactly."

Kelley and his wife often lie in bed at night figuring out plots. Kelley usually writes a story by "talking it" to his wife. She sits at the typewriter as he walks about dictating. But he writes his "really good stuff" in longhand himself.

He has met some challenges in his day.

"Once a magazine asked me to write a story called 'The Greatest Monster,' he recalled recently. "*Greatest*, mind you. That meant that there could be *nothing* bigger. Now, say I wrote about a monster ten miles high. Some guy would come along and write about one twenty miles high. There was a poser! I had to figure out a monster so big there can be nothing bigger. Well, there was only one answer, of course: I made the earth itself the monster. It was like a huge snake, see, curled up like an armadillo. It had already eaten a couple of its moons. Now it's waking up, with the war and the bombs and everything. I've never read about a bigger monster. If I do, then I'll have to try again. I'll make the planet Jupiter into a monster."

The kiss went down to my toes in a breathless, delicious shock. My knees knew an amazing weakness and my lips trembled as I returned the kiss. I'd been kissed a number of times before by a number of good-looking, eligible young men, but I'd never known lips like his. . .

Inevitably, Kelley was drawn into the vortex of the true detective story and the real confession tale. A host of Canadian pulps had sprung up during the war and were selling at hotcake speed to servicemen and others travelling about the country.

"They'll call you up just like I'd say to you, 'Go out and get a pound of hamburger,' and ask for three confessions and four detectives by the end of the week," Kelley reports. "Then they'll tell how many they want sexy, how many non-sexy and I turn 'em out."

For the true detective stories, he has a few newspaper clippings to go on and his imagination. He once wrote an 8,000-word true detective based on a 300-word clipping. For the confession stories, he needs only his imagination.

"I'm good on characters," Kelley says. "Some guys, if they want to say a girl's beautiful, they'll write a 200-word paragraph of straight description. I don't do it like that. I sneak it in in little bits. One time I might mention in passing that she has thighs like pillars of white ivory, then, later on, I'll sneak in the fact that her high-tipped breasts look like young pomegranates.

"I'm starting a detective yarn now. Who am I having the killer? A murdering fiend? No! A little defenceless old woman. That makes it more horrible.

"Say I want to describe a horrible, fiendish monster with slavering jaws and wild eyes: I wouldn't describe it at all! Instead I'd say it was so horrible I *couldn't* describe it.

"And here's another tip. Have the detective the murderer. That always fools 'em. I've done that several times."

Kelley admits that he has never yet made the reader the murderer, but he once wrote a story in which the author was murdered.

As for confession stories, he's not very proud of them. "Sickening! Sickening!" he says. "When they phone me up asking me for some more I *plead* with them not to give me any. 'NO! No!' I say. 'Make it all detective stories.' But it's never any use." Often Kelley takes his weekly output of detective and confession stories down to an editor and gets them accepted without anyone reading them.

She could not help but admire the utter fearlessness of the man advancing up the road in that ghostly pre-dawn light and so recklessly exposing himself to the gunfire of a murderer and racketeer. . . But if she was hoping that all this might end in romance, she was doomed to disappointment. "Knuckles" Kane lived only for adventure and was in the underworld. . .

Speed is a pulp writer's stock in trade. You have to be prolific, at half a cent a word, to pay for the week's groceries. Kelley wrote a 15,000-word novelette, *City of the Centaurs*, in one day. He wrote *The Tapestry Triangle*, a 40,000-word paper-covered book that was published in Toronto and sold in England, in one week. He was paid a flat $150 for it.

His 60,000-word novels take him ten days to two weeks, but he gets as high as one thousand dollars for them. In 1940 he supplied plots for fifty-two half-hour radio plays. (Somebody else wrote the actual scripts.) Kelley visited the radio station once every two weeks to dictate the plots. He'd figure out the first plot during a seven-minute streetcar ride, transfer to a second streetcar and have his second plot figured out by the time he reached the studio.

Kelley was recently asked which was his most fantastic story. He raced rapidly through half a dozen of his wildest plots, finally settling on one called "The Island of Death."

"You can't have *anything* more fantastic than that, where I have Death a beautiful woman on an island," said Kelley. "You know where her lover came from? She'd first met him two billion years before when he was shot down from a planet as a seed and it grew up in the shape of a person. You can't get anything more fantastic than that. Look at the Bubbling Grey Sea, the Brain of the Earth.

Look at the Board of Life—I had them all in that story. The Board of Life, that was a huge, gigantic board on the side of a black mountain—oh, a *tremendous* mountain: it had the Alps beat off the map. On this mountain there's a huge board with a billion little pinpoints of light. Each one of those lights is a human life. Each one of them goes out—pop!—that's somebody dying. That was 'The Island of Death.' It was well liked. Yes, they liked that one."

Peter Cartwright never quailed before any man. In a flash he seized the bully's hand, brought his great strength into play with a viselike grip that forced the other, screaming, to his knees. Peter then made the man pick up his Bible and return it to him. . .

Aside from his own work and the historical research he sometimes finds it necessary to do, Kelley does little reading. "I'm a great believer in Edgar Rice Burroughs," he says. "Know what he says? 'Read nothing. Learn nothing.' Well, Burroughs did all right."

Ultimately, Kelley has his eyes on Hollywood. "I have seven plots—seven wonderful plots," he says. "Unusual—distinctive. I can say, in all truth, that none of them has ever been used before."

One of the plots involves the unrequited love of a Siamese twin for a girl who makes her living putting her head in a lion's mouth. There's a subplot involving a professional dwarf suddenly faced with the tragedy of finding that he's starting to grow again. Kelley hopes to have Peter Lorre play the part of both Siamese twins. "They are joined at the waist," he explains. "Gad—can't you just see him?"

Meanwhile, Kelley continues to churn it out in an unending stream. He is spurred on by the fact that he has always sold everything he has written, with one exception—a story of Roosevelt's reincarnation within the body of a crooked U.S. president, four hundred years into the future. Roosevelt was alive at the time and the editor thought the story might be in poor taste. Kelley burned the 70,000-word manuscript in disgust. Shortly afterwards, the editor wrote that he'd decided it *wasn't* in poor taste after all. Aside from this regrettable loss, there is no evidence that the presses won't continue to gobble Kelley stories as long as his imagination and stamina hold out.

As part of the exhaustive research that went into the preparation of this article, it became necessary to challenge Kelley to make up a story on the spot. He rose to the occasion beautifully, beginning without hesitation.

"All right, there's this big dance going on, see, and there's this escaped criminal, a man with a price on his head, hiding among the dancers. Suddenly he meets this beautiful girl, and he's so struck by her he throws caution to the winds. Instinctively he senses there's something strange, something different about her. He's fascinated. He pursues her. Then she turns to him and says, 'I must leave now.' 'But, please—give me some clue as to where you live,' the escaped criminal pleads. Suddenly the midnight hour strikes and girl starts to run down the stairs. . ."

Thomas P. Kelley crouched forward, eyes alight, arms gesticulating, words worth upward of half a cent each pouring from him, as he moulded his own particular version of the age-old pulp story of Cinderella.

And the cloven-hoofed Wolves of Whorra were advancing to the attack, led by nine nude women who had been dead for a million years!

Make Way for the One-Eyed Monster

From *Maclean's*, June 1, 1949

THE CITY OF NEW YORK has always presented hazards to the visiting Canadian, but until last week I, for one, had never encountered any serious language barrier. It is now, however, necessary to warn the traveller who wanders into the tall jungle of Manhattan that he will almost certainly be faced with the sort of conversational gambit that was tossed at me during a small house party a few days ago.

"Say, Jack," said a man across the room, "did you catch Channel Nine last night?"

There was a general knowing giggle that left me blank.

Finally a friend came to my rescue by explaining that I was from the Canadian back country, had no knowledge of television, and therefore couldn't know that a group of college students were experimenting in a clandestine fashion with this particular TV channel. They had, my friends solemnly declared, been showing naughty and illicit Mexican-made movies to the delight of most of the television addicts in the New York area.

As there are more than half a million sets in greater New York, these addicts number well over two million. If a New Yorker isn't an addict he has a friend who is. The chances are that the friend spends most of his time hanging around the addict's house.

Men and women who have spent years fruitlessly Luxing their undies nightly, or reading Dale Carnegie until they can recite him backward without winning a solitary friend or influencing a child of five, have suddenly found themselves being treated like Harry Truman the day after the election simply because they have acquired a TV set. "In the old days," one of this happy breed confided to me, "we never used to see *anybody*. Now we have a wide and influential circle of friends."

We may soon expect this sort of thing in Canada, now that the CBC has announced its own TV plans. Within eighteen months the Joneses next door may have their first receiver. When this happens the things that are going on in New York will become part of the Canadian social pattern.

New York is history's first TV town. At the moment it has the greatest number of televiewers per square rod and is the only area in the world where you can choose between five separate programs from five separate stations (six, if you count Channel Nine).

In this teleconscious town, where the natives speak glibly of "similcasts" and pugilists wear specially striped telepants for clearer reproduction on the cathode tube, the visiting fireman inescapably finds himself, like a Wells time traveller, viewing with some awe the picture of our future society.

The terms "mores" and "folkways" crop up whenever TV is discussed. "Television will undoubtedly have a profound effect on our social mores," five or six New York televeterans told me. Already the effect is being felt.

A man I know who owns a set swears that he has known a man intimately for a year without once seeing his face. "He comes into our room in the dark, sits down in front of the set, stares at it until the show is finished, gets up and puts his hat on and leaves before we get the lights on again," he told me.

A friend of mine in Manhattan, who is trying in his own puerile way to stem the wave, refuses to buy a receiver. "This monster will devour us all unless we resist it," he told me seriously. "I refuse to have my life dominated by a ten-inch picture, blurred at the edges."

But the wave is already lapping at the ankles of this Canute. Sundown finds him fidgety; dusk comes and the telelust is on him; night falls and a milky way of telescreens wink on. He phones an acquaintance who owns a TV set, leaps into a Yellow Cab, trundles across town and meekly takes his place with the other pilgrims before the shrine.

The televirus is creeping inexorably across the city. A big indoor pool is now advertising "Swimming with Television." In the bars, where TV has been the greatest thing since the free lunch, a new social stratum has emerged that places the scotch-and-soda drinkers close to the screen and the beer and ale men well to the rear. On the Avenue of the Americas a fund-raising organization has tried to attract attention to itself by building an entire $15,000 house on a vacant lot. To attract attention to the house they've turned on a TV set on the walk in front.

The clifflike apartment blocks that girdle the city are rapidly sprouting the new foliage of the TV aerial, and the small talk around town is peppered with tributes to the new gods of the television era: a puppet named Howdy Doody, a wrestler who calls himself the Golden Superman and a none-too-successful radio comedian named Milton Berle who is currently the hottest thing on television.

Berle prepared himself well in advance for his teledebut by rendering his schnozzle more photogenic. A plastic surgeon pared it down, and Berle liked the effect so much he has since given further "schnoz trims" (as *Variety*, the show-business bible, calls them) to his friends for Christmas.

TV advertising is already overtaking radio advertising in the New York press. In one tabloid I counted a total of four full pages of TV ads compared with about two and a half of radio. There is, however, a better indication of the astonishing strides that TV has made in the past year: a swaddled infant in the advertising world, it has quickly lent itself to the same comparatives that have long been a part of the soap and cigarette hucksters' vocabulary. Each TV manufacturer now announces unequivocally that his set gives a bigger picture than that of any competitor.

"You're really socially ostracized if somebody has a bigger screen than you," a man with a twelve-inch screen told me the other day. "They'll desert you like flies." As the average televiewer today has only a ten-inch screen, this man feels fairly safe for the moment, but there's a rumour that a fellow down the hall is thinking of buying a set that makes my acquaintance start up all beady with sweat in the dark of the night.

I had a glancing encounter with TV when my wife and I dropped around to the apartment of a New York magazine man. Our host was a moment or so late getting up from the office and, as his wife was in the kitchen, his ten-year-old daughter opened the door. The child surveyed us with a dazed look and then, as if drawn by a magnet, returned without a word to a low settee in the hall, sat down beside her eight-year-old brother and began to stare fixedly at the wall. Our hostess presently appeared and explained her daughter's actions. "They're waiting for Howdy Doody, you know."

I then saw what it was the two children were gazing at. Opposite the settee squatted the Monster, its great square Polyphemus eye returning the unwinking gaze of the youngsters. From its flat cranium there protruded two great beetle-like feelers, knobbed at the end. Later I learned this was a built-in antenna, but at the moment the whole machine bore an uncanny resemblance to one of the Insect Men of Mars.

On the screen a black-and-white cartoon was reaching a violent climax. The children watched it with sober interest. It had the jerky movements, the crude drawing and the simple story line of the early vintage animateds and reminded me nostalgically of the first cartoon I'd ever seen—Oswald the Rabbit in *Mississippi Mud, circa* 1927.

The cartoon seemed to be shown from under a pool of gently rippling water, and it had some of the qualities of an aluminum engraving because of light contrasts. Our host, who arrived at this moment, apologized for this. "Honestly," he said, "the television picture has the same clarity as a modern motion picture—except at our place."

We moved into the drawing-room, but the children remained behind, still staring fixedly at the eye. "Do you like this better than the radio?" I asked the little girl by way of a parting shot. She gave me the withering glance I deserved. "The thing seems to act on the children like a . . . a soporific," said our hostess. "Anodyne," quickly corrected her husband, who works for *Time*.

The next day we attended a "television evening" at the invitation of a friend named Jim who has a friend who has a set.

"Always a crowd at good old Al's," Jim told me as we arrived at Al's apartment. "We're here in good time."

We were indeed. Al and his wife were half through supper, and Al waved us toward the TV set and continued eating coleslaw. The set, a console model, formed the focal point of Al's apartment and performed the same function as a fireplace in a pre-TV room. Facing the set were three occasional chairs in a row behind which was a chesterfield, all arranged in theatre fashion. A newsreel, made up of films taken the previous day, was just finishing, and presently a placard appeared announcing the beginning of the Milton Berle show.

The entire show took place on the stage of a theatre, curtains closing after each item and parting to reveal new scenes. Four gas station attendants, standing before a painted gas station, gave a visual singing commercial about a motor oil, and Berle arrived a moment later, wearing a toga and wig and driving a Roman chariot with four horses.

"Isn't it awful what you got to go through for a lousy $15,000 a week?" he asked an unseen audience, which laughed madly at him.

After some more of this patter Berle introduced an acrobatic team of four men. Once again I had the feeling of nostalgia that the old-time cartoon had given me. Here, by means of this bright new medium, I was being introduced to a vaudeville act apparently identical with one I had last seen at Shea's Hippodrome in Toronto, *circa* 1930.

"Are there television shows all day long?" my wife was asking.

"Right from 7 a.m.," said our hostess happily. "That's why our kitchen looks the way it does."

Berle had returned *sans* toga and was introducing a man who he said had developed a new spring suit. The man walked across the stage wearing a suit to which giant springs were attached.

Then Berle introduced his first guest star, Key Luke, the Chinese movie actor. Luke and Berle went through some patter, then reappeared in Chinese dress and began to talk in pidgin English. "Who was that mandarin I seen you with last night?" Luke asked.

"That was no mandarin," returned Berle, "that was a ukulele."

There was some more of this (Berle donned a false nose at one point). Then Berle introduced his second guest, Ethel Merman, the Broadway musical star.

"Hey, they finally got Merman," shouted Al. "They finally got her for $5,000. They've been trying to get her on TV for a year and they finally did it."

Miss Merman appeared in a black evening gown, which the ladies were quick to criticize. Something about the lighting gave her face a soiled appearance, and a white, horizontal line near the neck of the dress served to accentuate the flattened, somewhat obese look that the screen tends to give to TV actors.

"Poor Ethel," clucked one of the ladies. "She has no TV future."

Ethel sang a song, then she and Berle appeared dressed in turn-of-the-century motoring costumes (Berle also wore a tremendous moustache) and went through a patter routine before a painted replica of an early-vintage auto. "What kind of automobile is that anyway?" Miss Merman wanted to know.

"It's a Hardly Able," Berle answered.

The man who gave the commercial appeared dressed as an old-time bowler-hatted street hawker (selling motor oil) and went through a sure-fire vaudeville routine that at one point involved a tried and ancient wheeze in which a man enters, gyrating from side to side, and announces that he's a clock. "What time is it?" asked the hawker.

"Eight o'clock," said the clock.

"But I've got half-past eight," said the hawker.

"Then I must be slow," said the clock and speeded up his clock movements to the delight of the invisible audience.

I could be wrong, but I thought I detected on the faces of both these men the same look of fierce delight that had ennobled the countenances of the four acrobats. The look seemed to say, "We told you so. We always knew vaudeville would be back."

Berle and Miss Merman wound up the show with "Varsity Drag," *circa* late 1920s—Berle dressed in blazer and wide-bottomed trousers, Merman attired as a flapper.

By the time this hour-long show was over I found that I had been enjoying myself hugely. The telecast has borrowed virtually nothing from either radio or the movies and most of its material and format had been dredged out of a nostalgic past. There was only one thing missing.

"Hey," Jim said. "They didn't throw any custard pies tonight. Usually they throw pies or squirt somebody with a seltzer bottle."

"They threw ketchup," said his wife cheerfully. "That announcer threw a rubber meatball soaked in ketchup."

We watched for a couple of hours more. Then Al turned off the set and said, "Now comes the horrible moment. We see each other." We had been sitting in the dark for the entire evening.

"If you should have a feeding problem about the time your daughter's one," Al's wife was saying to my wife, "just let her watch Howdy Doody. Honestly, you know, you stuff the food in their little mouths and they don't even know they're eating."

"The trouble is getting them to bed," said Al. "The kids never want to go to bed any more."

"It's different from radio," Jim said. "The trouble with television is that all the shows can be considered kids' shows."

At this point I noticed we were all still sitting theatre fashion and that the three persons in the front row were twisting around awkwardly to talk to the three in the rear. This was adjusted somewhat, but for the remainder of the televisit something of this orderly theatre-row effect remained.

A couple of days later we returned to Toronto, a town were TV has yet to make its mark. In our apartment we have two small radios, one for the living room and one for the bedroom. We always thought they were pretty good to have around, but now, somehow, they've taken on a shoddy, almost nineteenth-century look. And when we twist the familiar knobs to tune in the familiar programs we feel rather as Henry Ford must have felt when, after taking the first whirl in his new horseless carriage, he was reluctantly forced to step back into a buggy and jolt off down the rutted road.

The Real War in Korea

An editorial from *Maclean's*, August 1, 1951

I N THE GATHERING DUSK of Korea's weary, bloody war, some things were clear and others still clouded. Certainly the Chinese, some of whom had Spanish-American War rifles and some of whom had only clubs, were moving back up the peninsula through villages roasted by our napalm and cities crumbled by our shells. The long lines of refugees were on the move again, and the rice was green only in those paddies that had survived the tread of marching feet. People were saying that we'd won the war.

But had we? Can you win a war in this tragic year of 1951 as you win a prizefight, by brute force in the fifteenth round?

To answer that question you've got to think back to what the war in Korea was all about. The initial objective was clear enough. It was, as Corporal Karry Dunphy of the Pats put it, "To resist aggression and all that sort of thing."

But surely this is a negative objective. What have we done in Korea that is positive? Sure, we're winning the old-fashioned war of brawn. But what about the newfangled war for men's minds? Have our actions in Korea made more friends for the Western world? Have we been able to convince the Koreans themselves that the phrase "our way of life" is something more than a slogan? Have we succeeded in selling our brand of democracy to this proud but unhappy race?

It is terrifying to report that the answer seems to be a flat, unqualified No!

If we had gone into Korea as an invading army of conquerors with the express purpose of humiliating the citizenry we could have done no worse than we have done in the name of the United Nations, the Western world and the democratic way of life.

I have some vivid memories of Korea, and many of them I wish I could forget. There is the memory of the old Korean who stumbled unloading a crate from a c-54 in Pusan, and of the little pipsqueak of a GI private who seized him by the faded coat lapels and shouted in his face, "You sonofabitch—if you do that again I'll punch you in the nose!" There is the memory of the wretched young man with his feet half eaten away, dying of gangrene and refused medical assistance by a succession of MOs because he was a Korean and didn't count. There is the memory of the Canadian private who emptied his Bren gun into a Korean grave, and the memory of the GI in the bus at Pusan who shouted loudly at a comrade about how much he hated the gooks—and the look on the face of the Korean bus driver who overheard him.

And always there is the memory of the crowded streets and the khaki river of soldiers flowing through them, many of them drunk, not a few of them arrogant, most of them with too much money to spend: a shifting montage of jeeps driving lickety-split down narrow lanes built for oxcarts, of voices cursing at the men who didn't move out of the way quickly, of faces leering and winking at the women, of hands dispensing the largesse of democracy—a piece of gum here, a piece of chocolate there—to the ragged hungry children begging on the curb.

There is above all the memory of the serious young Korean university graduate gazing solemnly and sadly at me across the remnants of a chow mein dinner that had cost the equivalent of two months' wages in Korea, and saying, "You Americans are so stupid. You have made prostitutes of our women and beggars of our children. Surely you are not going to make the mistake of thinking the Koreans love you?"

We were eating in a native restaurant because this young man could not eat with me in the officers' mess where all other war correspondents ate. Yet he was an accredited war correspondent, too, who wore the United Nations patch and uniform. But he was a Korean. Sorry.

Surely this illustrates the stupidity of our policy in Korea. We not only go out of our way to insult a group of Koreans, but we single out newspapermen—the very people who can interpret, or misinterpret, our way of life to their countrymen. In Korea we have given very little thought to anything but the military expediency of the moment, whether it encompasses the breaking of dikes on a paddy field or the tacit support of a government that is about as democratic as Franco's.

The great lesson of the new decade is already clear: that the ends of military expediency are not enough, that you can't burn away an idea with gasoline jelly but can only destroy it with a better idea. But this lesson hasn't been put into practice.

Our soldiers are sometimes referred to as "the ambassadors of democracy," but the painful fact is that they lack both training and talent for ambassadorship. They have been taught how to fight and they fight well. They have not been taught how to act and they act badly.

It seems to me there are two basic principles we must accept. One has already been suggested in these columns by Lionel Shapiro: that these days it is as important to teach a soldier how to get along with other people as it is to teach him the first and second stoppages on the Bren gun. This will take more than just the odd lecture and the occasional pamphlet. The idea needs to be drilled into the troops as surely as the manual of arms.

The other thing we must understand is that we all share some of the responsibility for what has happened to the Korean people and their land. No matter who is to blame, it is we who must rebuild this wretched country, for victory will rest in the end with the side that gains the trust of the people.

I believe this is the only practical aim we can follow in Korea if we are to come out of this business with our heads up and our ideals unsullied. The fact that it is also the moral course is perhaps an added argument in its favour. If we succeed with it we may yet make "our way of life" seem worthwhile to the people who've had it inflicted on them for the past twelve months.

Hindmarsh of the Star

From *Maclean's*, April 1, 1952

I N THE RANKS OF THAT VAST army of men who at one time
or another have worked for Harry Comfort Hindmarsh, the
presiding genius of Canada's largest newspapers, the *Toronto
Star* and *Star Weekly*, there circulates an intriguing but untrue story
that illustrates the awe in which he is held. The story has it that
Hindmarsh has sent for an old employee to tell him he is fired.
When the old man reaches Hindmarsh's office and hears the news
he thanks him profusely.

"What are you thanking me for?" growls Hindmarsh. "It's
Christmas Eve! You've been here forty years! Can't you see I'm
cutting you off without a cent?"

"I realize that, Mr. Hindmarsh," says the old retainer, tugging at
his forelock, "but when I first heard you had sent for me I thought
you were going to *sell* me."

In some sections of the newspaper fraternity, where Hindmarsh
is regarded as an ogre, this sort of thing is believed as gospel. In others where he is revered almost as a saint, it is dismissed as calumny.
Around this almost legendary figure, whose name and reputation
are inseparably enmeshed with the newspapers he controls, the
winds of controversy blow with gale force. But if an occasional gust
disturbs the impassive calm with which, from the pinnacle of his
office, he views the world around him, he does not show it.

In his forty-two years at the *Star*, in which he has risen from cub
reporter to president, Harry Hindmarsh has neither answered his
critics nor coddled his admirers. His detachment is such that he has
never publicly displayed any of those passions of hate, love, anger,
frustration, reverence and awe that he has inspired in others and on
which the *Star* itself has thrived for half a century.

Even to the closest members of his staff he is an unknown quan-
tity, a creature of myth and fable, whose own picture has appeared

only once in his newspaper. Few men know him well. He has seldom called anyone who works for him by his first name. He is "Mister" to all; all are "Mister" to him. When he eats in the restaurant below his office he eats alone, a little before the rush hour, a silent figure at an empty table.

There are few neutral opinions about this huge, brooding man of sixty-five with the small, heavy-lidded eyes, the close-cropped white hair, and the plodding gait. He is still held in awe by most. Of the fifty-five newspapermen and former newspapermen interviewed during the gathering of material for this article, fewer than half a dozen would allow themselves to be quoted directly about him. But whether they respect or hate him, almost all newsmen who have crossed his path are secure in one opinion: he is the greatest editor they have ever worked for.

Under Hindmarsh's peculiar genius, the *Toronto Star* has gained its reputation for a relentless coverage of the news unequalled anywhere, as well as for some of the most erratic journalism extant. Money is no object to him, distance no obstacle. Reporters have flown off to Persia on a whim or phoned Montevideo on a hunch. Under his aegis *Star* men have hired everything from tugboats to airliners to get the news. One man hired a railway train and returned to the office aghast at what he had done. But Hindmarsh raised his salary ten dollars a week.

Many have hated his guts. One reporter tried to kill him with a foot-long pair of copy shears. Hindmarsh at no time changed expression or took his hands from his pockets as underlings leapt to his rescue. Ernest Hemingway wanted to punch him in the nose. When the Star Building was erected on King Street in 1929, one wag suggested that a motto be carved around it: Every Man for Himself and the Devil Take the Hindmarsh.

But *Star* reporters have always worked for him like beavers. "You really live a story with the Big Guy," one ex-staffer recalls. "When a hot story was breaking he'd come out of his office to take control and a sort of aura would form around him." In moments of crisis he is the calmest man on the floor. As managing editor he used to deliver in his deep, slow voice an unending series of instructions that might dispatch a dozen reporters to a key spot, some on the dead run. But he himself never spoke above a low, conversational level. "It was like joining a religious order," another old reporter says. "When you worked for Hindmarsh you couldn't help yourself: you just lived, ate and breathed that goddam *Star*."

The *Star*'s greatest scoop occurred just after Hindmarsh became managing editor in 1928, and it illustrates the lengths his men went to to get the news for him. The German aircraft *Bremen* had crash-landed off the Labrador coast after history's first successful east-west crossing of the Atlantic. Bush pilot Duke Schiller was expected to return to Lake St. Agnes in Quebec with first news and pictures of the event. It was the greatest story since Lindbergh, and the press of the continent dashed to the lake to meet him.

But the *Star* was ahead of them all. Before Schiller got away to Labrador it reached him with an offer of $7,000 for his story. To get his men to Lake St. Agnes at once, Hindmarsh hired a special train. The *Star* reporters fought off six American newsmen who tried to climb aboard. Then at Murray Bay, the nearest telegraph outlet, they tied up the line by ordering the operator to wire a copy of the *New Republic* back to the office.

Schiller finally flew in carrying one precious roll of film. For a single picture a New York tabloid was later to offer $20,000. An American reporter got the film first, but Fred Griffin of the *Star* seized him and physically tore it away. He put the film on a *Star* plane, which flew off for civilization. The plane was forced down at Quebec. The *Star* hired a train to speed the film to Montreal. At Montreal it was printed, and Roy Greenaway of the *Star* hired a taxi to drive the 350 miles to Toronto. The taxi drove at sixty miles an hour through a raging blizzard. At one point the steering wheel came off. Greenaway and the driver rammed it on. At another point the taxi hit an oncoming car.

"We're from the *Star*," cried Greenaway.

"It's all right," said the other driver. "I'm a friend of Mr. Atkinson [the *Star* publisher]."

Shortly before 11 a.m. the pictures arrived at the *Star*. They appeared on the paper's front page that day, giving it a twenty-four-hour beat on every paper in the world.

Hindmarsh's news imagination often nudges the bizarre. In July 1926, fifteen youths were plunged into Balsam Lake in northern Ontario, when their war canoe capsized. Eleven drowned. Hindmarsh's reaction was immediate. "Reconstruct the tragedy," he said to the first reporter back from the scene. Dutifully, thirteen reporters went out, hired a war canoe, paddled it into Lake Ontario, capsized it and plunged into the icy waters while photographers snapped the scene.

"News," Hindmarsh has said, "is the greatest gamble in the world." Once he sent Gregory Clark and photographer Norman James to British Columbia with orders to get a story—any story. They ran into a major air crash and came up with exclusive interviews with the survivors. He has never had much sense of geography. One reporter remembers being in New Orleans on a story. He got a call from the *Star*. "Hop up to Chicago." In vain he protested it would be cheaper and swifter to send a man from the office.

Many of the *Star*'s great stories have been the result of Hindmarsh's analytical mind. Once he sent a reporter to cover the murder of three little boys who had been shot in their sleep by their twelve-year-old sister. He was not satisfied with the reporter's story. "There's something behind this," he said. Further digging revealed the girl had been fascinated by her father shooting pigs through the eyes. She had re-enacted the scene in her sleep. It was another Hindmarsh scoop.

Hindmarsh's "hunger to know what is happening," as one of his reporters calls it, his "childlike wonderment in the little things" is reflected in the heavily scrawled suggestions on *Star* galley proofs, which he reads carefully. His attention to small detail has always been a source of wonder. He gives his men explicit instructions on what to do, where to go, what questions to ask. During the kidnapping of brewer John Labatt, when Toronto was being combed for suspects, one *Star* man was assigned simply to stand across from the

Royal York Hotel until 4 a.m. and note whether anyone who looked like a gangster walked in the side door.

Hindmarsh has always felt that a picture is worth ten thousand words. Reporters ransack the homes of the slain to get photos of the victim. One *Star* reporter was told by the widow of a man impaled on a picket fence that there was only one available photo of the victim, showing him as a child. "It's all right," said the reporter cheerfully, "we'll paint a moustache on."

Hindmarsh is so insistent on harsh black-and-white contrast in his pictures that photographers have carried rolled-up bed sheets with them to get the stark, simple backgrounds he likes. He also insists that the faces of the subjects show. A *Star* photographer once took a touching photo of a returned soldier, his face buried in the bosom of his two little girls. It won prizes, but the *Star* wouldn't use it: you couldn't see any faces.

Hindmarsh chooses pictures with the speed of light from the stacks set before him. He chooses the sugary *Star Weekly* cover paintings in similar fashion. One reporter once brought him a painting as a Christmas present. Hindmarsh thought it was for the *Weekly*. "Take it away!" he rumbled after a swift glance.

At one point the *Weekly* decided to run reproductions in colour of famous paintings. Hindmarsh selected a man to choose them. "But Mr. Hindmarsh," the reporter protested, "I know absolutely nothing about art."

"Fine," said Hindmarsh.

"But there's something else," the reported added. "I'm colour-blind."

"Excellent!" boomed Hindmarsh. "You're the man."

This contempt for the public was apparent in another Hindmarsh innovation—the symposium. Reporters would select dozens of names at random from the phone book and ask such questions as "Do men make more fuss over pain than women?" The paper found this a useful tool in editorial campaigns. "Hindmarsh trained us to ring up people and get them to say, 'Yes, you are quite right,'" one former symposium expert recalls. Last summer the *Star* attacked the Toronto City Council through the symposium technique. One man told a reporter he thought the council was inept. "That's the exact word Mr. Hindmarsh wants us to use," said the reporter gleefully.

Hindmarsh's disdain for the public has been matched by a cavalier attitude toward the great byline writers who have worked for him. He was once asked why men like Ernest Hemingway, Morley Callaghan, Pierre Van Paassen, Gordon Sinclair, Gregory Clark, Jimmy Frise and Matthew Halton had all left his employ. "They all got too big for their britches," Hindmarsh said.

Two of the greatest legends surrounding Hindmarsh concern the departures of Hemingway and Van Paassen. Hemingway worked for the *Star* between 1920 and 1923, and there are several versions of the reasons for his departure.

The Gordon Sinclair, or popular, version is that Hemingway, after returning from Spain, was assigned to write a promotion story on a white peacock and refused in a spectacular resignation that, when pasted on the notice board, measured five feet in length.

The J. Herbert Cranston, or authorized, version differs. Cranston, a former *Star Weekly* editor who knew Hemingway well, says that Hemingway had received some documents from an Italian diplomat he was interviewing that he promised faithfully to return. When he found that Hindmarsh had flung the papers in the wastebasket he quit.

The Hindmarsh version is that Hemingway was sent to northern Ontario to cover a labour dispute. His dispatches so favoured the strikers that Hindmarsh wired him to start reporting the news. Hemingway returned in high dudgeon, stormed into Hindmarsh's office, gave him a half-hour tongue-lashing, and then quit.

There is probably some truth in all three versions. Hemingway seems to have quit over a variety of things. He did post a long critique of the *Star* on the notice board, and he certainly hated Hindmarsh. "Working for him was like being in the Prussian army under a rather poor general," he once said. At one time he planned to write a novel about Hindmarsh to be called *The Son-in-Law*

(Hindmarsh had married the daughter of *Star* owner Joseph Atkinson). Years after he quit the *Star* he wrote to the struggling Newspaper Guild announcing that he was enclosing a cheque for one hundred dollars "to beat Hindmarsh." There followed four pages or so of comment and then a final sentence: "On second thought I'm making it two hundred."

The popular legend about Van Paassen is that Hindmarsh, on being told by two Catholic priests that the correspondent was covering the Spanish war from a Paris apartment, secretly got on a boat, went to Paris, walked in on Van Paassen, said two words, "You're fired!" got back on the boat and came home. Actually, though Hindmarsh did go secretly to Paris he didn't see Van Paassen. On his return he fired him by letter, giving no reason, but enclosing a cheque for one thousand dollars. Van Paassen's dispatches, which had been markedly anticlerical, disappeared from the *Star*. Van Paassen still regards the whole affair with bewilderment. *Star* men, he says, kept popping up wherever he went while he was in the paper's employ, apparently checking up on him. Once he came out of Ethiopia and was accosted by a missionary who said, "I'm a friend of H.C. Hindmarsh. Have you *really* been in Ethiopia?"

When Hindmarsh considered that one of his "prima donnas," as he called them, had grown too big for his britches he brought him down a peg. Footloose Gordon Sinclair, back from a world tour, found himself writing obits. Hemingway, back from Spain, Greece and Turkey, was hauled out of bed at 4.30 a.m. to cover minor fires. When the late and great Fred Griffin, a fiery Irishman, grew temperamental, Hindmarsh chopped his salary.

"Hindmarsh is always sympathetic to someone in trouble," Sinclair said the other day, "but he doesn't respect strength."

A shy youth who became a big man physically and financially, Hindmarsh has a gruffly paternal attitude to the men who work for him. To the weak ones he is like a father, half indulgent, half stern. There are numerous instances of *Star* reporters whom Hindmarsh has bailed out of debt. It is his custom to have all the man's bills brought to him. He totals them carefully, checks to make sure there are no more, then signs a cheque for the entire sum. His only stipulation is that the man involved keep quiet about it. Hindmarsh has sent sickly wives of staffers to Arizona and paid for their children's operations. One woman prays for him every night because he saved her husband from alcoholism and took him back on the paper.

But he insists on doing things his way. When *Star* men get sick they often find Hindmarsh selecting the doctor and prescribing the treatment. Once he called in Morley Callaghan and told him in a fatherly way that he had been smoking too much and staying up late at nights.

"But you're *wrong*, Mr. Hindmarsh!" said Callaghan emphatically.

"You're fired!" rumbled Hindmarsh, who doesn't like to be told he's wrong.

Callaghan was fired five times from the *Star* but never actually stopped work. "The trouble with you, Mr. Callaghan," Hindmarsh said to him once, "is you've never been broken to harness."

When Matthew Halton wanted to write a book, Hindmarsh, who felt that a man's every waking moment should be devoted to the *Star*, refused him permission. Halton indicated he would anyhow and was fired. Then Hindmarsh made him a present of $10,000 and agreed to buy an article a week from him at a sum that exactly equalled his staff salary.

It was precisely this dominant attitude that made the *Star* the dominant paper in the news field. Hindmarsh has never allowed anyone—man or newspaper—to get the better of him. When George McCullagh bought the *Telegram* and announced he would "push that Communistic rag [the *Star*] off its pedestal," the *Telegram* began to beat the drums for a serialization of Dickens's *Life of Christ*, an old circulation-getter that the *Star* itself had published decades before. Hindmarsh promptly called in a reporter. "Get me a life of Christ by 5 p.m.," he said in the same slow voice in which he had once told a city editor to "get me an elephant." The reporter got a life of Christ and the *Star* got it into print a full day before its rival. Since then its circulation has risen steadily. The *Telegram*'s hasn't budged.

The sharp edges of Hindmarsh's many-sided personality have left their mark on everything with which he comes into contact. The desire to dominate, the almost fanatic attention to detail, the insatiable and childlike curiosity have all had their effect on his family, his private life, the people who work for him, the political party he supports, the church he goes to and the town in which he lives.

It is impossible to divorce his private existence from his newspaper, for the two are impossibly tangled. He lives at Oakville, some thirty miles along the lake from Toronto, and Oakville to the *Star* is the most important small town in Canada. It chronicles the town's events in minute detail. When British American Oil began building a refinery near the Hindmarsh home, *Star* reporters combed the area gathering critical opinions charging that it would pollute the beaches.

Hindmarsh is a member of St. John's United Church, Oakville. Once when the church was looking for a new minister, teams of *Star* reporters combed the province for a likely candidate. The teams were usually three strong: a reporter, his wife and a shorthand man. The shorthand man took down the minister's sermon verbatim. The reporter wrote a memo on his appearance and popularity. The reporter's wife wrote a memo on the minister's wife. From this, the new man was chosen.

When Hindmarsh became president of the Oakville Golf Club, he called in some of his executive staff and urged that they take things easier. "Get out in the fresh air. Play golf!" said Hindmarsh. They dutifully swelled the membership of the Oakville Club. One or two actually attempted to play golf. In their absence a big story broke. A memo from Hindmarsh told them to stay at their posts from then on.

Many old-time reporters have memories of curious assignments involving homework problems for Hindmarsh's four children. One man had to comb through all English exam papers of the Oakville high school for a decade and find out what six essay topics were assigned most frequently. He then had to prepare essays on all topics, written in the style of a teenage girl. These were for the "guidance" of one of Hindmarsh's daughters who was having trouble with the subject. Hindmarsh went over this homework as carefully as he did *Star* galley proofs. Sometimes he would call in a second reporter and ask for a rewrite.

He is nothing if not meticulous. One reporter was called in to select a hired man for the Hindmarsh home. He interviewed sixty-three prospects before he got the right one. Once, planning a vacation to the Bahamas, Hindmarsh had a reporter check the average temperatures for a week. One evening Hindmarsh visited the new home of his son-in-law Ab Fallon. He discovered one of the bookcases only partially full. He produced a tape and measured the gap. Next day he sent down to the *Star* library for four feet eight inches of books.

He takes a microscopic interest in the details of his reporters' private lives. One reporter sent him a memo announcing he was to be married. He got back four closely typed pages from Hindmarsh giving detailed advice on how to start a home: the exact brand of refrigerator to buy, the kind of furnace to install, and the section of the city in which to settle.

"He warms his hands over the fires of other people's lives," a former employee has said of him. "He lives vicariously in the lives of his reporters," another comments. Certainly Hindmarsh, who sends people to the ends of the earth, seldom stirs from the steady day-to-day routine that takes him from home to office and back again. Such is his isolation from the world and the men around him that few know his history or background. Perhaps this is purposeful. One reporter was so terrified of Hindmarsh he was physically unable to speak to him. Then one day he was told Hindmarsh's nickname at school had been Dogmeat. This regained him his voice.

Hindmarsh is a big man who weighs 220 pounds, stands six feet three inches and walks without swinging his arms. Many of his staff believe he is German in background, perhaps because he looks like

Bismarck without the moustache. Others are certain that he was a foundling or a stepchild. Neither belief is true. He was born of Canadian parents in Missouri, the son of Harry Frank Hindmarsh, a telegrapher. His father's people came from Margate, England. His mother's family, the Comforts, were from New England.

The father impulse is strong within him possibly because he never knew his own father. Hindmarsh keeps his own family closely around him on his twenty-two-acre estate. One son and two sons-in-law work at the *Star* and live nearby him along with twelve of his fourteen grandchildren. Only his eldest boy, John, rebelled, quit the newspaper and went off farming by himself. It was a blow to his father.

Hindmarsh's own father died young of tuberculosis. All his life Hindmarsh, who was only two at the time, has lived in the shadow of this. He has a fear of chest colds and will go home at once at the sign of a sore throat. The *Star* has long advocated compulsory x-ray examinations for TB. Hindmarsh has a hypochondriac's interest in doctors and diagnosis. New medical discoveries fascinate him, and the *Star* covers them with gusto. (It got the first newspaper story on Banting's discovery of insulin.) Hindmarsh always asks to see the complete reports of medical conventions, and he sends men about the country on the hunt for new miracle cures. He is as careful about the ailments of his staff as he is about his own weight and diet. He once ordered a rotund reporter to lose weight and to make sure had him weighed daily on the scales in the circulation department.

Hindmarsh's mother was a strong-willed woman with a fierce, possessive love for her boy. After her husband's death she moved back to her former home of St. Thomas, Ontario, where her father, Hiram Comfort, a woollens merchant, was the richest man in town. She inherited his wealth and used some of it to indulge her son. (His was the finest cornet in the collegiate band.) Years later when Hindmarsh moved to Toronto she moved with him. She couldn't bear to see him marry. When his betrothal was announced she conscientiously redecorated the house for his bride. The night before the wedding she fled to California.

In her later years she unaccountably took to drink, and this too had its effect on her son. Around the *Star* there is a saying that if you take one drink, you're fired; if you're a hopeless alcoholic, your job is secure. All his life Hindmarsh has tried to save his men from drink. Homewood Sanitarium in Guelph and Shadowbrook in Toronto have been called Star Annexes. At present five *Star* reporters are taking daily Antabuse treatments. Hindmarsh himself has had only one drink in his life: once when he caught cold he took desperate measures and accepted a glass of whisky.

In St. Thomas, Hindmarsh, living alone with his mother, grew up a shy and somewhat lonely boy. Some of the shyness is still in him and partially explains his remoteness from others. He was fond of cats, dogs and music and played the violin, bugle and cornet. He was taunted for playing with girls, and this his pride could not stand. He lay in wait for one girl and gave her a thrashing. He still loves music and recently instituted the *Star* hour of recorded music, which runs 365 days a year on a Toronto station. Hindmarsh personally selects it himself, mainly from pieces he remembers as a boy. The program is rehearsed and played daily into his office loudspeaker.

At the University of Toronto he became a leading figure on the campus. In his sophomore year, the third-year students warred with his class. Hindmarsh refused to let them get the better of him and led his fellow students in an attack on the third-years, trapping them in a ravine, daubing them with ink and shoe polish and shaving their heads. He and Norman Lambert, now a senator, were suspended for two weeks as a result. He became a successful debater, president of the History Club, vice-president of his class, a member of the Literary and Scientific Executive and editor of the *Varsity*. Some of his classmates were later to provide grist for the *Star* mill. Two were hanged for murder, one killed himself, one absconded with a client's funds and one, Vincent Massey, became Governor General.

The quotation underneath his picture in the university yearbook would baffle many a *Star* reporter today. "For this," it read, "was the gentlest man and the meekest that ever sat in hall among ladies."

Hindmarsh had taken a year out to work on the *Detroit News*. His first assignment was an interview with a gypsy king. The king wouldn't talk until Hindmarsh paid his daughter a quarter. Since then he has never hesitated to spend money to get exclusive stories. He transformed the *Varsity* from a literary weekly to a daily paper, complete with big pictures on the front page, in which can dimly be recognized the techniques he was later to perfect. The power of the Press fascinated him. "Be he a veritable pygmy," he wrote. "the newspaperman may quiz the grandest minion of the law with impunity. Mention the magic word 'reporter' and this dweller on Olympus becomes as other men are."

On graduation he went to work for the *Globe*. Once when a sensitive reporter balked at covering a hanging, Hindmarsh volunteered. On the gallows the prisoner confessed to two more murders. After he dropped, Hindmarsh leaned over the trap and watched fascinated as his toes and fingers twitched their last. Then he rushed below to watch the body cut down. His report was so enthusiastic that Toronto reporters have ever since been barred from covering hangings.

Hindmarsh joined the *Star* in December 1911. Two years later, at twenty-six, he was city editor. In 1915, Joe Atkinson, disturbed at the young men flocking about his daughter Ruth, remarked that "next Sunday I'll bring a *real* man out." The man was Hindmarsh. Ruth rebuffed him at first: she felt her father was thrusting him at her. But Hindmarsh courted her ardently. Eventually they married and have had a close and happy married life. Atkinson told Hindmarsh to find another job; he didn't want a son-in-law on the *Star*. Then he changed his mind. Hindmarsh stayed on. For more than thirty years he was literally at Atkinson's beck and call.

The gentlest man and the meekest was now having the iron boiled into his soul by John R. Bone, the *Star*'s scholarly looking but tough managing editor. Bone looked like an elderly Arrow collar man with his pince-nez and slicked-down hair, but his appearance belied him. The picture that dominated the wall of his office was anything but scholarly: a huge copy of a New York tabloid's famous photo of Ruth Snyder dying in the electric chair. He rode Hindmarsh hard. When he died in 1928, the new managing editor's character was cast in a permanent mould.

He was now, to all intents and purposes, the dominant personality on the dominant newspaper in Canada. But there was one man he could never dominate, and that was his father-in-law. Atkinson was always as close as the buzzer on Hindmarsh's desk, and before the shrill, carping tones of the publisher, the big man was submissive. He complied promptly with Atkinson's demands, which often meant stopping the presses. But he accepted these rebukes with the same impassive spirit that has characterized his career. Sometimes, after berating an underling, he would remark, in his slow way, "Well, he's had his for today; we all get our share of that." In the hours off the paper he had little social life. He didn't like the embarrassment of Atkinson tracking him down for an impromptu conference wherever he might be.

The greatest division between him and his father-in-law was over money. Hindmarsh, brought up in comparative luxury, was a spender. Atkinson, who went to work for a living at fourteen, was a saver. When Hindmarsh plunged on a big story, Atkinson made him recoup next month. To do so he had to fire men and cut salaries. A proud man, he took the brunt on his own shoulders. "If you have something unpleasant to do, do it at once," he has said. In 1930 he gave thirteen men their notice on Christmas Eve. It was to plague him for years. Each Yuletide a group of ex-employees would send him a Merry Christmas telegram, collect.

But a greater blow came in 1948. Unknown to Hindmarsh, the *Star*'s great writer-and-artist team of Gregory Clark and Jim Frise had decided to go to work for the Montreal *Standard*. Their names and faces were familiar to millions through their Greg-and-Jim feature in the *Weekly*. Their whole lives had been bound up with the paper.

On the train back from Montreal one October evening, the two old retainers sat glumly. The die had been cast: they were leaving the old sheet. Finally Frise broke the silence. "Greg," he said, "somebody has got to tell Hindmarsh."

"I suppose so," said Clark.

After another silence, Frise spoke again. "Would you tell him, Greg?" he asked.

"Okay, Jim," said Clark.

More gloomy silence. Finally Frise spoke. "Greg?"

"Yes, Jim?"

"Tell him on Christmas Eve."

Today, the buzzer no longer sounds in Hindmarsh's office. Last winter he stunned the organizers of a Community Chest cocktail party for the Press by accepting an invitation that for years he had ignored. He and his wife arrived and drank ginger ale. He has taken to appearing at other functions as well. But he turned down, rather wistfully, a testimonial dinner that a group of ex-staffers wanted to give him.

His staff, organized by the Newspaper Guild immediately after Atkinson's death, is now the best paid in Canada. Experienced reporters get upwards of $100 for a 37½-hour week, plus overtime. "It's the best thing that ever happened to the *Star*," Hindmarsh says today.

The raffish crew who passed by the score through the *Star*'s office has been replaced by serious young men in double-breasted suits and horn-rimmed spectacles. Hindmarsh believes in hiring only university men, preferably editors of the *Varsity* or graduates of journalism faculties. "The cult of the prima donna is dead," he says.

He still occupies the same office, just off the editorial rooms. Like his character, it is a strange blend of the spartan and the sentimental. The walls are bare of pictures except for one of his old friend Senator Lambert and one of the Star Building. The office is furnished with the original chairs and chandelier that Joseph Atkinson started his career with. On his desk, with a clock, two statuettes of dogs and a humidor filled with the Bachelor cigars he constantly smokes, is an inkstand made from the original stone that went into the Star Building. In it is a huge pen, a foot long, which holds an entire bottle of ink and has awed *Star* reporters for almost forty years. It was given him by his mother when he first became city editor.

In this redoubt he spends the greater part of his waking day. "He only feels secure in his office," an acquaintance says. He arrives at nine and begins sending out memos with the huge, interlocking initials "HCH," which are looked on as law at the *Star*. He reads everything that goes into the paper. Nothing is purchased for the *Star Weekly*, no picture chosen without his okay. Indeed, the *Weekly* has no editor-in-chief other than Hindmarsh. He even chooses the sweaters sent out to poor children by the Star Santa Claus Fund. Social workers have occasionally differed with him on this score but, as always, the big man is adamant. During the recent Royal Tour he was down at the office by 5 or 6 a.m. to choose the day's pictures and put them on the engraver's enlarger himself.

And yet he still does not exercise supreme control over the paper that has been his life. The ghost of Atkinson still haunts the *Star*. Hindmarsh is president of the Star Publishing Company charged with "supervising the carrying out" of the decisions of the board of five directors that Atkinson's will set up to govern the paper. Hindmarsh is one director. The others are Frederick Tait, business manager, Alex Stark, *Star* lawyer, young Joe Atkinson and Ruth Atkinson Hindmarsh. All but Mrs. Hindmarsh, who serves without a fee, draw an annual $25,000 in salary.

The *Star* itself is owned by the Atkinson Charitable Foundation, which to date has distributed $336,867 to some forty-two worthy causes, mainly research foundations, universities and hospitals. Atkinson conceived the idea in 1927 after Hindmarsh asked him not to leave his money to the Hindmarsh youngsters for fear it might spoil them. The foundation was set up in 1942 but didn't operate extensively until Atkinson died. Its formation has been as controversial as the man who created it. The retroactive Charitable Gifts Act passed by the Ontario Conservative government after Atkinson's death seems to be aimed directly at the Liberal *Star*. Under its terms the foundation must sell 90 percent of the *Star* by 1956.

48

In the law, Harry Hindmarsh faces the greatest battle of his career. Freed from Atkinson's restraining hand, he has brought the full force of the *Star* to bear upon it. During the Ontario election campaigns the *Star* has smote the Leslie Frost Conservative government, which passed the Gifts Act, hip and thigh. At the peak of election campaigns the paper has carried little else but political news dominated by flaring headlines and full-page photographs, frankly pro-Liberal. Hindmarsh has written the most controversial headlines himself.

One was a frank appeal to the voters:

**Support hospital plan
and insure your health
ELECT WALTER THOMSON**

Another read simply "May be your mother—Thomson," and was accompanied by the greatest foofaraw of pictures and political eulogy yet seen in Canadian journalism. The *Star* somehow contrived to give the impression that the Conservative government was driving old ladies into insane asylums.

Since Atkinson's death *Star* readers and reporters have become resigned to this sort of thing. During the federal election, which the *Star* covered with fifty reporters and photographers, Hindmarsh wrote another headline in the *Star*'s clipped style, which read:

**Keep Canada British
Destroy Drew's Houde
God Save the King**

The final line was too much for Alex Stark, a staunch Baptist who felt it was vaguely blasphemous and perhaps unpatriotic as well. He persuaded Hindmarsh to change it to Vote St. Laurent in the second edition. St. Laurent won the federal election, and Hindmarsh has felt ever since that the *Star* was largely responsible. He has less to say about the provincial results. The Liberals elected only seven men, and Walter Thomson, their leader, was himself beaten. This débâcle was blamed on the *Star* by almost everybody. The paper's circulation declined by seven thousand for the first time in the peak month of December. If Hindmarsh was shaken by the result, he did not betray it. His explanation for his paper's wild behaviour was simple enough. And in it was echoed something of the personality of the youth who refused to let the third-year gang get the better of him and the man who wouldn't be dominated by prima donnas. Some people, Hindmarsh said, had the idea that the *Star* was afraid of the Conservative government of Ontario because it hadn't been attacking it as violently as it had when George Drew was premier. In the election campaign he wanted to make one thing clear: the *Star* did not support the government that passed the Act designed to crush it. The *Star* was afraid of no one.

In this, at least, Harry Hindmarsh, the gentlest man and the meekest, succeeded.

La Chasse

From *Mayfair*, October 1953

THIS IS AN ACCOUNT of an expedition I recently made into the eighteenth century through the good offices of a friend with diplomatic connections. The place: the little village of Chantilly, France. The time: early November. The occasion: the opening of the most exclusive hunt in all France, presided over by the Marquis de Roualle.

Every year, for God knows how many centuries, the Roualle dynasty has been stage-managing the various ancient ceremonies that have to do with the pursuit of noble stags by men in brocaded coats on horseback. *La chasse* is the symbol of all that is traditional in France, or, if you want to be nasty about it—all that is decadent. It involves the "best" families, on horseback, the cream of French society and the diplomatic corps in shiny, chauffeur-driven automobiles, and the local townspeople on bicycles.

Our day began, of all places, in church, in one of those graceful Gothic monuments to an earlier age when men of unlimited faith stretched tall spires toward the heavens in architectural supplication. Here, beneath a delicate lacework of vaulted stone, the ceremony of blessing the hunt took place. The marquis himself met us at the door and the marquise took us to our seats, which were reserved, as in a theatre. The marquis is a big man with clear, cold eyes of icy blue, hair that was once jet and is now silver-grey, and the fine regular features one associates with the aristocracy. He was wearing the costume of the hunt—the beautifully tailored breeches, the beautifully polished boots, the dark blue coat with the crossed horns woven in gold brocade on the lapels, the bright silver scabbard at his belt. The marquise is a pert little woman with lips that turn up and small eyes that perpetually twinkle in the French manner. She was wearing a simple blue suit and a dark blue hat low over one eye.

Around us, crowded into the narrow pews, were stationed the witnesses to the events of the day. The grey morning light, filtering through the slender windows, cast its soft halo over the dark morning coats, the polished Sam Brownes, the glinting rank badges of the attachés, the well-scrubbed craniums of the elder statesmen. The perfume of evergreens with which the chancel was garlanded lay heavy in the air, and upon the whole company was levelled the glassy gaze of half a dozen mounted stags' heads.

From the side a group of little choirboys in white and scarlet trooped in like sheep, with their shepherd, a bent old man in a cocked hat and dusty epaulettes, leading the way to the centre of the choir. Now from the Gothic heights behind us there suddenly blared a fanfare of horns. High in the choir loft were huntsmen sounding their call, and in through the great doors came more huntsmen, and some huntswomen, in the scarlet or blue of their particular hunt, mounting into the seats of the choir, the hunters in scarlet on one side, the hunters in blue facing. In the centre, between the little boys, stood a single beagle, with the single letter "R" shaved into the hair on his ribs. He neither moved nor twitched nor quivered.

The service began. The huntsmen in the loft again sounded their horns, the choirboys sang, a priest prayed, another made a short sermon in French regarding the glories of the chase. In the choir, the aristocratic faces inclined slightly toward him in silent agreement. Here were the features of the blooded French: the hair jet-black, the nose straight as a ruler, the nostrils sensitive, the moustaches clipped, the lips pursed, the chin firm as granite. Here was the head held high, the back straight, the eyes so clear they seemed to be unseeing. The women, who were beautiful with a cold, passionless beauty, wore their tailored tunics like men. But one, out of the corner of her eye, kept watching with warmth and feeling her two small children in the second pew.

The service ended, the horns sounded, the hunters withdrew, the multitude followed. We circled round the church and through a forest of Ionic and Corinthian pillars, burst into a circular amphitheatre from which sprouted the wings of what I took to be a palace but which were, in reality, the stables of the Marquis de Roualle. In this baroque setting a second service took place. The flock of choirboys appeared through the archway, the hunters sounded their horns and a priest blessed the swarm of squirming hounds (each marked with the shaved "R") and the group of passive horses.

This done, the multitude wandered forward, through a Romanesque archway that was crumbling slightly, and there, spread out before us, stretched the domain of the Roualles. A sere heath sloped gently down for a quarter of a mile to a delicate forest that stretched off as far as we could see into the grey autumn haze. Down on the left, near the forest's edge, squatted a fairytale palace, complete with towers and minarets and all the rococo accessories of its time. The shaved hedgerows of a formal garden arched outwards from it, and a beautifully manicured lake embraced it gently. There was, I think, a small drawbridge and certainly a magnificent stone entranceway and an intricately wrought iron gate.

But the horns were sounding again. Past us in stately procession moved the mounted hunters, acknowledging the greetings of the crowd, moving without hurry toward the woods beyond. The throng broke for the parked cars, the cars disentangled themselves from each other, the townspeople threaded in and out between them on their cycles and the whole gave pursuit. A quarter of a mile farther on everyone stopped again. The hunters got off their horses, the marquis talked to the marquise, walked to his station wagon and changed his coat. The hounds bayed and strained at their leashes. The hunters remounted and headed down a long forest avenue. The cars all started up at once and scuttled off down another road. I rode in a low black car with an ambassadorial flag flying from the fender.

We came to a clearing in the forest. The cars entered from one direction and presently the hunters came down their long avenue, still at a stately walk, from another. From this clearing in the private forest of the Marquis de Roualle, the avenues of trees stretched off, like the rays of the sun, in all directions, straight as a shaft of light. The yellow leaves still clung to the brittle branches, which arched high across the avenues like the Gothic windows in the church we had left.

Now dogs, hunters, people, cars and bicycles were jammed together in the clearing. Diplomats in black berets began to produce flagons of wine and heavy cheese sandwiches. Their wives produced thin-stemmed glasses of wine and delicate little sandwiches. Hunters came and went on horseback. Several young women in black riding-habits and veils, with features of porcelain, floated past on sidesaddle. I was beginning to experience the same feeling of confusion that a Frenchman might feel at a Grey Cup football final.

A bulky man in a black beret and wearing great horn-rimmed spectacles was introduced. He was the ambassador to somewhere or from somewhere, a genial man with a little English and a good deal of French.

"You have the principle of *la chasse*?" he asked.

"I do not comprehend too well the sport," I told him.

"I will enlighten you, *alors*. They go now, *les chasseurs*, to see a group of animals. I believe they know in advance where they are. On sighting these beasts, they signal to the others with the horns. Then they seek to detach from the main body a particularly fine specimen of a stag. This is most difficult, you understand, because the stag does not always wish for this. Once the stag is separated from his companions the hunters give chase with the dogs. The animal eludes them. But the hunters do not despair. When one has seen him he sounds upon the horn as a signal to his comrades. They gallop to the spot and the chase continues. All day they chase and we follow in the cars to watch. Naturally they do not always chase too hard for they do not wish to capture their quarry too soon."

I was beginning to get hungry, for it was now one o'clock and as yet the hunt had not really begun. My friends suggested we seek out a small bistro in a nearby village where hunting could be done quietly and without undue exertion. But first we had to escape from the forest. As the low little car slipped down the avenues, past the gesticulating townspeople on their bicycles, red-coated men and women on horseback began to pop out in front of us. Uniformed men, apparently placed there for the purpose, halted us. Ahead, the perfectly rigid figure of a hunter on horseback sat still as death in profile across the roadway. Somewhere through the trees there floated the ghostly call of the horn. The hunter trotted off the road and down one of the innumerable pathways that spiderweb the woods. Our car moved on.

We found our bistro. We ate steak chateaubriand and drank Nuit St-Georges '45. Across from us sat a middle-aged couple at a table for four. Two of the four seats were occupied by a pair of handsome black poodles, who sat at their places as rigidly as the huntsmen on the horses.

The proprietor of the bistro collected rare books. He brought some first editions down for us to look at. They were thick little books with heavy, brittle, embossed paper, delicately wrought covers and raised backings. Like the ritual we had watched that morning they were a link with another age, when men took a century to raise a church spire, when each book was wrought as carefully as a piece of sculpture, and red-coated horsemen cantered through private forests chasing a single stag according to a careful set of rules.

It was dusk when we rejoined the milling group in the forest. Again we were in a clearing, with long avenues radiating from it like the spokes of a wheel. It might have been the same one, but there were many. The spectators had formed a tight circle from whose centre there rose the melancholy sound of a dozen horns played in unison. We had missed the kill. Already the fallen stag had been carefully dismembered—the hoofs and horns preserved, the meat distributed. What was left was the property of the dogs.

We pushed our way to the forefront. In the centre of the tightly pressed circle were the hounds. They were eating something, tearing and rending and tossing their heads as they cracked the bones between their teeth. On the ground was a shapeless mass of scarlet flesh, and it was at this horror that the hounds were tearing while the light grew dim and the horns of the hunters wailed out through the forest.

They stood, the hunters, in three tight groups around their grisly prey, the groups forming the three apexes of an equilateral triangle: one group in scarlet coats, one in blue coats, and a third in blue coats with gold braid.

The group in the brocaded coats raised their curved horns to their lips and as if on signal blew out the notes of their hunting song—a mournful lilt that seemed to echo across the chasm of the centuries. When they had finished, the second group began with their own song, and then the third. Then it began again. In the group of scarlet-coated hunters, standing at the very forefront, was a bowed old man with white hair and a sunken face veined with innumerable blood vessels. His features were set in an expression of majesty and determination, and as his cheeks distended and as the horns blew out it seemed as if the most important thing in the world to him was to stand in that forest blowing his horn across the carcass of a dismembered stag. He was still blowing as we left, the car lights glinting on the silver scabbard at his belt—and for all I know he may be blowing still.

We drove through the gathering gloom to another house of the Marquis de Roualle with the sound of the horns ringing in our ears. On our right as we drove for miles the lands and forests of the marquis stretched out from behind their stone walls. The mansion we now entered was in keeping with our day: oak panelling, crystal chandeliers, fading tapestries, marble fireplaces. In front of one of these stood the marquis himself. He had changed his coat again and was now wearing a longer and richer garment of pale pink satin, still reminiscent of the hunt.

There was champagne and pâté in the dining room and a great throng of people pressing toward the bar in much the same way as they do at a cocktail party in Canada. I fell to talking with one of the huntsmen, an amiable nobleman who asked me if we had similar affairs in our country. I tried to explain the Grey Cup final but gave it up.

"Alas," he said, "you are viewing here a dying sport. Only the wealthiest families can afford it now. Each year a few drop out. Each year there are fewer horses . . . fewer hounds . . . fewer hunts. It is a great credit to the marquis that he maintains the old traditions. How long will it continue I cannot tell. You will excuse me? I have the grand thirst."

He left me and presently we left the *grande maison* of the Marquis de Roualle—left him still standing before his marble fireplace in his faded pink satin coat, gallantly kissing the hands of the ladies and bidding goodbye to his guests. We drove again down the road that skirts his lands, past the private forest so silent now, past the rococo palace and the grey old church of Chantilly and out onto the flat, hard road where, at 100 kilometres an hour, we flashed on to the bright new lights of Paris.

My Entrée into Buckingham Palace

Address to the Empire Club, Toronto, March 25, 1954

I MUST CONFESS TO SOME slight feeling of schizophrenia because of the varied interests of this audience. Should I talk to the members of the Empire Club about the Empire? Or should I address my remarks to the writers and journalists here and give them the lowdown on the best way of getting into Buckingham Palace without a program?

I wish, really, that somebody had given me the lowdown before I commenced the researches for my book. Because it's not so easy to get into Buckingham Palace. Early in the game I went to see the naval officer who, because of his twenty-five years in the silent service, is press secretary to the Queen. He very charmingly said that he would help me in any way he could. What could he do?

I said, "I'd like to see around the palace."

A look of pure horror crossed his face.

"See around the palace?" he said. "See around? My dear chap—nobody sees around Buckingham Palace!"

I went away from there, and I got a book on the palace. And I discovered that the Royal Philatelic Collection is housed at the far end of the second floor, and it occurred to me that anybody going to see the royal stamps would also cut himself in on an unofficial tour of the palace. So I phoned the keeper of the royal stamp collection, and he said that he'd be delighted to show me around. I told him I was from *Maclean's*. I didn't intend to give the impression that *Maclean's* is a stamp magazine, but I must confess that if he got that impression I didn't correct it. At any rate, the next day I toured the palace on the way to the stamp room. And then I spent a pleasant two and a half hours looking at stamps. I don't collect stamps, but it was very interesting.

But there was one part of the palace I didn't see, despite the very kind remarks that some people have made about my researches, and that was the backstairs. I never got near them. And of the hundred-odd interviews that I had in preparing the book, you'll be interested to know that only one was with a palace servant. I didn't intend to interview any palace servants, but a newspaper friend of mine insisted I go through the ritual. He arranged for us to meet this man in a pub called the Bag o' Nails near the palace. You know every royal servant is forbidden on pain of dismissal to talk to the press. But it was at once clear to me, on entering the Bag o' Nails, that the entire clientele consisted equally of Buckingham Palace servants and of newspaper men who were interviewing them.

I must say the proceedings that followed reminded me of those interviews we read about with Igor Gouzenko. The man we were to see sidled up and sat down with us. There was some guarded conversation, and then he looked over his shoulder, turned pale, and said, "Quick, we're being watched!" And then, pausing only long enough to knock back a flagon of mild and bitter, he led us out a side door, through an alleyway across some cobblestones and into a second pub. And here I again tried to ask him some questions. And he was just about to answer when he suddenly dug me in the ribs, put a warning finger to his mouth, knocked back his pint of mild and bitter and off we went again. Very exciting! But not very rewarding.

As you can see, gathering material about the Royal Family has some elements of the cloak and dagger about it. One thing I learned early in the game was that to get to see anybody in a high place, on this subject, you had to know the password. I remember I was trying to reach a man in a high financial institution who knew a great deal about the Duke of Windsor. Let's call him Gattling–Fenn; it was a name rather like that. I finally got through to his secretary's secretary, and then with a great deal of difficulty I got through to *his* secretary.

I said, "My name is Berton, I'm from *Maclean's*, I'm researching the Royal Family and I want to interview Mr. Gattling–Fenn."

She said, "I'm sorry, Mr. Maclean, but Mr. Gattling–Fenn isn't in, he doesn't know anything about the Royal Family and if he did he wouldn't tell you."

A long discussion followed. It got me nowhere until I finally used the password.

I said, "I'm a friend of Beverley Baxter's!"

Instantly there was a click on the line, and a voice said, "Gattling–Fenn here!"

Now I should have used the password again. But I didn't. I started all over again, trying to give him my name and my purpose.

He said, "I'm sorry, Mr. Maclean, but I'm afraid I can't help you. I don't know the Royal Family—why don't you go up to Buckingham Palace and let them show you around."

I said, "I've tried that. It didn't work."

He said, "Well, Mr. Maclean—what did you say the name of your magazine was again?—Toronto, did you say?—I'm afraid I don't recall it; well, anyway, I can't help you."

So then I sprang the password again. I said, "I'm a friend of Beverley Baxter's."

"Oh, Bax!" he said. "How is the old boy? I say, you must be from *Maclean's* magazine! You'd know Floyd Chalmers, Napier Moore—all that crowd. How are things on University Avenue?

"Why," he said, "I'll bet I can tell you what you're here for! You'll be doing something about the Royal Family: Coronation Year! Well, I can help you. I know the Duke of Windsor, you know! Why on earth don't you come to see me?"

So you see what I mean about the password.

The Edwardian Imperative

From *The Royal Family*, 1954

1. The Jersey Lily

SHE CAME FROM THE ISLAND of Jersey in the channel to London in 1877 with an obscure husband and a single black evening gown, and within a week she had taken the city by storm. She had classical features, a translucent skin, straight fair hair, a white throat, and eyes that no one could forget.

She did not tighten her waist in the fashion of the day. "To see her walk," Lady Oxford later wrote, "was as if you saw a beautiful hound upon its feet." When she entered a drawing-room all conversation ceased.

She was the greatest feminine phenomenon of her age. When her portrait was hung in the Academy they had to rope it all around to protect it from the enthusiastic crowd that constantly surged about it. She herself had to give up walking in the streets because of the mobs who surrounded her.

One day a woman wearing a similar black dress in a public park was mistaken for her. So great was the press of people that she was whisked, suffocating and insensible, to St. George's Hospital.

Men fought over her. She was to be seen of an evening in a polished silk hat and a skin-tight riding-habit mounted upon a spirited chestnut in Rotten Row. One evening she was riding with the Earl of Lonsdale when she noticed a man of her acquaintance at the railing and stopped to speak to him. The Earl was infuriated. There were words. The Earl leapt from his horse and over the railing, sprang upon his rival, and knocked him down. It enhanced the Jersey Lily's reputation.

Whistler, Millais, and Burne–Jones all painted her portrait. Oscar Wilde wrote a poem to her and later a play for her called *Lady Windermere's Fan*. Women wore Langtry shoes and Langtry hats, which she unconsciously inspired by twisting a piece of velvet into a toque and sticking a quill through it.

The Old Queen had received a present of a beautiful white she-ass from Egypt, and she wanted to give it a suitable name. She wrote to Lord Cromer and asked him what the Egyptians usually called these animals. Lord Cromer replied that every she-ass in Cairo was called Mrs. Langtry.

The old Queen simply had to see her. She astonished all her court by staying up late at a reception instead of turning the presentations over to a daughter. Then the reason was espied. Mrs. Langtry was at the end of the line.

Mrs. Langtry captured London.

Albert Edward, Prince of Wales, captured Mrs. Langtry.

2. Guelpho the Gay

"We all feel motherless today," Henry James wrote to a friend in Paris. "We are to have no more of little, mysterious Victoria but instead, fat, vulgar, dreadful Edward."

Fat he most certainly was. In an age of gargantuan appetites, he was king of the trenchermen. He could look up from a monstrous dinner and say, plaintively, "What—only five savories?" He could stride into the Hôtel du Palais in Biarritz, seat himself at a table announcing he wasn't hungry, then trudge steadily through course after course, leaving those about him gasping for breath, to inquire with a wounded air when the fruit came round, "Is there no cheese?" At night it was the custom to leave a cold chicken or a plate of sandwiches beside his bed. They would be devoured by the time morning tea with its accompanying platter of biscuits arrived.

But he was not vulgar and he was not dreadful. His succession came as a breath of tropical air to the chill and arid atmosphere of the Victorian court. In his youth they had called him "Guelpho the Gay," and he was all Hanover.

He came to the throne an old and ailing man in the twilight of his days, subject to deep periods of melancholy, bitterly mortified by the years of rebuffs from that same mother who had whispered his name on her deathbed. From her he had never known the respect that he was to insist on from others. "She does not much like the child," Greville the diarist had written, and when he was still in his frocks she had scooped him up and slippered him while the court watched. For the rest of her life she continued to submit him to various public slipperings of one form or another. When he was thirty-three and setting off to tour India, she lectured him on the details of what he should eat and how he should behave on Sunday and ended up by admonishing him to be in bed by ten. After Albert's death she developed what Lord Palmerston called "an unconquerable aversion" for him. To the end of her reign clerks in the foreign office were employed altering copies of the dispatches she had signed to keep all delicate or important matters from him, and he, like the lowliest of her subjects, had to depend upon the press for his information. She did not even bother to inform him that she had been made Empress of India, a breach that was heightened by the fact that he was in India at the time. She told Gladstone that she doubted her son's fitness for high estate.

His upbringing was so badly handled that it can stand as the classic textbook on How Not to Rear a Child. Albert and his punctilious mentor Stockmar were terrified that the boy would develop the pleasure-loving instincts of the Hanovers, and as a result he was kept in a state of protective custody for all his formative years. At the age of seven he was taken from his governess, and from then on he was denied all feminine influence and all companionship with boys his own age. Albert personally supervised his training (with the gloomy Stockmar at his elbow), and one of the first things he banned was toys, for he felt they contributed nothing to a child's development. Bertie's first tutor was a young man named Birch who did not see eye to eye with these dictums and was therefore quickly and summarily dismissed. Bertie was despondent: he had liked Birch so much that he was in the habit of writing him affectionate little notes and hiding small presents under his pillow. The new tutor, Gibbs, was cut from different and more mediocre cloth. He believed in manners, dress, morality, duty, and not much else.

The Coburg blueprint for Bertie's education was simple: he was to spend every waking hour of the day improving himself or being improved. Walled off from the outside world in White Lodge, Richmond Park, he was surrounded by a bleak company of aging soldiers and greying clerics who forbade him to speak to anyone outside the immediate household. He must keep a daily diary, which was read regularly by Albert and Stockmar. They had a habit of inserting biting comments on its composition and making suggestions for rewriting portions that did not appeal to them. He must write regular letters to all his royal relatives in which were to be inserted proverbs or Biblical quotations. He was not to lounge or slouch or even put his hands in his pockets or make jokes or read novels, even those by Sir Walter Scott. He was to study music and art and have poems, plays, and improving books read to him at all hours. In other words, he was to have everything a growing boy should have, except love, freedom, and gaiety. It is not surprising that when he grew older he went off in pursuit of all three.

Bertie's third tutor, Colonel Bruce, a disciplinarian, arranged his day like an army syllabus. Before breakfast he was to memorize classics and prepare exercises; after breakfast he was to take lessons in Italian; between eleven and twelve came the study of the classical languages; and after lunch he was steered through museums and art galleries. He studied French from five to six and music from six to seven. All of this was supposed to produce a model youth, a second Albert. But Bertie was strangely stubborn in his resistance to it all. He was a frail, nervous boy, subject to fits and tantrums that nobody professed to understand. When he was fourteen his parents commented bitterly on his obvious lack of knowledge. When he was sixteen he asked to be allowed to join the army, but Albert wouldn't hear of it and spoke at length of "the temptations and unprofitable companionships of military life." When he was seventeen he received a birthday present of another lengthy memorandum that began with the words "Life is composed of duties. . . ." Bertie read it and burst into tears. Metternich saw him about this time, when Bertie was in Europe, and remarked that he had a pleasing personality but "an embarrassed air and is very sad."

He was packed off to Oxford and then to Cambridge. The memoranda regarding his conduct increased in detail and in length. The terrible vision of George IV still hung like a ghostly ogre over all of Albert's dictums. As Prince of Wales, this Hanoverian rake had gone about in a black velvet coat glittering with pink spangles and shoes with high scarlet heels. Bertie therefore must wear sombre clothing. And the former Prince of Wales had been addicted to practical jokes, so Bertie must be cautioned against such frivolities. And he had played cricket. Bertie must not play cricket. It was far too democratic a game, anyway, for it tended to place a prince on the same level as the rest of the world, and that would not do. There were only two games he could play: croquet and tennis. There were other precepts. Bertie must not smoke. Bertie must wear a special academic gown so that his fellow students would know who he was. Bertie must sit in a special seat at lectures. Bertie must not mix with his fellows. He must live by himself, surrounded as always by the dry old men who were his only boyhood companions.

Occasionally Bertie managed to evade his jailers. Once he escaped from Cambridge, boarded a train, and headed for the freedom and anonymity of London. But his absence was discovered and his route traced. Albert was telegraphed, and when Bertie got off the train he found a royal carriage waiting for him with orders to proceed directly to the palace.

Yet through it all Bertie continued to resist every effort to cast him in the Coburg mould. They sent him to Italy to improve his mind, but the only thing that intrigued him was a trio of portraits of beautiful women in an artist's studio. They sent him to Egypt to see the pyramids, but he sat on the cold stone, plunged into a copy of *East Lynne*, and spoke bitingly of "mouldering stones" and "tumbledown old temples." They gave him such a diet of improving books that he never again picked one up. They made him concentrate so hard that in later life he was never able to stay with any subject for more than half an hour. They made him so lonely that in his after years he could never bear to be alone again.

He began to look and act suspiciously like a Hanover. He had the Hanoverian eyes and the Hanoverian tendency toward plumpness. He had the Hanoverian passion. He had a charm and ease of manner and a complete absence of that shyness that was a Coburg quality. He did not wear spangles, but in his adult years he affected a variety of advanced dress that became popular style. And almost to the end of his days he was addicted to practical jokes—to the hiding of dried peas in friends' beds and the thrusting of burning cigars into their outstretched hands.

For Albert the Good, who had succeeded in making his queen and his eldest daughter over in his own image, had failed utterly with his heir. It was not the only failure of the Coburg training plan. Albert's daughter Victoria, who became Empress of Germany, tried it with her son, with similarly lamentable results. "The dream of my life was to have a son who should be something of what our beloved Papa was, a real grandson of his in soul and intellect," she wrote to her mother. The son turned out to be wilful, hot-headed, and mischievous with an appetite for flattery and an almost unbearable pride. At the age of four he was crawling about sinking his teeth into the bare shanks of his kilted relatives, and later, as Kaiser Wilhelm II, he continued to bite off more than he could chew.

After Albert's death it was thought proper that Bertie should be married. He did not particularly want to wed, but his mother felt that he should become domesticated as soon as possible, before any more regrettable Hanoverian tendencies began to appear. A list of suitable royal young women was drawn up, but Bertie never got past the first one, Alexandra of Denmark, a princess of great charm, great simplicity and dazzling beauty. They were married in 1863, and Bertie was on his own at last; but it would not be quite accurate to say that he settled down. Released from his gilded cage, he soared on full wing in pursuit of forbidden pleasures.

His great town home, Marlborough House, and later his country estate of Sandringham, became an axis around which a new society revolved within the larger perimeter of Victorianism—a society that was known at first simply as the Marlborough House set, but was later to take on the permanent label of Edwardian. It was a loose and lively society dedicated to aristocratic pleasures—to enormous pheasant shoots, yachting parties, twelve-course dinners and masked balls; to baccarat, billiards, good cigars, fast horses and dazzling women. Needless to say, it did not play chess. Everything it did was on a prodigious and exotic scale, and at its head was the bearded and debonair figure of Albert Edward, whose name was already invading the music halls:

As I stroll along with big cigar and promenade the Strand,
The ladies say "How grand! Oh doesn't he look gay?"
And in upper ten society, I hold a mighty sway.
I'm the bosom friend of Albert, Prince of Wales.

He set the fashion. The Norfolk coat, the Homburg hat, and the dinner jacket all swept into popularity because he was among the first to wear them. Paris overflowed with Prince de Galles cigars, suspenders, wines and brandies. When Albert Edward began to drink an obscure German wine called hock, it became popular almost overnight. When he got rheumatism in his shoulder and began to shake hands with one elbow close to the waist, everyone started to shake hands that way. He invented a cocktail, which everybody drank: rye whisky, crushed ice, square of pineapple, piece of lemon peel, dash of Maraschino, some champagne and powdered sugar. The boy who had been prohibited from smoking now puffed on Egyptian cigarettes especially put up for him by Laurens. And when he entered White's club and found that smoking was prohibited, he simply organized a club of his own, the Marlborough, opposite his own home. Here, if not at his mother's court, he was king.

"His menus for breakfast were almost appalling in their length and solidity," a commentator wrote in 1885. At one breakfast he consumed mutton chops, oysters and asparagus. His sideboards groaned of a morning with galantines, cold pheasants, grouse, ptarmigans, hams and tongues, which his guests could sample between the hot courses of porridge, omelets, whiting and devilled kidney. His dinners ran up to twelve courses. Lamb would follow quail and chicken and turkey would follow lamb. There would seldom be fewer than three desserts (peaches and cream, soufflé, Venetian ice). In the middle of the meal there would be a breathing-space, and Albert Edward would eat a *sorbet* to cleanse his palate and smoke a Russian cigarette. Then he would plunge in again, and after the cheese and fruit he would smoke an enormous Corona-Corona.

In the field, portable stoves were trundled out to keep the luncheon dishes hot, and steaming cups of turtle soup were brought round to the hunters. For hunting was the great love of Albert Edward's life, and he came to be one of the better shots in the realm, though his accuracy was marred by a certain restlessness and impatience, which characterized his entire life.

The Edwardian hunts were as prodigious as the Edwardian meals. Every year ten thousand partridges were raised from eggs and set loose in the Sandringham coverts. The prince's larder held six thousand birds and was exceeded in size only by that of his friend the Baron Hirsch, in Hungary. In a single shoot, the prince and his friends would knock down three thousand birds or six thousand rabbits and in 1885 sixteen thousand birds were killed in one season on the Sandringham estate.

The prince shot stags in Berzencz, bears in Slavonia, crocodiles on the Nile, flamingoes, spoonbills and storks in Egypt, and an enormous bat in the tomb of Rameses IV. He stuck pigs in India, bagged a tiger in Nepal and an elephant in Ceylon, and sent them all back, mounted, skinned or tanned, together with sloths, cheetahs, leopards and deer, to England. When he went to India in 1875 he took along three horses from his stable of sixty that had been especially trained, by a series of visits to the zoo, to take no notice of wild beasts and reptiles. His hunting camps on this occasion were like great cities, populated by twenty-five thousand souls as well as a variety of animals: two hundred and fifty camels, one hundred horses, sixty teams of oxen and more than a hundred elephants.

It was hard to keep pace with this indefatigable prince who was filling the vacuum in his life with an enormous capacity for luxury. Lord Hardwicke, the inventor of the polished silk hat, tried to keep up with him on his tours of India and Africa and as a result lost a good portion of his fortune. Another long-suffering crony, Christopher Sykes, actually went bankrupt through entertaining the prince, as his nephew later recounted, and the prince had to pay his debts for him. For it was a costly matter to satisfy his tastes. The Duke of Sutherland once gave a Nile party in his honour, and the liquid provisions placed upon the steamer for this occasion included three thousand bottles of champagne, four thousand bottles of wines and liquors, and twenty thousand bottles of soda water.

The entertainment of the prince at a country home required an enormous outlay. A complete suite of rooms had to be placed at his disposal, including bathroom, dressing-room, bedroom and sitting-room, and it was the custom to call in upholsterers and decorators to transform these to the royal taste. Telegraphic arrangements had to be made as well as arrangements to house the rest of the prince's considerable entourage. He brought his own chef, two valets, and always a footman in scarlet livery who personally served him at the table. The prince himself chose the guests and the menus and, from the moment he arrived, he, and not the owner of the house, acted the part of host.

In the great rambling mansion of brick and stone that was Sandringham, the tiger skins and boars' heads mingled with the yachting and racing trophies against a background of crimson silk screens, dusty gold hangings, upholstery of blue brocade, and the inevitable conservatory stuffed with palms and wickerwork. Long into the night the guests danced while the prince pumped a barrel organ, and sometimes there would be sleigh-ride parties with Albert Edward and his friends tobogganing down the great staircase on tea trays.

For Bertie of Wales was seeking the childhood he had never known. He was an avid tricyclist and one of the first royal personages to buy a motor car. He loved to pour a bottle of brandy over the head of his sombre companion, Sykes, and roar with laughter as this unfortunate and snobbish man, without changing expression, let the liquid trickle slowly through his beard and remarked quietly, "As it pleases Your Royal Highness." There were other amusements involving Sykes. He was hurled under a billiard table and prevented from escaping by the prince and his companions who poked at him with billiard cues. He was dressed in a suit of armour for a fancy-dress ball, then locked out and left to clank about in the public thoroughfares. The prince watered his bed with a sprinkling-can and soaked his head with a soda siphon and thought it all capital fun. There were other jokes involving animals, which the prince and his great crony, Lord Charles Beresford, indulged in: poultry doped and tied to bedsteads, live donkeys dressed up, hoisted into private chambers and slipped under the blankets.

In Paris, which became his favourite city, there were more erotic amusements. "The Prince of Wales is leading a very dissolute life here," Lord Clarendon reported to the ambassador in Paris, "and so far from concealing it his wish seems to be to earn for himself the reputation of a roué."

His portly figure, perfectly turned out, became a familiar sight along the boulevards and in the Moulin Rouge, where his incognito was respected and the star attractions were Yvette Guilbert and La Goulue, later to be immortalized by Toulouse-Lautrec. From his headquarters in the staid Hotel Bristol he made his way to the Café Anglais and its famous private dining room "le Grand Seize," with its crimson wallpaper and golden hearth. He even appeared on the stage in Sardou's *Fédora*, taking the part of a corpse half hidden from the audience while the great Bernhardt wept across his body.

Back in London, his little single-horse brougham clipclopped discreetly over the London cobbles as he sought out the kind of womanly affection that had been denied him in his boyhood. He found it in a galaxy of professional beauties of whom Lillie Langtry was the crowning ornament.

After Mrs. Langtry there were other conquests, and some defeats. One high-bred beauty refused to be seen with him when he came calling in his little brougham. In vain he urged her not to mind the gossip. People, he said, were always saying things about him, and he didn't care a bit. "Perhaps not, sire," came the cool reply, "but so far they say nothing about me, and I don't mean that they should."

He needed the company of attractive and brilliant women, and although his wife, Alexandra, filled the first requirement, she did not fill the second. She was an unworldly and almost childlike woman who had been brought up with great simplicity in the little yellow palace of her father, Prince Christian, an impoverished cavalry officer. There, in Copenhagen, Alexandra knitted her own stockings, sewed her own dresses, and always waited on her parents' guests. Occasionally Hans Christian Andersen came and read aloud to her from his fairy tales. Now, in her fairy-tale existence with a Prince of England, she never quite lost her simplicity of being. She loved to turn cartwheels, which she accomplished with great elegance, and she was fond of simple jokes. She was delighted when one of Lord de Grey's footmen dropped a tray of valuable china, and it became the custom on subsequent visits for Lady de Grey to have a tray of cheap and brittle china ready that could be smashed by a footman, to Alexandra's great glee. In Marlborough House, in the middle of a wall of bookshelves, she had a secret door installed behind the false façades of books bearing such names as *Look Within, The Hidden Door,* and *Open Sesame.*

Her generosity was as fabulous as it was naïve. She had a drawer stuffed full of five-pound notes, which she dispensed on impulse. She was a target for any charlatan, for she would answer any letter begging for money with an immediate cheque, regardless of its authenticity. She was told once that one such letter was from a professional beggar who made a habit of preying on the gullible. "If that is the case and no one else will help him, I must send the poor man ten pounds," Alexandra replied. She was equally kind to animals and would stop her carriage to upbraid anyone she saw mistreating a horse or a dog. When her own pets died, she buried them soberly in the grounds of Marlborough House and erected small tombstones to their memory. She had a way of treating crowds as if they were all personal friends, and she would often appeal to the people closest to her carriage to look after their children when the throng pressed close.

She was fabulously unpunctual, a failing that drove her meticulous and fanatically precise husband into towering rages. She even kept him waiting for his coronation until, it is said, he hammered on her door and cried, "Alexandra—if you persist in being troublesome you shall not be crowned at all!" Generally, she was twenty to thirty minutes late for dinner, and in later years, when she lived alone as a widow, her household was in a state of perpetual chaos. Often she would not sit down to lunch until three-thirty in the afternoon. Her room and her desk presented a similar spectacle of confusion, littered with books and pictures and miniatures and curios, bottles of scent, gold pencils, souvenirs and bric-a-brac. For everything she was given, no matter what its intrinsic value or beauty, she formed an attachment, and could not part with it. It was the same with her children. She could not bear to see them grow up and leave her, and when they did she could never quite get used to the fact that they were adults. When her eldest son died suddenly of typhoid fever, she followed the Victorian tradition of locking up his room and keeping it exactly as it had been in his lifetime.

She was a dazzling beauty, even in later life when she had grown deaf and lame. Her brows never wore a frown nor bore a wrinkle. She had a perfect oval face, sloping shoulders, an exquisite carriage and she wore jewellery as if she had been born with it on. She was perhaps the most popular woman in the realm, and it was because of her Danish background that the prince could never see eye to eye with his pro-Prussian mother on the question of Bismarck's annexation of the Danish provinces of Schleswig and Holstein. It helped turn him against the Germans, and it was the wedge that broadened the gap between himself and his nephew the kaiser.

But Alexandra, beauty though she was, did not fill the vacancy in Albert Edward's life. All his days he pursued the will-o'-the-wisp of feminine companionship. It is possible that he found it at last in Alice Keppel, a woman described by Hugh Walpole as a "sergeant-major with a sense of humour." This genial, handsome woman, who seemed to have no enemies, became his constant companion and whist partner, keeping up a brilliant line of conversation that ran all the way from the politics of the day and the price of stocks to the latest scandal.

The prince's defection from Victorian proprieties, while they were always discreet, could not but become matters of public knowledge and discussion, and it is ironical that in each of the two public scandals in which he was involved he should have been cast in a minor role.

The first came in 1871 when Sir Charles Mordaunt of Walton Hall, Warwickshire, applied for the dissolution of his marriage with Lady Mordaunt on the grounds that she had committed adultery with Viscount Coles, Sir Frederick Johnstone (both friends of the prince) and "some person." That person was the prince himself. He was summonsed as a witness in the court case, where a series of perfectly respectable and innocuous letters between himself and the lady in question were produced. This, coupled with the fact that Lady Mordaunt was found insane, served to clear him of any culpability. But his very presence in the witness-box created an unfortunate impression in the public mind and added fuel to the fires ignited by the republican clubs then springing up all over England, attacking the queen and her family. It was, curiously, another accident that restored the prince to popularity. He came down with an attack of typhoid fever that almost took his life, and the queen came out of her self-enforced seclusion to stay by his side until the crisis passed. This sentimental spectacle of a mother's vigil and a son's anguish struck the imaginative nation, and when the prince finally came out of his coma and was reported to have asked for a glass of beer, this completely English action caused universal rejoicing.

A much more notorious scandal was the so-called Tranby-Croft affair, which took place twenty years later, in 1891. It took its name from the country residence of a wealthy shipowner named Arthur Wilson. It was here, during a game of baccarat at which the prince was a player, that Sir William Gordon–Cumming was accused of cheating. Sir William signed a paper promising never to play cards again, and the others thereupon undertook to keep the incident a secret. But the story leaked out, and Sir William brought an action for slander against the principals in the baccarat game. In the subsequent court case, Albert Edward again appeared as a witness, and it was his testimony that largely influenced the jury to find in favour of the defendants. The prince had not observed Sir William cheating, indeed he had hardly been brought into the matter, but he said he believed the testimony of his friends. Sir William's defeat had a Victorian air of melodrama about it: he was ruined forever socially, but his sweetheart, who had stood stoutly at his side throughout the affair, married him at once. The trial was almost as disastrous for the prince. The general public considered it monstrous that he should gamble at all. The great journalist W.T. Stead, in his *Review of Reviews*, invented what he called a prayer gauge by which he calculated the exact number of fervent "amens" that had been voiced in the churches of the land, on the prince's behalf, during the half-century of his life—all apparently to no avail. The archbishop himself felt called upon to ask the prince to renounce gambling. Victoria summoned him for one of those icy, earwigging interviews he dreaded so much. Worse still, the Kaiser, who was forever seeking a chance to be one up on his uncle, sent along a sickeningly moral little note on the evils of gambling that drove its recipient into a white rage. When he visited the Duke of Richmond's home he was met with a polite request: "You can do as you like, sire, when you are under my roof; but no baccarat!" It was at this time that the public prints announced, with raised eyebrows, that he had attended thirty plays, twenty-eight race meetings and forty social affairs in the space of nine months. And yet there was little else for him to do. He could not take his proper stance beside the throne because the occupant refused to permit it. When he came to the throne, at last, it was almost too late.

He was not a profound man, but he fitted the mood of the age that took his name. He knew everything, as Gladstone remarked, except what was in books. He placed more emphasis on outward and visible signs than he did on inward and spiritual graces. He was a fanatic on matters of dress and appearance, on decorations, ribbons, orders and medals. He could spot a faulty decoration instantly, no matter how obscure. A motion picture, one of the first, was made of his coronation, and during its showing his picture was thrown on the screen, reversed. Instantly his guttural German voice could be heard booming out his only comment: "Decorations on the wrong side!" Once, when a Swedish diplomat wore one of his orders the wrong way, the king, on saying goodnight to him, whispered a single phrase in his ear, "Hunt and Roskell, 25 Old Bond Street." The puzzled minister visited the premises of these court jewellers and at once discovered what was wrong.

As prince, and later as king, he kept two valets working full time, and he insisted that those around him observe all the proprieties of attire. (He himself used up two dozen pairs of gloves a year.) At one affair an admiral's daughter appeared in a dress that showed about an inch of ankle, and he administered a husky reproof. "I am afraid you must have made a mistake. This is a dinner, not a tennis party."

He believed in discretion. As prince he once gave a dinner at Marlborough House in the course of which a member of the company told a bawdy story. In the middle of it two women slipped in to listen. At once the prince invoked the frigid punishment of sending for the man's carriage. On another occasion a companion make a joke involving the Deity. He replied icily that "that is a name which should never be mentioned in jest." When Leopold II arrived for his coronation with a retinue of mistresses, the king let it be known to the Belgians, through his prime minister, that he would never again receive their monarch.

For he was a believer in etiquette and good form. He loved the race track, but never on Sundays. He knew a great many divorcees, but he would not receive them at court. He had a violent temper, but he never let it show in public. His rages came like sudden gusts and vanished as easily. He is supposed on his accession to have seen a bust of John Brown, his mother's ghillie, and smashed it in a fit of temper, for Brown had once been rude to him. At card games he would often swear violent oaths at his partners on losing a hand, for though he played rather badly, it depressed him to lose. Once, on shipboard, he grew suddenly angry at the design of a special star which was supposed to accompany the Order of the Garter being presented to a non-Christian prince, and he threw the whole thing out of a porthole.

But in public he was always pleasant. He was a stickler for etiquette and propriety and for the outward preservation of those Victorian values that seemed to him to be eternal. Women were important to him, but he always regarded them as playthings. It horrified him to think they might get the vote, and he was even reluctant to eat venison if he thought the stag had been shot by a huntress. He was punctilious about the dignity of his own position. The story that he sent for Mrs. Langtry's carriage and ended his alliance with her because she dropped a piece of ice down his neck is only a legend, but if she had performed this breach of etiquette that is certainly what he would have done. He never opened any of his vast correspondence; a servant stood behind him with a knife and decorously slit each letter. He never handled used money, only newly minted coins, a situation which sometimes caused embarrassment when he was gambling for high stakes. He was once playing billiards with a friend and asked him to hand him a package of cigarettes. The friend complied, whereupon Edward at once reproved him. "You should have handed me that on a tray," he said.

He had the grand manner and could freeze a man with a glance—but he preferred to be amiable. His courtesy was unfailing. To people who he knew would not accept a tip he would offer his "portrait" on a new gold sovereign. He had the carefully developed ability to walk between two lines of men, shake hands with each one, and pass a word or so with those he knew best without ever breaking his stride. One of his most treasured possessions was a solid-silver inkstand presented to him anonymously when he was Prince of Wales. He had been walking in Piccadilly when he saw an aged and blind beggar trying to cross the road. No one paid any attention until the prince happened along, took the man's arm and steered him through the traffic. The following day the inkstand arrived engraved with the words: "To the Prince of Wales from one who saw him conduct a blind beggar across the street. In memory of a kind Christian action."

He was a born diplomat. He could make pretty compliments in three languages, and he never had the slightest trouble making graceful little extemporaneous speeches. The quality of being able to look amused and diverted at all times made his first tour of Canada and the United States as a young man an instant success. Half a million people gave him a frenzied ovation in New York, and when he left, a man in the crowd shouted: "Come back in four years and run for president!" He had no racial or religious or national prejudices, and he numbered Jews, Catholics and Americans among his friends, a radical procedure at that time for a prince of the blood. These friendships often stood him good stead. One close crony was Sir Ernest Cassel, the great Jewish financier who had risen up from a bank clerk. He lent the prince half a million pounds at 2.5 percent, then told him how to invest the money and as a result brought him to the throne solvent.

The giving of presents was Edward's greatest joy, and the finest present he felt he could give was a medal or decoration. It pleased him to see men wearing as many as possible. He was a considerate host, always placing books and hanging pictures in his guests' rooms chosen carefully to fit their tastes. For he was a man who liked life to slip by smoothly and easily. He wanted everybody to be friends, with him and with each other. When he was attacked by republicans like Sir Charles Dilke and Keir Hardie, he went to see them and won their friendship through sheer charm. (He read the

77

radical paper *Reynolds News* every week of his life.) He had a knack of resolving arguments among his companions, and it is not surprising that after he ascended the throne he brought this happy facility into world politics. They called him Edward the Peacemaker.

He earned this title through three diplomatic turning points in his reign: the peace with the Boers, the Entente Cordiale with France, and the Triple Entente with France and Russia. His own part in these matters has often been overrated, for it is probably that they would all have come about without his presence; but in each instance he did play his part. It was he who opposed a policy of unconditional surrender, therefore making possible a practical ending to the Boer War. His own cordial treatment of the czar, which included investing him as an admiral of the Royal Navy, helped cement relations with Russia. But it was in Paris that he enjoyed his greatest triumph. His state visit to France after his accession to the throne met with a chilly and hostile reception, and there were cries of *"Vivent les Boers!"* as he passed by. He got an equally frigid treatment when he went to the theatre, but an incident during the entr'acte melted the ice. He purposely left his box to mingle with the hostile crowd, where by chance he espied an actress whom he had seen perform in England. He made his way to her, extended his hand and in a voice that all could hear he said, "Oh, mademoiselle, I remember how I applauded you in London. You personified there all the grace, all the *esprit* of France!" The story raced through the city and next day all Paris was at his feet.

But if he is to be credited with the *ententes*, he must also be charged with his part in the alienation of Germany, for since the Schleswig-Holstein incident he had developed a strong dislike for the Prussians and a congenital distaste for that arrogant posturer, the Kaiser. Yet even here he did not let his feelings show in public. The Kaiser had been made an Admiral of the Fleet by Victoria, and this had caused him to strut so much that the yachting season at Cowes was rendered all but unbearable for his uncle. In June 1904, the Kaiser, wearing his British admiral's uniform, gave a banquet at Kiel aboard the Imperial yacht *Hohenzollern* at which the king was a guest of honour. In the course of a toast to his uncle's health, he made a sword-rattling speech in execrable taste about the greatness of the German fleet, which all present expected would inflame the king to a white incandescence. But instead of a stinging reply he spoke to his nephew almost paternally, with an unruffled air of great condescension. "The interest . . . which for many years I have taken in" (here he paused slightly) "*yachting* . . . exercised too great an attraction to allow me to miss the opportunity of convincing myself how successful Your Majesty has been in inducing so many to become interested in the sport in Germany."

It is ironical that the reign of the Peacemaker should have ended on the eve of war. The dawn of this brief eleven-year period had been marked by the king's own depression at his mother's refusal to let him serve and the last-minute postponement of his coronation by a sudden attack of appendicitis. ("Will my people ever forgive me?" he cried as he was taken into the operating-room.) The twilight of the reign was marked by even deeper melancholy. Acute and unexpected attacks of gloom had been marring his health for some years, and now in 1910 he entered upon a struggle with his prime minister, Asquith, who wanted him to create enough Liberal peers to ensure the passing of the budget by the House of Lords. This increased his morbidity and it is said that he was dissuaded from abdicating only with the greatest difficulty.

He was occasionally superstitious, and it was always his habit on midnight of New Year's Eve to order his house cleared of guests and servants just before midnight struck. Then he would be the first to enter the door, leading Alexandra by the hand. But in the opening moment of 1910 he was forestalled in this custom by one of the younger members of the family. "We shall have very bad luck this year," the king said. It was a gloomy prediction but an accurate one. Before the year was out, he was dead.

Like his mother before him he stubbornly resisted death when it came. "I shall work to the end!" he declared as his strength failed. Now his queen, who had been a philanthropist all her life, performed one crowning act of philanthropy. She sent for his mistress,

Alice Keppel, and led her by the hand to the dying man's bedside so that in his last moments he might be happy. But he was already too far gone to recognize either woman, and before the day was ended, the Peacemaker was at peace. Halley's comet was in the sky, and throughout the realm people were preparing for the end of the world. In a way they were right. Gathering on the horizon were the clouds of a war that would destroy forever the measured, voluptuous, easy world of Guelpho the Gay.

Shopping for a Coffin on the Avenue of Life

From the *Toronto Star*, September 26, 1958

THE OTHER DAY Byng Whitteker, the radio announcer, and I went shopping for our coffins.

We had been talking about the grisly business of modern funerals and so decided the best way of saving our wives a deal of trouble and money was to make the arrangements in advance, as cheaply and simply as possible.

So we went shopping for our coffins on a sunny, September afternoon, feeling very much alive and a little sheepish.

We visited one of the town's finest funeral homes, and we had a talk with a pleasant, matter-of-fact young man who might easily have been an encyclopaedia salesman or a sports-car salesman or anything, in fact, except a coffin salesman.

But the pleasant young man would not sell us a coffin, for he said we were much too healthy, and the price of funerals was rising, and if people bought now and took delivery later, the funeral directors would go broke.

But we asked, just out of curiosity, what the cheapest possible funeral would cost, and he told us if you really wanted that sort of thing you could get it for about three hundred dollars. Not that they made any money on that kind: the overhead was too high. Most people paid at least six hundred, and there were plenty who paid five thousand or even fifteen thousand and got beautiful, beautiful coffins of solid bronze. In funerals, the young man said, the sky was the limit.

Well, Byng and I said, suppose you wanted a *really* cheap funeral: just a plain pine box and a quick, unescorted trip to the graveyard. No cosmetics.

Well, said the young man, he supposed you could get a plain box, but you would have to get somebody else to drive you to the cemetery for *they* certainly wouldn't do it, not with their overhead.

The public, he said, likes a lot of frills. Why, outside in the drive-way were three Cadillac hearses worth fourteen thousand apiece. Fords would do as well, but the public had to have Cadillacs.

And who was to say the public wasn't right, the young man said. Most people really wanted to be buried "decently and properly." There was that outfit down the street, "the put-'em-in-a-box-and-take-'em-to-the-grave society" he called it, who were all for these cheap funerals. But, the young man confided, when the president of that society lost his nineteen-year-old daughter last year, he had changed his mind and buried her in the conventional manner, "decently and properly."

"And that's exactly what you or your wives will do, gentlemen," he said. "If your wife were to die tomorrow would you *really* put her in a cheap box and ship her to the graveyard? Come on, now, would you?"

We gave no answer. The mournful strains of the funeral parlour organ accompanied us through the door and into the bright sun-light of St. Clair Avenue. The first crisp scent of fall was in the air, and we agreed that it felt good to be alive. So we decided to walk west to Avenue Road, for on a sunny day this happens to be one of the most rewarding walks in Toronto. In the space of sixteen blocks there are three parks and a ravine, and much open space, and some good gardens, and walls clothed in Virginia creeper, and solid, Georgian buildings that were once stately homes but have now become little brick hives in which doctors of every species try to keep you from the funeral parlour down the street.

St. Clair, indeed, has become the Harley Street of Toronto, and a remarkably cosmopolitan one as the doctors' names testify (Nishikawa, Glionna, Ngai, Miyake). You can uncover every kind of healer there, from chiropractor to gastroenterologist (stomach doctor to you). Every bodily need is catered to: you can be embalmed, or confessed, or psychoanalysed, or pumped out. And I would be willing to bet that one of these austere, ivied façades hides a fancy bordello, or its facsimile, for St. Clair is an extremely democratic avenue.

We stared over the rim of the little ravine, alive with drifts of goldenrod and small, bright patches of Michaelmas daisy; and we strolled past Sir Winston Churchill Park, alive with Crusader petunias; and we stopped briefly at Timothy Eaton Memorial Church, where the elms form a perfect Gothic arch as if in sympathy with the board of directors.

There was a wedding here: women in lacy white, men in pearl grey (the kind of men who buy bronze coffins), arranged on the lawn like chess pieces. A little farther on an expectant mother scaled the ramparts of a doctor's stone castle. Down the street romped chubby infants performing impossible feats with hula hoops. And through it all wound the black serpent of a funeral cortège, with the headlights of the fourteen-thousand-dollar Cadillacs glowing eerily in the sunlight.

And all this symbolism of life and death and birth and consummation was not lost on two robust men who had been shopping for their coffins.

We kept walking till we came to the Unitarian Church, "that outfit down the street" the young man talked of. In we went to see the Reverend Bill Jenkins, who helped found the Toronto Memorial Society, which the young man spoke of by a different name. It is a non-sectarian group, trying to restore dignity to modern funerals.

Well, we learned some interesting things here. We learned the society has never had a president, or even a director, with a nineteen-year-old daughter, dead or alive. We learned you *can* arrange for your funeral in advance. We learned you *can* have a really inexpensive funeral, for about two hundred dollars.

Though the society's original plan was to give its members this kind of minimum service, the members themselves don't want it. They prefer to spend an extra hundred or so on a slightly better coffin and a wee bit of embalming.

We told Bill Jenkins what the young man said about being buried "decently and properly."

"I'm glad he didn't say it to me," Jenkins said, "because I buried my mother in the plainest coffin and sent her to the grave without fuss. Some of my relatives haven't spoken to me since, but that was the way she wanted it, and that was the way I wanted it. And it was done decently, and with dignity, too."

We said goodbye and walked out again into the sunlight of St. Clair, the Avenue of Life, each preoccupied with the problem of death, each pondering what we would really do were our wives to die tomorrow.

Across the way, in another of St. Clair's little parks, was the gay figure of Peter Pan, the boy who never grew up and needed no funeral. The statue is moulded from the same metal as the rich men's coffins, but in this case I think the bronze is put to a nobler use.

A Report on Torture as Practised in Modern Canada

From the *Toronto Star*, November 20, 1958

For they starve the little frightened child
Till it weeps both night and day:
They scourge the weak, and flog the fool,
And gibe the old and grey. . .

  – Oscar Wilde, "The Ballad of Reading Gaol"

I N THE LAST WEEK of October of this year, four mental defectives were brutally and painfully tortured within the walls of
Kingston penitentiary by a method that reaches back to the
days of rack and thumbscrew.

The torture was quite legal and was approved by the authorities
in Ottawa. It was duly reported in the civilized press of this civilized country. The headlines were minor ones and there was no
outcry.

The method of torture, which was not reported in the press,
was, roughly, as follows: The prisoners were taken to a room that
contains a device known in prison parlance as "the machine." It
resembles two long ironing boards formed into a large V under
which are supporting legs that can be folded so that the machine
can be moved quickly out of sight of visitors.

The prisoners were stripped and blindfolded; then each was
made to lie face down on the machine with his legs resting on the
arms of the V, and his chest and body resting on the part that is
joined. He was securely strapped so that he could not move.

Each man was then beaten an unspecified number of times (the
authorities would not reveal how many) by a guard who wielded,
at arm's length, a heavy length of leather strap, perforated so that
the perforations bit into the flesh.

I do not know how it was in this instance, but in most cases a prisoner is not able to work for several days after receiving such a beating. In some cases he has to be sent to hospital.

These four convicts were strapped because they had attempted to escape and held three prison officials as hostages with knives against their throats.

I say that they were mental defectives for two reasons: First, they were working in the toy repair shop, which is earmarked in Kingston for occupational therapy. Inmates do not work there unless they have a psychiatric history or are undergoing treatment by a psychiatrist. Secondly, the warden himself, Walter F. Johnstone, described all four as "on the lunatic fringe."

It is hard to believe that in this year of 1958 we are still treating people of unsound mind by beating them. I say "treating" because I presume the prison authorities were not moved by any base motives of revenge but really because the infliction of bodily anguish on these men would have a therapeutic effect.

That is the more charitable of the two explanations, though it does not, or should not, bring any of us much comfort.

I do not propose here to review the impressive body of evidence that suggests that physical torture does not deter sane men from crime (let alone mental defectives) but, in point of fact, embitters them to the point where they become confirmed enemies of society.

I do not propose to point out that the majority of men beaten in penitentiaries have already been beaten in the reformatories and before that in the training schools with no salutary effect.

For even if it could be proven that the whipping of a human being to the point of hospitalization was statistically effective in moderating criminal tendencies, I should be opposed to it.

I oppose the torture of human beings, sane or demented, not because of what is done to the tortured, but because of what is done to the torturer. And we are all torturers, each one of us in this free democracy, as long as we condone torture and maintain it as law on our statute books.

It does not matter that the torture takes place in a darkened cell behind stone walls where the sounds of the blows are muffled and the victim's groans are faint. They are loud enough for each of us to hear, echoing down the corridors of our conscience.

The guards in Kingston, who are ordered to perform this cruel duty on a rotation basis, must pay a fine if they refuse; and many do refuse, for the whip works its subtle poison on the man who wields it as much as on the man who suffers it. But no one of us can really purchase escape from the whip; we must each pay a fine whenever that whistling thong lacerates the flesh of a fellow-human. For with each stroke we surrender up a small piece of our mortal soul.

I have often thought, in this connection, of the Germans during the days of Hitler who claimed that they did not really know what went on behind the grey walls of the concentration camps and the gas chambers. But they knew all right; deep in their hearts, they knew and preferred to forget.

And we know, too, though we seek not to know. The telltale prickings of our conscience can be seen in the use of the word "paddle," which is a euphemism for the instrument of torture. It conjures up a comfortable picture of a child gently suspended on its parent's indulgent knee.

But the object of the exercise is far more hideous, and each of us secretly understands this quite well: It is to inflict the kind of pain that will cause grown men to cry aloud in anguish.

Here, from an eyewitness, is a description of the marks left upon a man by this so-called paddle: "They were about two and a half inches wide and were crisscrossed on both sides of the buttocks. The skin was not broken, but rather seared as if the outer skin had been stripped off, leaving the inner skin exposed. You will see such a mark, smaller of course, on a person whose bare arm has been rubbed by an electric emery wheel in motion.

"The next morning these marks were black and blue and the welts were puffed up as a black eye is puffed.

"The prisoner, in this case, was a grown man who had led a fairly tough life. If a younger, less-hardened man were strapped as he was strapped, I have no doubt the punishment would draw blood."

These particular scars mercifully have long since healed. But there are deeper scars on society, and there is no man, unless he is without conscience, who cannot feel their pain.

Requiem for a Fourteen-Year-Old

From the *Toronto Star*, October 5, 1959

In Goderich town
The sun abates
December is coming
And everyone waits:
In a small, stark room
On a small, hard bed
Lies a small, pale boy
Who is not quite dead.

The cell is lonely
The cell is cold
October is young
But the boy is old;
Too old to cringe
And too old to cry
Though young—
But never too young to die.

It's true enough
That we cannot brag
Of a national anthem
Or national flag
And though our Vision
Is still in doubt
At last we've something
To boast about;
We've a national law
In the name of the Queen
To hang a child
Who is just fourteen.

The law is clear:
It says we must
And in this country
The law is just.
Sing heigh! Sing ho!
For justice blind
Makes no distinction
Of any kind;
Makes no allowance for sex or years,
A judge's feelings, a mother's tears;
Makes no allowance for age or youth
Just eye for an eye and tooth for a tooth—
Tooth for tooth and eye for eye:
If a child does murder
The child must die.

Don't fret—don't worry . . .
No need to cry
We'll only *pretend* he's going to die;
We're going to reprieve him
By and by.

We're going to reprieve him
(We always do),
But it wouldn't be fair
If we told *him*, too.
So we'll keep the secret
As long as we can
And hope that he'll take it
Like a man.

And when we've told him
It's just "pretend"
And he won't be strung
At a noose's end,

We'll send him away
And, as like as not,
Put him in prison
And let him rot.
The jury said "mercy"
And we agree—
O, merciful jury:
You and me.

Oh death can come
And death can go
Some deaths are sudden
And some are slow;
In a small, cold cell
In October mild
Death comes each day
To a frightened child.

So muffle the drums and beat them slow,
Mute the strings and play them low,
Sing a lament and sing it well,
But not for the boy in the cold, dark cell,
Not for the parents, trembling-lipped,
Not for the judge, who followed the script;
Save your prayers for the righteous ghouls
In that Higher Court who write the rules
For judge and jury and hangman, too:
The Court composed of me and you.

In Goderich town
The trees turn red
The limbs go bare
As their leaves are bled
And the days tick by
As the sky turns lead

For the small, scared boy
On the small, stark bed—
A fourteen-year-old
Who is not quite dead.

Operative 67's Vain Attempts To Buy a Vacuum Cleaner

From the *Toronto Star,* December 15, 1959

O
PERATIVE 67 HAS HAD some tough assignments in her career: taking dancing lessons at Arthur Murray's, jousting with TV repairmen, and so on. But these have been mere child's play compared to the task that she was given three weeks ago.

"Operative 67," I said to her, "here is an advertisement of President Electric Limited, 420 Dupont St. It seems they are emptying their warehouse to make room for new 1960 merchandise. To do this they are offering tremendous savings on their present stock of brand-name appliances.

"Here, for instance, is a 'famous name brand vacuum cleaner' that they are offering at the ridiculously low price of $12.95 each.

"Now, Operative 67, here is your assignment: *Try and buy one of these vacuum cleaners*. Go! Do not darken the door again until you have it."

Yesterday the Operative returned, wringing her hands and weeping into a large handkerchief.

"I've failed you, chief," she sobbed. "I've done everything possible. I've even signed a conditional sales contract. But I can't get the vacuum cleaner. They just don't seem to want to sell it to me."

The Operative's story is a lengthy one, but I shall try to condense it here to essentials.

At 12.30 on November 25, Mr. P. Leufer of President Electric arrived at the Operative's door, carrying the $12.95 machine with him in a cardboard box. He gave a brief demonstration.

"Fine!" said the Operative. "I'll take it!" and she handed him fifteen dollars.

Mr. Leufer said he was awfully sorry, but he didn't have any change. He said, however, that he would have the machine shipped COD. It would take a week or ten days.

The Operative said she wanted the machine right away so she could clean her apartment. Mr. Leufer then said he had a bigger and better machine out in the car. She could have *that* right away. The Operative said well, couldn't she just clean up her apartment with the little machine? No, said Mr. Leufer, firmly, running out to the car and getting another machine. This one, he explained, cost a bit more, $200 actually. He showed her how beautifully it worked.

The Operative said she'd prefer to have the little $12.95 machine if it was all right with him.

"Well," said Mr. Leufer, "when I told you this big machine was worth $200—well, it isn't really. Actually, it's only $169.50. However, there's a special on right now, and you can have it for $149.95."

Operative 67 said she wanted the little machine.

Mr. Leufer, battling manfully, offered to throw in a box of flatware free if she'd consent to buy the big one. The Operative refused. Well, said Mr. Leufer, he'd sell the flatware to another customer for $20 and she could have the machine for $129.95. A steal!

The Operative said she wanted the little machine.

Well, said Mr. Leufer, she could have the big machine for $109.95 in cash. He'd claim it had a scratch on it and tell the company he was selling it as a demonstrator. Sorry, said the Operative, the little machine, please.

Mr. Leufer began to attack the little machine. Look, he said, it's got no filter to catch the dirt that sifts through the bag. And the motor isn't sealed off like in the *good* machine. Also, he warned the Operative it would have to be serviced at least three or four times a year; the dust was always getting into the grease on the bearings. Not only that, but she couldn't operate the machine for any more than twelve minutes at a time: the case got too hot.

"I don't care," said the Operative doggedly, "I still want it."

So, finally, Mr. Leufer brought out a contract for the Operative to sign. The contract stated that she had received and paid for a machine at $12.95. Mr. Leufer explained, however, that she wouldn't actually get the machine for some days because the one he had with him was a demonstrator. The machine would be sent COD.

No money had changed hands, and Operative 67 still had no machine; but President Electric had a contract (in quadruplicate) in which she acknowledged that she had bought one. Mr. Leufer went away with his big machine and the Operative reports that he was just a little bit annoyed.

Twelve days later the Operative phoned President Electric and asked where her machine was. It took her a while to get to the right man. This man tried to explain to her what a fool she was to buy the little machine (which is called the Ideal) instead of the big machine (the President).

"Why, for the time you use the President you probably used up a dozen machines like the little Ideal. And by the time you add money to it in cleaning and oiling and service you'll spend *twice* as much as the President costs you. If something breaks on it, you have to pay for it yourself. If a hose breaks, you pay $5.50; if the motor burns out, you pay $17.00. You got to get it serviced at least twice a year—that costs $6.00. And in a year or so you'll be looking for another vacuum cleaner."

Operative 67 said she still wanted the $12.95 machine.

The man said the little machine wasn't strong enough to remove anything but surface dirt from a rug. It couldn't remove sand or grit or anything like that. The Operative said she didn't care; she wanted it.

Well, okay, said the man on the phone, but it would take quite a while. There might be trouble at the border; the machines came from Japan, and there'd be a delay in orders and so on.

The days went on and on. The Operative phoned again and asked for her machine. This time she got a different man and a different story. No, he didn't know when she could get her machine.

He would have to check with the shipping department. Sorry, the stockroom was closed. Tomorrow? He couldn't really say.

The Operative offered to come down to the office herself and personally pick up the machine and pay for it. No, said the man on the phone, that wasn't possible. The machines were shipped directly from the manufacturer. Who was the manufacturer? "Anglo-American" of Toronto. "Don't worry," the man said, "we'll ship you the machine just as soon as we can."

But the days drift by and the machine doesn't come and No. 67 is in despair. For the first time as my operative, she has failed!

Is the Press Too Sensational?

Address to the Empire Club, Toronto, January 21, 1960

I AM HERE BEFORE YOU TODAY to talk to you about the terrible sensationalism of the daily newspapers in this country.

I was discussing this whole thing on a radio panel a while ago. The subject of the discussion was the title I have chosen for this talk, "Is the Press Too Sensational?" The first panellist, who is a bearded intellectual, said, "Yes, it certainly is—flaring headlines about inconsequential subjects"; and the second speaker, who is a former newspaper woman, said the same thing; and the third speaker, who is a housewife, said the newspapers blow up these stories of violence out of all proportion to get circulation and so on; and then I was asked and I made myself very unpopular by saying, "No, the Press is *not* too sensational; I don't think it is nearly sensational enough."

But I should explain that my definition of what true sensationalism is, is slightly different from the accepted clichés. I happen to believe that it is the subject matter of a newspaper story that makes that story sensational, and not the way it is handled on the front page. You can take any newspaper story and make it *look* sensational. For instance, suppose that Allan Lamport, exhausted by his work on the TTC, decides to take a holiday in Bermuda; normally that is a two-paragraph story buried among the classified ads. But suppose the *Toronto Star* decides to make a big, front-page story out of it—flaring, 196-point headlines:

LAMPORT LEAVES FOR BERMUDA
"Not Coming Back for Two Weeks"
Says Controversial TTC Commissioner

Well, that story looks sensational, and a lot of people will rush out and buy newspapers and read it, and they will be very disappointed.

Of course, that is not true sensationalism. It is phony sensationalism. That kind of story does not really cause any sensation at all because it just is not sensational no matter what you do with it. My feeling is that, by and large, the daily newspapers of this country do not carry enough stories on their front pages and elsewhere that are really sensational, or that cause a sensation.

The fact is that most traffic accidents and most drownings—yes, and most murders—no longer produce sensations. We know in advance that there are going to be so many every year. Just as we know that there is going to be a squabble in the TTC regularly every month. I suggested the other day that a really sensational headline would be:

NO SQUABBLE IN TTC TODAY

My newspaper thought I was being funny, but I was deadly serious.

What is a truly sensational story? To start with, it is a story that people do not expect to read. It is usually a story that is not on the surface, in other words a story that takes time and effort and money to uncover. A plane crash these days is not a sensational story. But if a newspaper goes out and discovers the reason why the plane crashed—it may be that the pilot was worried about his wife's illness, or it may be sabotage, or it may be a defect in the plane's construction—well, that story is likely to be sensational.

I will give you an example of what I mean. Last March an unknown Toronto organization called the Freedom Foundation got itself in the news because it distributed a rather silly pamphlet saying that fluoridation was a Communist plot. Miss Phyllis Griffiths of the *Telegram* dug into this story over a period of several days and discovered that the people behind this same foundation were mixed up in a gold mine in British Columbia and were raising money from the foundation members in a very dubious manner. She produced a series of front-page stories that the *Tely* properly ran under big headlines. These stories were truly sensational.

98

Now this is the sort of thing I am talking about, and I say there is not enough of it in this country. Why not? Well, there are several reasons, but the main one is that it is cheaper and easier not to be sensational. It is simpler just to sit in the office and let the news roll in—as, indeed, the radio stations do. And it does roll in. It comes in off the CP wire and off the UP wire and off the AP wire. It comes in the form of handouts and press releases and syndicated articles you can buy for a song. A handful of men can today put out a newspaper that touches all the bases and that covers all the superficial news of the day. Now if that newspaper has no competition to keep it on its toes it will thrive and, as it does not spend very much money, never gets into trouble or controversy, never expresses a distasteful opinion or goes out on a limb or makes anybody mad, it will make a lot of money. And that is the situation in many cities in this country today, where there is no alternative means of communication.

I am always amused by newspaper publishers who write editorials, or get somebody to write editorials, demanding freer competition in some field, and praising the principle of free competitive enterprise to the skies. And then you find that all the time they have been writing these editorials, they have been trying to buy up the other paper in town, or the paper in the next town—or the local radio and TV station—so there will be no competition and they will have everything their own way.

There are precious few cities left in Canada where there is open competition between the newspapers. Let us look at the major cities: Victoria, two papers, both owned by the same interest; Vancouver, two papers, both owned by the same company; Edmonton, one paper; Calgary, two papers in competition; Regina, one paper; Saskatoon, one paper; Hamilton, London and Windsor, one paper; Winnipeg and Ottawa, two papers in competition; Toronto, three papers, all in competition; Montreal, two English-language papers in competition; and finally, east of Montreal, no competition. In this rapidly growing country the number of newspapers is diminishing and the control of these papers is falling into fewer and fewer hands. There are only five cities left in Canada where the newspapers are competitive.

But this is not the whole story. In many cities the chief means of communication are controlled by one source. In the United States there are seventy-three communities where the radio station, the TV station and the local newspaper are all in the same hands. The situation in Canada is comparable.

We have sixteen cities in this country where a newspaper owns a radio station, and in most cases it is the only newspaper in town. We have eight cities where a newspaper owns a television station, and in every case it is the only television station in town and in all but one case the only newspaper in town. And we have seven cities in which the newspaper owns the television station and a radio station as well.

Now we find, in the hearings before the Board of Broadcast Governors, several applications by concerns that already control radio or television stations or newspapers and sometimes all three.

One of the companies applying for a private TV licence in Vancouver already has interests in both Vancouver newspapers and two of the three private radio stations in the area. One of the members of this group, the Southam Company, owns seven daily newspapers outright and has substantial interests in four more, together with heavy interests in three TV and three radio stations. It is applying for further TV licences in three Canadian cities in which it also controls newspapers.

Frankly, I think this situation is unhealthy. I think if a newspaper does something infamous, the TV station or the radio station ought to be independent enough to rake it over the coals. The newspapers all employ TV critics. I would like to see a television station independent enough to employ newspaper critics. Somebody who will say: "Berton wrote a lousy column today; he is slipping"; or "Nathan Cohen hasn't fulfilled his promise"; or "The story on the front page is a lot of nonsense." Then the public will get a fighting chance of learning—and learning it from more than one source— what is going on. We might then have some true sensationalism on our front pages, and on the back pages, too.

Now there are some people, of course, newspapermen among them, who believe that if a newspaper enjoys a monopoly, it can do a better job for its readers. It does not operate under the pressure of the deadline; it is not forced to shovel the news into print at high speed; it can spend more time in a leisurely and thorough manner getting things right, instead of getting them first. These are valid arguments, but I do not see them working anywhere. The best reporting is being done in those cities—and this is the chief argument—where the competition is the fiercest.

The fact is that if a newspaper hasn't got somebody across the street continually keeping it on its toes, it tends to get flabby. The publisher thinks twice before he will foot the bill to send one of his own reporters to Washington or Ottawa. If there is a scandal in the city council, there will be no excessive haste to unearth it because the paper will know that nobody else is going to bother to unearth it. And the fact of the matter is, in most cases, it won't get unearthed at all. And the readers won't complain because they won't know what they are missing—they won't have any yardstick to judge the paper by. What they will probably say is, isn't it nice that we have a solid, respectable, unsensational paper? Because you know a lot of people are like that Social Committee of the UN the other day that said reporters should merely gather the news but they should never seek it out. Lord help us all if reporters became that passive.

There are some other dangers in newspaper monopolies that conspire against hard, objective, searching reporting. Here is an incident that happened recently in a Canadian city where a monopoly position prevails. A well-known city businessman was charged with and found guilty of drunk driving. Now when anybody is found guilty of drunk driving, the newspapers report it, as they report any other crime, and they name the man involved. This particular newspaper had run editorials on the evils of drunk driving. But the advertising manager went to the city editor and said, "You cannot publish this story." The city editor said, "I do not take my orders from you." So the advertising manager went to the publisher, and the publisher said to the city editor, "I am sorry, but we are not going to run this story." I should add that the businessman in question was a heavy advertiser.

Now if there had been any competition in town the following things might easily have happened: first, the opposition paper might have got wind of the story and revealed that its rival had suppressed it, thereby embarrassing its rival no end. Secondly, the city editor, who is a good one, might have quit and gone to work for the opposition. Neither of these things could happen, however, because the opposition paper was under the same ownership. This is a tiny example of the sort of thing I am talking about, but it is an indication of the stultifying effect of monopoly on the press.

Now we do not have that situation in Toronto. This is the only city in Canada that has three English-language newspapers all under separate ownerships and all competing with each other like mad. We hate each other! And I think that is wonderful. The papers here are all vigorously independent, and because the superficial news is always covered first by radio and TV, there is an honest attempt being made here now to get behind the headlines and tell the public things they do not know and cannot get elsewhere.

There are some disadvantages to this hectic competition, and the thing is not perfect. When you get really fierce competition, the newspapers tend to arrange their front page for the benefit of the opposition newspapermen and not for the readers. I remember in Vancouver, in the old days when competition was really rough—it is not any more—there was a small fire on one of the docks, and the managing editor said to me, "Get a car and six other reporters and three photographers and go down there and run around taking pictures and writing in your notebooks like mad." He said, "That will scare the wits out of the opposition." And, of course, it did. They thought it must be a big story, and they phoned for reinforcements and spread it all over the front page when it should have been two paragraphs inside. That is what I mean about putting out a newspaper for rival newspapermen and not your readers. And I would be the last to say that does not happen here sometimes.

Also, it seems to me that editors tend to think in terms of clichés of two generations ago. When the motor car was a novelty, a traffic accident was big news. When our population was smaller and there was no radio or TV, a murder was always big news. That is less true today. I am convinced that the public does not want so much to know what has happened—it already gets that instantly on the radio—it wants to know why it has happened and what is behind it. And this, often enough, provides the real sensation.

Some of the best reporting being done in the three Toronto papers does not appear on Page 1 at all, under flaring headlines—it appears on the page opposite the editorial page, Page 7, where background stories are published under the bylines of reporters who take their time and use their heads. Many of these stories are truly sensational, and some of them are disturbing. But my only complaint is that there are not enough of them. Yet there are more in this town than elsewhere because when one paper starts something, the others have to follow suit even if it costs money and time and effort.

It is no coincidence that we have in Toronto the only newspaper in Canada that has two of its own men in the Far East, the *Globe and Mail*; in fact, this paper has the only correspondent in Red China of any North American paper. And as a Toronto journalist and a Canadian, I am proud of this even though it is not my paper. Of course, the *Star* used to be the one paper with a Far Eastern correspondent. It is the same correspondent. As a matter of fact, the *Globe* stole him from us, and more power to them for it. It is always a healthy situation when a newspaperman has an alternative job to go to; it makes him just a little more independent than he otherwise might be, and independence is the lifeblood of our business. I hope the time will come when all the Toronto papers will have permanent staff members not only in Peking but also in Moscow and other capitals. As it is, there are more overseas correspondents from this town than from any other. In the towns where a monopoly exists, there aren't any; the newspaper readers there have to depend for their information on syndicated writers or press agency dispatches. I do not think that is any substitute for having your own man on the spot.

And so we return to the question, Is the Press Too Sensational? and my answer: I only wish it were. News, surely by definition, is that part of life around us that is sensational. The sensational findings of the archaeologists, for instance, have always been news. What I think the public objects to in newspapers is the attempt to make sensation out of something that really is not very interesting or very important, that is not, in fact, sensational at all. The advertising people, of course, were partially responsible for this. They use words like amazing, and wonderful, and sensational with absolutely no regard for their meaning. "Here is wonderful news of an amazing new scientific discovery that brings sensational results on wash day." And, we, of the press ourselves, have to take some of the blame. We have used the word "sensational" to describe events and discoveries and even speeches, like this one, that are something less than sensational.

Well, I happen to believe that it is an honourable adjective. I hope we can apply it properly and in its true meaning to more and more newspapers in the future. I should add that I hope there are more and more newspapers in the future, and not fewer and fewer. And, if anybody wants to call me sensational, and some people have, of course, I will not be the least bit upset or disturbed as long as my own brand of sensationalism falls within the definition I have advocated here today. And if it does not, I will be the first to know.

The Ultimate Lunacy
in the Case of Caryl Chessman

From the *Toronto Star*, February 22, 1960

I F THERE IS ANY LAUGHTER left in him, the man in Cell 2458, San Quentin, must surely be indulging himself today.

After eleven and a half years of reprieves, false starts, legal argument, press conferences, last-minute stays and final testaments, Caryl Chessman reached death's door on Friday, and once again the door stayed closed. Not because Caryl Chessman was found to be innocent, not because the conscience of the world dictated it, not because the Powers That Be were clement, not because a final legal loophole went unplugged, but simply because the State Department felt it politically inopportune to kill him for the moment.

In all the lunatic history of the death penalty, this, surely, is the ultimate lunacy. Caryl Chessman is being kept on ice for the convenience of a touring president.

It is a measure of the change in public attitudes that the recent outcry over Chessman should be so loud that it might even inconvenience a good-will tour in an election year.

Time was when we would have hanged Caryl Chessman on a public gibbet to the cheers of the populace and thought nothing of it—hanged him for any one of 350 offences, just as we once hanged small children for stealing silver to buy bread. For we believed, as the Chief Justice of the King's Bench himself believed in 1810, that death was the only real Deterrent to a theft of five shillings.

But we stopped hanging children, at last; and we stopped hanging grown men, too, for stealing or for picking pockets. You would have thought, as a result, that no highway would be safe from road agents, no alleyway empty of footpads, no public gathering free of those same pickpockets who had once done so well at the public executions where their colleagues were strung up.

Yet, I venture to say, you can drive the length of Highway 400 today without being accosted by a single highwayman. O'Keefe Lane, I understand, is empty of footpads, and I have had few reports of pickpockets at Massey Hall. Oddly enough, small children, though no longer hanged, are causing no major social problem by stealing money to buy bread.

Small children get enough to eat today, of course. The streets are brightly lit, thanks to certain work by Michael Faraday and Thomas Edison, and well patrolled, too, thanks to the invention, in 1829, of the uniformed city policeman. Is it possible that these things have proved greater Deterrents than the noose?

However that may be, the executions eventually moved indoors, out of the sunlit squares into the silent dawnlit cells. For we were all growing secretly ashamed of Public Death and wanted to be safely in our beds, out of sight and out of mind, when it occurred. (Though each of us knew it must be retained as a Deterrent.)

And that is why Caryl Chessman, when and if he finally goes to his death, will not ride down Sunset Boulevard in an open Cadillac and die on a scaffold at Hollywood and Vine, in full view of the TV cameras while the team of Chet and Dave describe the spectacle in all its Deterring Detail.

Yet, if Death is the ultimate Deterrent, surely this is the way Chessman ought to die—a public example to all who might wish to copy the ghastly pair of sex crimes for which he stands convicted.

But it is one of the grisly features of the Chessman case that death can be no Deterrent for those who imitate his folly. The law has since been changed and the supreme penalty abolished for crimes such as his.

Had Chessman been an ordinary criminal, without brains or funds, he would have been common clay these past eleven years. But Chessman was smart enough to write the books that earned him the money that bought him the high-priced legal help, that ferreted out the loopholes that have kept him alive in the death cell since 1948.

Thus, in this nagging case, we are faced with a series of paradoxes that makes us squirm uncomfortably in our seats.

The first is the old paradox by which a man of money and talent has been able to postpone the court's verdict for an unconscionably long time. There is little doubt that a poor man or a stupid man would have gone to his death long before this, unwept, unhonoured and uninterviewed.

The second is the paradox by which a man must die for a crime that no longer carries the death penalty. Why, we ask ourselves, are we killing Chessman? To avenge his victims? But even the supporters of Capital Punishment discard revenge. As a Deterrent? But it is no longer that. To be fair, then, to those who were convicted after Chessman but, lacking brains or money or luck, died before him? Perhaps; yet is it not passing bizarre that in order to bring justice to men already dead we must take another life?

Why the universal outcry over the case of Caryl Chessman, a convict undoubtedly guilty of a heinous crime? Why have our consciences been pricked by this particular man and not by others?

The answer is that, over eleven years, we have come to know Caryl Chessman, like it or not. He has written books and given press conferences and granted interviews and generally acted, not as a cipher, but as a human being. His tortured, hawk-nosed face stares out at us, year after year, from the newspaper pages. It is the face of a man of long acquaintance.

We cannot bear now to see him dead for the same reason that we can no longer bear public hangings. We want our legal murders committed before we rise, behind closed doors—committed on faceless criminals by a faceless hangman without even the press on hand. Chessman has got a little too close to us for comfort; he refuses to die quietly and gracefully and anonymously. He embarrasses us as he now embarrasses the President of the United States.

And so we return to the ultimate lunacy and the ultimate irony and the ultimate savagery of the Chessman case. His life has been spared, perhaps for good, in the hope that this act will prevent hot-blooded Latins from hurling jeers or worse at the distinguished representative of a friendly nation.

And so I say, if the man in Cell 2458 has any sense of jest left in him, he must be smiling now over the fact that while his death could never be a Deterrent, his life, it is hoped, will be exactly that.

Mr. Jack Kent Cooke's
Amazing Mystical Conversion

From the *Toronto Star*, March 28, 1960

LTHOUGH ITS SIGNIFICANCE went largely unreported, it seems to me that the chief diversion offered the general public during the hearings in Toronto by the Board of Broadcast Governors was the conversion of Mr. Jack Kent Cooke, the well-known philanthropist, to the new religion of Canadian Culture.

I attended some of the sessions in the Oak Room of Union Station, and though Mr. Cooke did not win a private TV licence, he certainly held the limelight—and held it in the face of some pretty tough competition. There was Mr. Mavor Moore, giving one of the finest dramatic readings of his career, Mr. Johnny Wayne of the Ed Sullivan show, the comedy team of Eugene Forsey and Emlyn Davies (who *should* be on the Ed Sullivan show), Mr. Joel Aldred, the wealthy car salesman, Sir Ernest MacMillan, Foster Hewitt and a cast of hundreds.

I have never seen so many Distinguished Canadians gathered together under one roof. One noticed, in the box seats, such eminent figures as Sir Robert Watson–Watt, the inventor of radar, John Fisher, the inventor of Maple Syrup, Dr. Reva Gerstein, beautiful girl psychologist, and Larry Henderson, beautiful boy newscaster. All of them were involved in the applications.

In these hearings for a TV franchise, Virtue predominated, as Mr. Cooke was to illustrate. Words like "public service," "community interest," "cultural fabric" and "educational responsibility" were studded like sequins through the briefs and submissions. One heard practically nothing about Old Movies, TV Westerns, rock 'n' roll or Mighty Mouse. The accent was on Canadianism and the Arts. Buffalo was the wicked villain, and everybody, Mr. Cooke included, was trying to out-CBC the CBC.

Name-dropping was honed to a fine edge. Every applicant worth his salt managed to sprinkle the names of a score of leading Canadians through his opening remarks. One man got Cardinal McGuigan and Rabbi Feinberg into a single sentence. Another, who had a book publisher on his board, managed to toss off the names of our leading novelists.

By the time Mr. Cooke got up there were no big names left. *Who's Who* had been exhausted. The *Social Register* had been squeezed dry. Undeterred, Mr. Cooke entered the witness box alone—a man who had received the Message and seen the Light. He was dressed in his best suit, a dark conservative number with matching vest and four-in-hand, as befits a Patron of the Arts and a Champion of Culture. There he stood—a so truly blue Canadian that he may easily replace the beaver, the maple leaf and the New York Rangers as a symbol of the nation.

Now you may remember, a while back, that there was some whimpering and hair-rending by the private interests over the BBG's insistence that all programming be 55 percent Canadian in content. I'm happy to report that the carping has ended. Indeed, the applicants at the Oak Room were falling all over themselves to top this figure. It remained for Mr. Cooke to lead the field with 64.4 percent "the instant the station opens."

If Mr. Cooke came to the hearing under certain disadvantages, he turned not a hair. He is the sole owner of CKEY, a radio station that has devoted 58 percent of its time to popular records, more than 20 percent to commercials and less than one-half of 1 percent to public service, children's programs, drama, interviews and documentaries. Yet here was Mr. Cooke promising to deliver great gobs of these things on the screen. The only item missing was *Great Hymns of All Time*, but another applicant proudly unveiled that the following day. (P.S. He won the licence.)

Until his recent conversion, Mr. Cooke was a member of the You-Gotta-Give-the-Public-What-It-Wants School. The closest he got to culture was when he described the Fabulous Sixty tunes on his station as "the folk music of the American continent." He once ran afoul of the Fowler Commission for broadcasting too many commercials. But now here he was talking about a TV station as "the servant of the community" and referring, disarmingly, to one commercial announcement every fifteen minutes.

I don't know if Mr. Cooke has undergone some kind of mystical experience or not, but surely this is the greatest about-face since the days of the Apostle Paul.

"For many years I have observed with deep sympathy the efforts of educational groups in the field of television," said Mr. Cooke earnestly. Well, he was prepared to devote two hours a day, six days a week, to pure education. "And I promise you, gentlemen, that is a minimum!"

With that Mr. Cooke began to reel off the names of organizations that would help him in his work: the Toronto Symphony Orchestra, the Art Gallery, the Royal Ontario Museum, the Opera Guild, the National Ballet, etc. A titter rippled across the audience; they had heard all those names in previous verbal briefs.

Later Mr. Cooke was asked if he had actually approached these various cultural groups. He said he hadn't; they were being bothered by all the other applicants. He planned to wait until they were a little less busy.

One got, next, a fascinating insight into Mr. Cooke's new concept of programming. I do not recall that he mentioned the Top Sixty Tunes, but we did hear about live music, concerts and live union actors (whom Mr. Cooke has never employed). There was talk of a weekly ninety-minute drama "from the great classics of literature—English, French, Greek. . . ." There was a mention of a panel discussion on democracy; there was a reference to a conversation program between a man-and-wife team, discussing such topics as how to fix a leaky drain, the problem of juvenile delinquency, their personal concept of Arnold Toynbee and so on.

Well, Mr. Cooke's performance only served to point up the overall air of unreality that hovered over the proceedings before the BBG. Everything seemed just a little too good to be true. Personally, I longed for some rascal to announce flatly that he planned to produce a blood-and-thunder drama of the Living West. Sandwiched in between the endless Chopin recitals, the wholesome children's programs, the religious choirs, the earnest panel discussions and the National Ballet, it would have come as a breath of fresh air.

This, however, no one could afford to do, the climate being what it was. Oddly, the one note of reality was introduced by Mr. Cooke himself when, in an unguarded moment, he described the private licence as a "rich plum."

And that really was what all the talk about culture and all the breast-beating about Canadianism and all the name-dropping in the Oak Room were actually about.

Toronto's Changing Image

From *The New City*, 1961

W HEN PEOPLE SPEAK of Torontonians in the mass they usually mean Old Torontonians, forgetting that the Old Torontonian is almost extinct. The split between the natives and the newcomers is a very uneven one. As the metropolitan area has almost trebled in population since Depression days, the outlanders (as they are sometimes called) outnumber the native-born by almost two to one. Yet it is the Old Torontonian who has given Toronto its image.

The Old Torontonian of legend is a rock-bound Tory of sturdy Anglo-Saxon merchant stock, a Royalist and a Protestant, a blue blood, humourless and clannish to a fault. His anti-Semitism is apparent enough to the newcomer to be a continuing cause for comment, yet it is not so much an active form of race hatred as it is a passive acceptance of a belief that "those people"—the upstarts, the *nouveau riche*, the immigrant classes, the non-Christians, the non-Protestants, the radicals—do not really belong; they are simply not the Right People. You would not find their sons and daughters at Upper Canada College or Havergal; you would not let them into the best clubs because they are not True Torontonians.

The Old Torontonian is the truest of the blue. A believer in the sanctity of private property, he has none of the herd instincts of the invading horde. That is perhaps why, until recently, Toronto has been a city of single-family dwellings. Old Torontonians, rich and poor, have been brought up in individual houses—not apartments or boarding-houses, or duplexes or triplexes or flats or lodgings, or artists' attics or ribbon developments, but detached homes of solid brick or, at the very least, brick facing. We have the word of Hugh Garner, its chronicler, that Toronto's Cabbagetown district, once the largest Anglo-Saxon slum on the continent, was one of the very few in which each family owned its own house.

In the nineteenth century, along Jarvis Street and Queen's Park Crescent, where the merchant princes lived, these houses were truly baronial. Hart Massey's great mansion had twenty-seven rooms, eight bathrooms, eighteen mantelpieces and a pantry so large it was later rented out as a three-room apartment. The windows were leaded and stained, the walls frescoed, the ceilings gilded, the floors inlaid, the tile mosaicked. Moors came from Spain to garland the walls with arabesques. Craftsmen from Scotland fashioned the scrolled mahogany cabinets. The moulds for the bas-relief on the walls were instantly destroyed so they could never be copied. A conservatory, big as a nightclub, was hot with orchids. An organ, a fish pond, a fountain and an Otis-Fensom elevator were all part of the furnishings.

Some of the castle-like quality is still faintly present in Rosedale and Forest Hill and along Bayview and The Kingsway, where Norman turrets, square Georgian mansions and Tudor gables (their small, leaded windows invariably curtained) help preserve Toronto the legend. The houses are still being built faster than the apartments, and out in the great, grey expanses of Scarborough, East York, Etobicoke and half a dozen other suburbs, a kind of fruit-box architecture prevails: here are street after street of small brick bungalows, each identical with its brother, all seemingly stamped out by a giant machine and laid out in neat rows for sale.

Thus, the Old Torontonian looks at the world through a special window. As a property owner he is instinctively cautious. He is not one to make whoopee in local night spots. When he dines, he almost always dines at home, or in somebody else's home. He has little sympathy with anyone who wants to disturb the measured grace of his Sunday, which by happenstance as much as religious temperament he has made a day of quiet. He does not understand the needs or hungers of those who are imprisoned in small apartments or single rooms; indeed, he does not think of them at all.

Dr. Martin Loeb, a social scientist whose depth studies of various Torontonians are the basis of much that follows, recalls that in his boyhood days in Toronto apartment dwellers were something beyond the pale: one simply did not know them. There are still thousands of Torontonians today who do not really know their city: do not know what kind of people live there, have rarely if ever been inside a nightclub (unless one counts the gilded, high-ceilinged ballrooms of the Royal York or the King Edward), have never eaten at a foreign restaurant or explored the gaudier expanses of their own town.

Although the Upper Class Old Torontonian is staunchly Church of England (with all that the name implies), the middle-class Old Torontonian tends to be Methodist in background. Toronto owes much of its image to its Methodist merchants. Its reputation for commercial acumen as much as its reputation for Puritanism stems from its Methodist ancestry. The public tends to remember these traits and forget that Methodism also had a social conscience, which is responsible for the heavily liberal and progressive qualities in the Canadian political character.

The Puritan stamp of the Methodists is still on Toronto in various small ways. The curtains in Timothy Eaton's great stores are still tightly drawn on Sundays, and tobacco has never been sold within. The late Joseph Atkinson's *Toronto Daily Star* still does not accept liquor advertising, continues to delete all references to the joys of imbibing, real or fancied, and prefers to refer to all spirits as plain, beastly "booze."

The Massey family, perhaps the greatest that the city has produced, was solidly Methodist. One Massey, parching in the Sahara, preferred to flirt with death rather than drink the only available liquid—wine. Sunday was so sacrosanct in the Massey homes that you couldn't even put a roll of Brahms on the electric player-organ much less ride a bicycle on the streets. The only amusements allowed the young Masseys were charades, mimes and *tableaux vivants*; the ironic result was that an astonishing number, including the famous Raymond, ended up in the theatrical world that the Methodists so fervently decried.

The most famous of the Methodists, Egerton Ryerson, gave his name to the Methodist publishing house that earned an early distinction by forcing Robert Service, the Klondike poet, to tone down some of his more robust work in the days before the First World War. Such traditions die hard in Toronto. In the late fifties, the Ryerson Press was refusing to distribute, much less publish, the much more robust poetry of its protégé Irving Layton.

In addition to this Puritan heritage, two other influences must be considered in the historical background of the Old Torontonian. One is the influence of the United Empire Loyalists and the other is the influence of the Loyal Orange Lodge. Loyalty is the key word—loyalty to Empire, to Queen, to all things British and Imperial, to the Protestant Church, to tradition, to the old-established values. The political influence of the Orangemen in Toronto's past was overwhelming, the emotional influence of the United Empire Loyalists equally so. Both movements made for conservatism, indeed for Blimp-ism; both helped develop the Toronto attitude; both are long outdated.

Where is the Old Torontonian today? Occasionally a rare specimen is encountered in the panelled confines of the Toronto Club or perhaps at the Hunt Ball. When one of them gives away a bride, or brings a daughter out, or is buried at Timothy Eaton Memorial Church, his picture appears in the press. I understand that one or two are being mounted and stuffed for posterity at the Royal Ontario Museum. But the typical Torontonians today are the New Torontonians. They dominate the city.

The genus may be conveniently divided into two species: first, the native-born Canadians who have moved to Toronto from the other parts of the country; second, the immigrants who have arrived from overseas. Since the war years, more than half a million of the latter and almost as many of the former have descended upon the metropolitan area of Toronto, which now has a total population of one and a half million. I doubt that any other city on the continent has absorbed such a high proportion of strangers in a similar period. It is they who are determining the city's shape and future course.

These two groups of New Torontonians see the city from opposite ends of the same telescope. To most immigrants, the physical town is a disappointment after the great cities of Europe. But to the native Canadian it is likely to be the first really big city he has lived in (since the people of Montreal, the only comparable community, rarely move to Toronto).

To the man from the prairie village or the coastal town, Toronto is the Hollywood and the Detroit of Canada as well as the New York. Contrary to what he has been told, there is much more to do here than there was at home. With his seven channels of TV, he feels for the time that he is really in the centre of things.

The immigrant, and especially the foreign-speaking immigrant, views the city differently. He tends to find it cold and unfriendly, and he is not dazzled by its size. He is not used to this North American style of community, which is little more than a vast machine for working. He is used to downtown parks and squares, to broad avenues and boulevards, to open spaces of all kinds. He believes aesthetic standards are important, and he does not find them in Toronto, with its narrow streets, its constricted areas and its hidebound architecture. He is a "downtown" man, and in various small ways his influence is already being felt. Within a generation he will have changed the face and the feel of the city.

The immigrant also wants a freer, easier city. He is perfectly prepared to attend church on Sunday mornings, but in the afternoons he wants some entertainment. With 500,000 immigrants pressing in upon it, the traditional Toronto Sunday hasn't a chance. Already the bars and coffeehouses and foreign restaurants are blossoming, and there are even one or two sidewalk cafés straining to bloom, like roses in a desert. One of the reasons for Toronto's new theatrical revival is consistent immigrant support.

When people first move to Toronto, and this is especially true of native-born Canadians, they tend to rent an apartment—and apartment living is new to Toronto. In the metropolitan area there are now some 60,000 apartments occupied, and of these 45,000 have been built since 1946. Almost 200,000 Torontonians, therefore, now live in large apartment blocks of six or more suites, and this figure doesn't cover housekeeping rooms, flats above stores or boarding-houses. Another 200,000 live in boarding-houses. It's a fair guess that almost a third of the population consists of people who are not home-owners.

The apartment dwellers are changing the city, too. It has been discovered, for instance, that they eat in restaurants at least once a week, and this finding comes as a shock to some Old Torontonians who rarely eat out at all. That is one reason why the restaurant business has started to flourish in a city that, until recently, has never been famous for its cuisine.

A scientific study of the apartment dweller shows what a different animal he is from the home-owning Old Torontonian. People have to learn how to use the apartment approach to life—not an easy task when one considers the deep-rooted rural tradition in our culture: house living has a strong emotional attraction. The house is a status symbol in Toronto, standing for family, stability and worth. The apartment is only an address.

Life comes to the man who lives in a house, and he does not need to seek it out. But in Toronto, the urban apartment becomes a base from which one goes out to find life—to find clubs, restaurants, laundromats, parks, bars, nightclubs and friends. And so, as the apartments begin to rise, the city stirs restlessly.

"At some given point in the growth of a city," says the social scientists' report, "there is a development of rootlessness. Living in different places, moving from job to job and perhaps even from spouse to spouse is part of the cosmopolitan life. Perhaps the word 'disengagement' should be used. . . . One characteristic of the apartment dweller is his tentativeness. He is looking for a change. . . .

"Living in hutches rather than houses is still largely a matter of second choice in Toronto. Apartment living has not yet become an established custom. If one is not sure one is going to stay in Toronto, then an apartment provides a solution. The basic uncertainty comes from those who are always looking for the big chance—the young, socially mobile people. . . .

"One of the most striking characteristics of the apartment dwellers is their interest in occupational success. They see Toronto as a city of opportunity. In many ways this must be true, but it seems that if another place were to present equal or better opportunity they would likely leave Toronto and go to a new spot."

And so apartment dwellers, like the immigrants (and sometimes the two are the same) are a breed unto themselves, totally distinct from the Old Torontonian. They are young married people, many of them with children. They are a very active group, who go out on evenings and weekends, crazy about sports, movies, theatres and vacation spots. These are the people, generally, that one sees downtown of a Friday evening crowding in and out of the Yonge Street bars, listening to folk songs, poetry and jazz in the after-hours attic and cellar clubs, jamming Maple Leaf Gardens for the wrestling and the hockey, flocking to *avant garde* plays, horror movies, museum tours, dance marathons, pizza carnivals, photo nites, satirical revues, goulash parlours, sportsmen's shows, motoramas, Broadway musicals, ragtime concerts, Chinese restaurants, Italian song festivals, silent films, TV panels, baseball openings, Sunday symphonies, ban-the-bomb rallies, stripperamas, roller rinks, steak houses, prom concerts, picture galleries and taverns—all of which have become a part of life in turbulent Toronto.

These are the people one sees on weekends stretched out by the thousands beside picnic tables in the sunlit conservation parks that are scattered about the city's outer perimeter. I remember one Sunday in Albion Hills Park, walking along the creekside and hearing what sounded like a recording of a Verdi opera playing somewhere in the woods. It wasn't a recording. I turned a corner in the pathway and came upon eight Italian construction workers, stripped to the waist, each holding an illegal bottle of beer and singing in unison around a picnic table.

These people care not a hoot about tradition. They are not sentimental about conventional Toronto. The blue Sunday knows no stronger opponents. Accustomed to change themselves, they are eager to see their adopted city change. They want more subways, more parks, more slum clearance plans, more traffic planning, more big buildings, more theatres and restaurants. In short they want a big, cosmopolitan city—and that, inevitably, means more apartments.

And so the old stability symbols, of which the red brick house was the most important, are vanishing along with the old Toronto image. Large numbers of New Torontonians will have to find substitutes for these symbols of stability. "Learning these substitutes," says Dr. Loeb, the social scientist, "and putting them together is a way of life, is part of the process of becoming a big city."

The Berlin Wall Goes Up

From the *Toronto Star*, September 25, 1961

B ERLIN IS A DREAM CITY, in almost every sense of the word. Its people live in a daydream that is as noble as it is illusory— the daydream of ultimate togetherness. They live with nightmares, too, knowing that on both sides of the Wall, a rock thrown at the wrong moment could touch off an explosion that would be their end.

The town harbours all the eerie inconsistencies that are to be found only in dreams—walls that run through churches and international borders that literally cut farmhouses in two. Yet the city also has its dream castles, and these are to be seen everywhere. Most of the world's great architects have left their monuments in Berlin.

The bad dreams of childhood also linger. One turns a corner and comes upon a mutilated building, furry with the mould of sixteen years, and if one looks carefully one can still see, somewhere in the rubble, the broken outlines of an eagle clutching a carved wreath from which the inevitable swastika has been hastily chiselled away.

But more than this, Berlin has all the phoniness of a dream. The contrasts between the East and West sectors of the city are certainly striking, but it is dangerous to make assumptions, as some do, about democracy and communism on the basis of what is on display here. Both halves of the town are weirdly unreal. West Berlin, for all its tinsel trimming, is an artificial community subsidized by the West to the tune of almost $400 million a year or more than twice what it costs to run Metro Toronto. Without this pump-priming the town would collapse. East Berlin, on the other hand, has had the sustenance purposely drained from it by its conquerors, who operate on the conviction that the vanquished ought to be made to pay the piper.

Berlin remains—and this is sometimes forgotten—an occupied city, on both sides of the Wall. On the western side this occupation is largely technical, but legally the British, Americans and French are masters of their sectors as the occasional incident demonstrates. The commander of the French sector, for instance, insisted on banning Kirk Douglas's film *Paths of Glory* because it dealt with a particularly shameful incident in the French army during the First World War. (The theatre owners in the rest of West Berlin were delighted by the publicity.)

Thus Berlin is unlike any other city in the world. It has more policemen, for example, than any other city, yet it has few planned crimes and almost no bank robberies since the criminals have no place to escape with their loot.

It has the highest movie attendance in Europe, and this is a symptom of the great Berlin malady—finding some place to go. It could be far worse, of course, for Berlin is a vast metropolis. There are even fields of grain and corn studded with cattle and sheep within the city limits—enough to supply the western sector with 10 percent of all its food needs. Yet, in spite of this, Berlin inevitably suffers from its isolation. That is why West Berlin's TV station holds an annual drive to get the children out of the city and why weekend tours to West German forests are doing a thriving business.

Yet Berliners have always been a special breed of German. Hitler certainly had no love for this town, which was the last to accept him. The Berliners are known for a particularly ironic form of humour, and this has served them well in crisis. I was shown, with great glee, a new insurance company head office, the floors of which had collapsed. The company had sued its architect, who had fought back in the courts. After a drawn-out case the architect lost. Fortunately, he was insured against such disasters—with the same company. This kind of thing tickles the Berliner's fancy.

After sixteen years of isolation the Berliner tends to think of himself as a Berliner first, a European second and a German third. "Those West Germans are a real bunch of hicks," one young Berliner told me, insisting that this was a general attitude in Berlin.

Certainly there is a fierce civic pride. Few Canadians, I suspect, would consider Berlin a good place to live, but there's plenty of evidence to show that hundreds of thousands of Berliners would live in no other city. Indeed, a man who packs up is thought of as a bit of a quitter. This explains the significance of a sign one Berliner put on a moving van while I was in the city: "Yes, I'm moving," the sign read, "but only to another part of Berlin!"

The fierce and often sacrificial loyalty of the West Berliners to their town was graphically illustrated while I was there. Signs had sprung up reading A Ticket on the S-Bahn Buys Ulbricht's Barbed Wire. The S-Bahn, or overhead railway, is owned by the East Germans though it runs—and continues to run, Wall or no Wall, crisis or no crisis—all over Berlin. It is the cheapest and most popular form of transportation, being about half the cost of subway or bus. It is an important source of revenue to the Communists, who are eager for hard money—the westmark being worth four times the eastmark.

Yet after the Wall was built, thousands of West Berlin workmen started to pay double in order to avoid the S-Bahn. The last figures I received showed that 290,000 of them had switched to bus or subway, causing a minor transportation crisis in the city. Scores of buses had to be commandeered from all over West Germany to solve the situation, and these arrived complete with drivers to whom Berlin's streets were utterly strange. They were still sorting it out when I left.

For all these outward displays of bravado, one cannot escape the suspicion, reinforced by statistics, that Berlin is a dying city. There *has* been a retreat from Berlin, but it has gone unnoticed since the population has always been maintained at a steady level by the flow of refugees across the border from the Soviet sector. On the day before the Wall went up 3,700 fled from East Berlin. Now that flow has died to a trickle. Inevitably, it seems to me, West Berlin must decline.

This the Berliners will never admit, and one can understand and admire their refusal to come to grips with the unthinkable. West Berlin's morale rests on faith—the unswerving belief that what is going on within the city is in the nature of a holding operation, that the day is coming when Berlin will be the capital of a united Germany. Nowhere is this more graphically demonstrated than in the town-planning department, where everybody stubbornly acts as if Berlin were one city and autobahns are planned to encircle, not just a part, but the whole.

Thus, Berlin clings to its dreams, and tries to forget its nightmares.

How I Launched
My Professional Writing Career

From the *Toronto Star*, January 4, 1962

A ROUND THIS TIME OF YEAR, I always get to wondering about a man named Chuck Gunn and whether or not he ever married a girl named Elsie.

I knew Chuck at Vernon, B.C., when we were both taking Basic Training. He slept three or four bunks away, and my first memory of him is of a short, stocky figure hunched over a writing pad, desperately trying to think of something to write to his girlfriend back in Vancouver.

I had a small Hermes Baby portable that fitted neatly into a large army pack, and I was clacking away like crazy on it when I caught Chuck's haunted look. He had been trying all evening to write that letter, and so far he hadn't got much farther than *Dear Elsie*.

And that, friends, is how I broke into the professional writing game. Chuck paid me a dollar to write a letter for him. In those days I was hungry to write anything, so he really got his money's worth.

I cannot remember all of that first letter, but I recall certain passages. It was, of course, a love letter in the finest tradition:

I can feel the insistent thumping of my eager heart as it beats against the ribs of its human prison [I wrote]. *Please, please set it free before it bursts from its long incarceration!*

"What does that mean?" Chuck asked nervously.

"It means you're mad for her," I told him. And I wrote that her eyes were like deep pools of gold dust stirred by tiny winds, a phrase I had stolen from an old *Doc Savage* magazine.

"Her eyes are sort of blue," Chuck said. So I changed it to deep pools of forget-me-nots.

125

That first letter ran to seventeen pages, and I got sort of intoxicated by my own prose. I quoted Omar Khayyam whom at the age of twenty-one I had just committed entirely to memory. I sneaked in a lush line or two from Ernest Dowson, who is another poet for twenty-one-year-olds. (I told Elsie I was desperately trying to "put thy pale lost lilies out of mind.")

I am sitting here [I wrote] *in the fitful gloom of an army hut, alone with the leaping shadows cast by the flaring light of a pot-bellied stove, thinking of you. My new-found comrades sleep, but I cannot sleep because my heart is too full, thinking of our last parting.*

"What did you do at your last parting?" I shouted to Chuck, who had joined a poker game at the other end of the barrack room.

"I can't remember much about it," he called back. "I was a bit loaded."

. . . No doubt you thought me intoxicated, and I was—intoxicated with the perfume of you . . . rendered insensate by the presence of your being . . . reeling with desire, yet desperately afraid to bruise the fragility of that bitter-sweet moment. . . Yes, Elsie, I was drunk, shamelessly drunk—but not with spirits, unless you count the flaming spirit that would drive me into the haven of your arms. . .

"Do you really think she'll believe I wrote it?" Chuck asked hesitantly when I handed him his dollar's worth. I assured him that she would—and that it would be a revelation to her. Actually, a sinister plan was already half forming in my mind. *Why*, a little demon was asking me, *should all this lovely prose-poetry be put to the service of Chuck?*

Elsie's reply, which arrived a few days later, was, to say the least, somewhat dampening.

Dear Honeybun [she wrote]: *Thanks a million for your newsy letter of last week, with all the little "titbits" of gossip. It sure was good to hear from you, Chuck. I miss you, too, honey, so take care of yourself and come back real soon. — Elsie.*

"Well," said Chuck, much relieved, "she doesn't seem to have noticed that the style is a bit different." I gritted my teeth. Surely, I thought, this woman must understand that this clod couldn't have written all that sensitive prose?

Chuck gave me another dollar to answer Elsie and then went back to the poker game. Now my mettle was up.

Dear Elsie [I wrote]: *The vacuum left by your presence is almost unbearable. Companionship here is all but denied me since my army cronies are low people of undistinguished mien who much prefer playing poker and singing rowdy songs to intelligent conversation. In all this human desert there is only one man whom I am pleased to call friend. His name is Pierre and he is a good cut above the others here. Nobody can figure out why he is still a private since he obviously has the necessary qualifications to make a battalion commander. I find his conversation stimulating in the extreme, and his knowledge of Omar Khayyam is simply voluminous. He is tall and good looking and strong as an ox; yet, I think, he can be gentle, too. I was thinking of introducing him to you on my leave but fear to, since he is irresistible to women. Perhaps we may leave that matter in abeyance.*

But enough of him. Let us talk of you. Through the darkling window of this simple barrack room the questing moon stares down with unwinking eye—the same pale moon that at this moment kisses your own spun-gold hair. . .

And so on for seventeen pages.

"Listen," said Chuck, when he read the letter, "I'm not paying you any dollar to plug yourself. Also, her hair is kind of mousy brown."

"I'll let you have it for free," I said hastily, breaking the union rules. Chuck was in a hurry to get back to the game and couldn't resist the offer. So the letter was mailed, uncensored, and all that week I waited impatiently for Elsie's answer.

Dear Honeybun [she finally wrote]: *Thanks again for taking time out to drop me a note about all your "doings." The gang in the barrack room sound really cute. But your so-called friend, Pierre, sounds like a bit of a creep. The weather is quite nice here but cold at night. I miss you. Do you have to write such long letters? Love, Elsie.*

And that ended my proxy romance with Chuck's girlfriend. He went back to writing his own letters.

Dear Elsie: Not much to write about today. Hope you are all well at home. In haste, Chuck.

She answered in kind. I never did get to meet her, but then I really didn't try very hard. I don't think we had much in common.

For Whom the Bell Rings

From *Spring Thaw '62*, A Stage Revue

*A*T STAGE LEFT *is the suggestion of a living room: a chesterfield or low settee, occasional chair, coffee table, lamp and a white phone. Husband and wife sit side by side on settee reading. Wife occasionally looks at watch.*

At stage right is a phone booth. A few seconds after scene opens, it is spotlit and a young, slightly frantic man arrives, looking anxiously at his watch. He dials; phone rings in the living-room set. Husband absently reaches for it.

WIFE   (*quickly*): No. I'll get it. (*She seizes the receiver.*)

LOVER   (*in phone booth*): Anne? Anne, darling? Is it you, Anne? (*He is ardent.*)

WIFE   (*pleasantly non-committal*): Yes. . . This is Mrs. Jones.

From this point on the young man is always intense while the wife sounds as if she may be talking to a stranger or a girlfriend.

LOVER: Oh, *God*, Anne—for a moment I thought perhaps you wouldn't answer! I've been going out of my mind with loneliness!

WIFE: Well, I'm certainly interested to hear that.

LOVER: You do love me don't you, darling? Say it, please! I've got to hear it from you. Please, Anne.

WIFE: Yes, well I'm afraid that's not going to be possible at the moment. (*Looks at husband, who is reading newspaper.*)

LOVER: Is there somebody with you? Is that what you're trying to tell me?

WIFE   (*pleasantly casual*): Yes. Yes, there is. Mm hmm.

LOVER: Is it—is it *him*?

WIFE: (*Laughs.*) Yes, that's right.

LOVER: I *need* you! Do you need me?

WIFE: Yes. I certainly do. Mm hmm. Yes.

LOVER: When can we meet? Where?

WIFE: Well, I'm afraid I couldn't tell you at the moment.

LOVER: How about next Wednesday?

WIFE: Possibly.

LOVER: Tuesday then! Thursday?

WIFE: The latter.

LOVER: Where'll we meet, darling?

WIFE: Well, I don't think I could say, really.

LOVER: How about the . . . the King Edward?

WIFE: I don't believe so . . . no.

LOVER: Oh, of course—that snippy desk clerk.

HUSBAND (*looking at watch*): Anne, for God's sake, are you going to stay on that phone all night?

WIFE: I'll be through in a moment, Henry.

LOVER: God, he bugs me.

WIFE: Me too!

LOVER: How about the Park Plaza? It's central.

WIFE: That would be fine.

LOVER: The same time?

WIFE: Ah . . . possibly.

LOVER: A little later—is that what you mean?

WIFE: Yes. That's right.

LOVER: Half an hour later? An hour?

WIFE: The latter, more likely.

LOVER: Darling, I've been tossing and turning. . .

HUSBAND: *Anne!*

WIFE: Yes, well thank you for calling. It's been nice talking to you.

LOVER: I'm kissing you through the phone (*makes kissing sound in receiver*). Can you hear that?

WIFE: Yes. I believe I can. Well, goodbye.

LOVER: All right, darling, until Thursday.

She hangs up and lover goes off. Husband looks again at watch. Wife resumes place on settee and picks up paper husband has dropped. Phone rings again and she reaches for it, but he forestalls her.

HUSBAND: I'll get it. (*Picks up receiver.*) Yes . . . this is he. . . Well, I'm certainly interested to hear that. . . Oh. I'm afraid that's not possible at the moment. . . Er, the latter.

Wife looks up from paper and stares at husband on phone.

BLACKOUT

Seasonal Reflections of a Country Dweller: February; April; May; October; November

From *Fast Fast Fast Relief*, 1962

February

I LOOKED OUT FROM MY BEDROOM window a few mornings ago and got one of those small bonuses that are granted occasionally, like free coupons in a Lucky Pop, to those of us who live in the country.

The world that morning was chalk-white, like a high-key photograph, each pointed cedar in our valley tipped with frost, each apple tree in the wild orchard etched in alabaster against the pale blue of the sky. A spectral mist rose delicately from the ashen ground through the white trees; nothing else moved. It is on mornings like these, I thought, that one has no regrets about the rural life.

I have been living in the country now for almost eleven years, and I cannot conceive of any situation that would make me dwell again in the city.

"But that terrible drive!" my friends are always saying. "Twenty-five miles, twice a day! I don't know how you do it."

I do it gratefully, for I consider it a boon to be locked up in a car for two hours every day, alone with my thoughts, safe from the insistent knock on the door and the unremitting jangle of the telephone. For much of this time I pass through a rolling countryside that is never the same one day to the next. When one lives long in the country one becomes alert to the changes of nature, and so the wayside seems to be alive. The first russet tinge on the grey limbs of the apple trees, the first glow on the red ozier, the first yellowing of the willow branches, all these are observed and noted and compared with previous seasons. One can tell almost to the day when the blue chicory will flower in the ditches, or the sumac reach the sensual peak of its autumn scarlet. The sight of a red-tailed hawk on a treetop, or a catbird in the thicket sets up one's day. Even the frequency with which the jackrabbits bounce in front of the car or the field mice scurry from their grassy tunnels takes on significance, for these, too, have their cycles, and the country dweller knows which years they are at their peaks and their ebbs.

When I first moved to the country I announced in my naïveté that I would have nothing whatsoever to do with the land. But when you live close to the soil, and all around you the glistening fields are being tilled and seeded, you cannot long resist the urge to create. A tree becomes as sacred as a wayside shrine after you have planted one or two of them; topsoil becomes more precious than any treasure; compost, which has been the subject of endless comic essays, takes on a truly mystic quality.

We throw nothing away in our house that can be returned to the black earth. Dead leaves and old grass cuttings, the discarded tops of frost-killed annuals, kitchen refuse of all kinds (from coffee grounds to apple peelings), lumps of old sod, the carcasses of groundhogs and rabbits—all these are piled in one corner of the lot and covered in earth and turned over every so often until they assume the consistency of mush and are spread out, at last, to renew a tired plot that has had the sustenance drained from it. To this day I cannot pass a city garbage pail without flinching at the thought of all that potential plant food gone to waste.

I began gardening during my second summer in the country when I did not know a hyacinth from a tuberose. One learns by trial and error, like a Sunday painter—planting a clump of shrubbery one season and digging it up and moving it to a new spot the next. It has occurred to me since that gardening is the most satisfying of all the visual arts since it alone is four-dimensional. A painting is flat and unchanging, and even a piece of sculpture, though you can view it from every angle, is static. But a garden moves through time: it is never the same from day to day, from season to season, from year to year. Its very impermanence conspires against its enshrinement.

You cannot hang a garden in a picture gallery—even capture it properly in a photograph—and only in Japan are famous gardeners and gardens of the past preserved in memory and honoured.

Every gardener, like every chess player, is a forward-looker. He sees his handiwork not as it is but as it will be. He plants a small whip of locust or a maple sapling and sees it as a sturdy tree five, ten, fifteen years hence. In the late fall he looks out on his borders and sees, not a strip of black loam, empty of growth, but a garden ablaze with April's scarlet. For he knows that beneath the soil, row on row, lie the plump bulbs of the Red Emperor and that within each bulb, curled up like an embryo, is a tiny green miniature of the flower that will burst forth in Technicolour when the snow has fled. In the country you learn something of the art of patience. The trees will grow, in their own time, to shade the house; the flowers will open and the fruit ripen when they are ready and not one moment sooner. Every amateur, when he begins, tends to plant things too large and too close together. He soon learns to plant them smaller and farther apart and to bide his time; they will grow.

Before I lived in the country I was at odds with the elements. Snow and rain were my foes. I have long since learned to welcome them both. At the moment I have a pond slowly filling up, and each heavy snowfall brings it that much closer to completion. As for rain, there are summers when I have prayed for it. In the city, where the plots are small and the gardens smaller, one can afford to water with a hose. In the country there is just too much space, and you learn to leave the watering to nature. Thus, there is no sweeter music than the rumble of thunder on a hot summer's eve, and when the small rivulets of water stream across the cracked and wrinkled surface of the soil, like tears on an old man's cheeks, the heart leaps.

I would not recommend country life for all. Some people are urban to their fingertips, and the long silences that we experience in the night—the absolute absence of brakesqueal, for instance—would only unnerve them. We cannot pop into the supermarket next door, for there is none—only a general store a mile or so away;

nor is there a neighbour just across the fence; there is no fence, only a rolling expanse of pasture-land dotted with small trees that will in time become big trees. But there is also a valley with a river winding through it, and a clump of pointed cedars and a wild orchard; and when they turn chalk-white, as they did one morning last week, and the ghost of a mist rises through them, soft as a maiden's breath, then I would not trade the country life for the fanciest penthouse on Park Avenue.

April

In Vaughan Township this month the concession roads are dark torrents of mud. The fields, tawny with last fall's stubble, have scarcely started to show green. The woodlots, a-tangle with the carcasses of elms and beeches splintered by last winter's storms, are naked of bud. In the dark places of the forest there is still the occasional tattered patch of soiled snow.

Yet there are signs of a reluctant spring. In the brimming swamps, the first red-winged blackbirds are searching for nesting places. In the apple orchards the branches glow redly. Along the roadsides the dogwood has turned from brown to crimson, while each giant weeping willow seems enveloped in a cloud of yellow mist. For the sap is running, as surely as the rivulets that crease the bottom land along the Humber. On Amos Baker's farm last week you could see it pouring from the trees, drip-dripping into the pails, coursing through the plastic tubing toward the underground tanks, and bubbling and steaming in the 200-gallon vats.

There are more than three thousand maples on Amos Baker's woodlot, and they have been standing there unlogged since Indian times. When the peak of the syrup season is reached they pour forth their juices at the rate of eight hundred gallons an hour, and then there is no rest for anyone.

The peak was reached a few days ago. Early one morning Amos Baker, watch in hand, was out among his trees, a pink-cheeked

135

man with flowing white hair, dressed as always in a dark suit and wearing a high-crowned black hat. He was performing an annual rite: timing the number of drops of sap that flowed each minute from certain familiar maples. As the day progressed, Baker saw that the flow was increasing. At four o'clock, when the sap normally ceases, the gain continued and Baker then knew that the trees would run all night and perhaps the following night as well.

For three days and four nights Amos Baker and his sons stayed on the job without sleep, emptying buckets, filling the vats and tending the fires. It has been that way for almost a century and a half. Five generations of Bakers have boiled sap at the same spot near the corner of the venerable woodlot, which is Toronto's biggest source of syrup.

There are maples here that were fully grown and producing sap when Amos Baker's great-uncle bought the land in 1816. There are trees with more than one hundred holes drilled in them, all long grown over. Sometimes when an ancient giant is finally felled, Baker finds century-old wooden plugs hidden eight inches within the trunk. These go back to the days of the pioneers who believed that plugging the hole with pine wood kept the trees healthy.

Last week I went out to watch the sugaring at the Baker farm. My first view of it put me in mind of pictures in my old school geography texts. There behind the old stump fence rose the naked trees: the pines, pocked by the oblong holes of the pileated woodpeckers, the beeches, smooth and grey, the ash, the basswood and the oaks all rising from the soft carpet of leafmould—and of course the maples, each marked with its bright blue pail. Squinting back into the soft grey depths of the spring woods, you could see these splashy spots of blue, standing out like queer flowers in a desert.

Off to one side stood the sugaring shack, built thirty-three years ago on the site of a previous shack, the steam pouring from it in a sweet cloud. Here the past mingles with the future, for Amos Baker is a man who likes to link one generation with another. He has preserved the foundation of the first furnace built by his father when the black iron kettles went into discard sixty-five years ago. Today it forms the base for his glistening sap tanks.

The Bakers, being Dunkards, a sect very similar to the Mennonites, do not bother with movies, radio or television. But on that farm the most modern equipment is on display. Galvanized funnels, thirty of them, poke their snouts from the forest floor. These lead to a subterranean network of pipes a mile long that drains the sap into underground storage tanks of 7,000-gallon capacity.

Inside the shack a mechanical pumping system feeds the sap, three hundred gallons at a time, into vats heated by oil jets and so constructed (through a system of thermostats, gauges and siphons) that the entire process of syrup-making has become almost automatic.

And so it is no longer necessary to throw an egg into the simmering brew to get rid of black matter or to toss in a chunk of pork to prevent the lot from boiling over. Even the trees are drilled mechanically by a man with a one-horsepower gasoline motor on his back.

On this farm, which owes so much to the past (where the house dates back to 1853 and the Pennsylvania-style barn to 1820), progress is not an evil word. The blue buckets themselves are about to become obsolete, thanks to the miracle of polyethylene tubing known as "Maple Flow." Baker has already been testing hundreds of trees by this method of tapping sugar maples. There's no doubt now that in a few years every tree in his woodlot will be connected by several miles of transparent tube, so that three thousand trees will be placed in harness, all pumping their sap in unison toward the storage tanks.

Here, in this tubing, one can view the throbbing magic of spring. No human agency, no mechanical device sends the sap coursing through the tubes. It is the trees themselves that pump it. In the spring when the juices within the trunk are drawn skyward toward the branches, a hole is drilled in each maple and the tubing connected by airtight spiles. Thus the sap that escapes is forced from tree to tree by an inhuman pressure that sends it gushing from a tube at the far end by a force as inexplicable as gravity. You can see it with your own eyes, bubbling along like blood in a vein, the very heartbeat of nature laid bare.

And that is how it is on the Baker farm where, a century ago, there were no grocery stores and the only sugar on the table came from the enduring maples. In those times the Baker family made syrup for its own use; now they produce three thousand quarts a year, and the supply has yet to exceed the demand.

Everything on the Baker farm has changed, in a sense, since Jonathan Baker first hand-hewed timbers for his barn. Yet nothing fundamental has really changed. Each spring, when the roads are dark torrents of mud and the dogwood forms its crimson fringe along the byways, the ancient cycle of the sap begins again and no human force can stop it. It helps explain why the Bakers hold fast to their gentle religion, as plain and enduring as the trees themselves.

May

Yellow is surely the colour of early spring. We saw, last week, the dandelions in their legions start up from the pale earth, buttering the meadows and the sideroads. The awakening willows, genuflecting before the May breezes, have been clothed in a catkin mist. The very warblers, nesting in orchard and thicket, are dappled with the protective hues of forsythia and daffodil. In the cedar groves, the first wild flowers have burst forth in various shades of citron, sulphur, apricot and gold.

For more than a decade, at this season, I have driven west along the Maple sideroad and stopped just before reaching the Purpleville corner. Here, concealed from the speed-blinded sportscar set, lies a small cool glen with a gurgle of water at its base. Last Sunday, the floor of this shaded hollow was brilliant with the mosaic of marsh marigolds, sometimes called cowslips.

I know of no more luxurious sight in mid-May than these golden flowers. They are not marigolds, really, since the garden marigolds we know are properly members of the daisy family (and, to confuse matters further, the French and African marigolds are really natives of Mexico). Nor are they true cowslips. The cowslip beds on which Shakespeare's Puck was wont to lie were actually yellow primulas, the mainstay of the old-fashioned English garden.

The marsh marigold is a buttercup, belonging to that vast family of brilliant bloom, wild and cultivated, that includes such exotic specimens as the peony, the columbine and the delphinium. If you search the woods a month from now, in the low moist areas along the rivers and streams, you will see another member of the family—that lovely white-cupped flower called the Canadian anemone. I have watched such a clump growing larger year by year on a bank above the east branch of the Humber. It multiplies by underground roots and nothing—not even Hurricane Hazel, which once buried this particular patch beneath a foot-thick layer of sand—can stop it.

When I first moved to the country in 1949 I knew nothing of wild flowers; but you cannot live long beside the woods and meadows without learning, otherwise you have no business fleeing the city. A drive along the sideroad or a stroll beside a dark, meandering stream is enriched by a knowledge of what is going on underfoot. A copy of F. Schuyler Matthews's *Field Book of American Wild Flowers* is the only teacher you need. I carry one in the bulky sidepocket of an old army jacket I scrounged from a quartermaster in Korea back in 1951.

If you want to delve a bit farther into plant life, then get a copy of Taylor's *Encyclopædia of Gardening,* which in a single volume will tell you all you will want to know about everything that grows, here or in Zanzibar, wild or cultivated. Among other things, it will tell you in detail how to build your own wild garden where you can grow and study the plants that are indigenous to this part of the world.

It was from this encyclopædia that I first learned that the strawberry was a member of the rose family. Each spring at this time, when the first white flowers appear on the wild vines (as they did last weekend), I confirm this through observation. There is a kinship with the toothed leaves and the five-petalled flowers of the briar rose that is unmistakable. (Look at the flowers of the raspberries or the yellow cinquefoils and you will see a similar relationship.)

I know a secret bank, not far from the little community of Humber Trails, where the wild strawberries grow so thickly and so plumply that, if your eyes are wide open, you can spot them glimmering redly from your car. But, happily for me, most people's eyes are not open that wide.

In the untrammelled meadows, beneath the elms, in shiny, mottled patches you will find in bloom one of the earliest of the wild flowers: the delicate yellow adder's tongue or dog-tooth violet. I prefer the former name since it is more descriptive and since the plant is not a violet at all but a member of the lily family, growing from a small bulb like its distant relative, the tulip.

Ten days or so ago, I saw these shiny olive leaves, splotched as if with mud, poking up from the dry grasses. The plants were already in bud and so—impatient after the long winter—I broke one open and drew forth the yellow petals. There is no need now for such vandalism. You can see these flowers this very evening, blooming in the meadows by the score.

The true violets are also peeping out from the mosses this week. They will be with us in their various varieties for all of the spring and much of the early summer. For the past fortnight I have been watching the progress of the heart-shaped leaves on the edges of the cedar copses, hoping for the sight of a flower. Last Saturday I was rewarded by the glitter of pale blue and lavender, sparkling like jewelled pinpoints almost everywhere on the dark rim of the forest.

Did you know there were some fifty varieties of violets to be found in the woodlands of eastern North America? They are to be seen in almost every colour save red and orange. There are several small yellow varieties that bloom well into summer, but I prefer the local white variety, which is the *viola canadensis* or Canada violet. It is one of the loveliest of the wild pansies, being pale yellow at the throat. It comes about the same time as the wild geranium, or herb-Robert, that tiny five-petalled flower of purest pink that really is a geranium. (The potted geranium, however, isn't a geranium at all but a species of *pelargonium*.)

More spectacular than these, if you know where to look for it, is the flower of the mayapple or North American mandrake. At this season you may see these plants bursting from the ground in patches beneath the larger shade trees on the slopes of the hills. The huge leaves open slowly in the early spring like green umbrellas, but most people pass them by without realizing that beneath this canopy in late May or early June one of the handsomest flowers of all lies waiting to be discovered.

Hidden under each leaf is a large cup-shaped flower of purest waxen white that the casual passerby will never see. Nature, happily, preserves it as a small but satisfying reward for those who bother to use their eyes as they stroll through the awakening countryside.

October

It is at this season of the year, while we wait with mingled feelings of apprehension and anticipation for the first frost to blacken the zinnias and enflame the sugar maples, that we begin to understand the sweet-sadness of autumn. Only in October are the senses afflicted by the schizophrenia of regret and gratification. Of all the months—even more than May—this one, I think, was made for poets.

Each year about this time I stare out from my window upon a thicket of leafless hawthornes, the branches as grey as death but the tips still crimson-bright with berries. Behind the hawthornes, marching down the slope like guardsmen in a file, stands a row of elms, their yellow leaves bleeding from them in the wind. They are dying, these elms, not in the seasonal sense but truly, for the sickness is on them and there is no cure. They remind me once again that my plans for the summer past have not all been fulfilled.

Behind the elms, but masked by their screen, one can glimpse for five miles or more the smoky blues of the valley winding north and west. Each autumn, when the wind whistles down this valley and the leaves flee before it, the curtain parts, as in a theatre, and we see fully revealed the far horizons of our rural world. Then I renew a promise to myself that the following year I will explore with my children the entire valley on foot to discover where it leads and mark what lies along it. Eleven winters have passed and we have not yet explored more than two miles; there are so many things to do in summer when the days are hot and the leafy elms hide the far horizon.

Across the little river that trickles below us—beyond the apple orchard and past the pencil-points of the arborvitae—there rises a green slope dotted with beech and ash and pine. Each spring as the frost leaves the ground, I swear that I will cross over to that slope so that I may see what the world looks like from the other side. Yet I have never quite achieved this. One is halted in one's excursions by the sight of a frog glistening on the river bank, or a clump of wild strawberries glowing in the sedges, or a blue heron eluding the eye-glass—or simply by the desire to sit in the moist heat on a log by the river and leave the scaling of slopes for another day.

Now that the chill is in the air and the mosses firm and almost crisp beneath our tread and a sense of remorse heavy upon us because we have left undone those things which we ought to have done, we may actually achieve our goals, but I cannot be certain of that. I suspect that we may never know what it is really like on the far side of the valley and that subconsciously we may not even wish to know, since knowing would dry up our sense of wonder.

Besides, there is so much to be seen and so much to be remembered on our own side of the slope. After eleven years, every worn stone, every eroded crevice, every battered log, has a special symbolism. There is, for instance, protruding from the shallow river a great flat rock. I never visit it (and "visit" is the proper verb) that I do not recall with pleasure those moments of relaxation many years ago when I, younger and more active, was helping with my own hands to build a house and, bone weary from the toil of it, would slip down through the cool forest and wade out into the brown waters and sit panting on this sun-warmed rock, sucking on a beer bottle, with my legs draped in the rustling waters.

A few yards away, reclining on the bank, there is a log as thick as a man's torso, still firm but grey with age. The eldest children never see it without exclaiming, "There is the log where we had our lunch that time!" Then returns the memory of a day so long ago (was it only nine years?) when there were only two of them, and we three made an excursion into the forest with our lunch in a paper bag— the lunch consisting of a single chocolate bar; and how we trudged and toddled down the little path, long since overgrown, that led past the young wild raspberries and along the river bank, the two little girls chattering like birds and tripping occasionally over branches; and how we came to this log, caught in a tatter of sunlight, and so by dint of clambering and hoisting got on top of it and sat there, the three of us in a row, carefully dividing our chocolate bar into equal segments and munching it cheerfully in the quiet of the forest.

I do not know why that particular excursion should be memorable. Perhaps it was because we found a bottle gentian growing all by itself in a small clearing where a little sun had reached it. (I have not seen one since.) Perhaps it was because our ages were all exactly right. All I know is that, try as we may, we have not been able again to recapture exactly the mood of that moment. Yet when we stumble through the encroaching thickets, the log is always there to recall it for us.

In the wooded slopes above the river there is a V-shaped chasm that cuts like a wound through the black wall of the cedars. It was the hurricane that caused it on that October night eight years ago— mangling a clump of silver birches and making a ruined rubble of the river bank. I remember then gazing in despair at this desecration and cursing the cruelty of nature, but one learns forbearance as one grows with the trees. The gap thus broken in the forest allowed the sun to leak in so that the sharp edges of the scar have long since been blurred with new growth. And so it has become a pleasant rite each year to go down to this place and watch the drama of the young saplings struggling toward the sky.

Thus does our valley change from season to season and endure from decade to decade. At this time of year, fearful of further procrastination and mindful of the fleeting of time, we hurry to make our final pilgrimage—to visit old landmarks and remark on new transitions. Here a bank has caved in, changing the shape of the new river. Here a tree has tottered and died, altering the profile of the forest. The slim young raspberry canes have become a tangle, devouring a pathway. The poplar seedlings have grown faster than the children, and almost as straight. But my rock still sits out in the river and our log still lies along the bank and the soot of old bonfires still darkens the pasture-land. Each recalls for us a memory or a meaning that brings its own satisfactions and that is why, though we honestly try, we have never quite reached the end of the river, and that is why we have yet to discover what it is like on the far side of the valley.

November

In the town where I was raised, the first snow of winter has already started to fall. It comes early in October in thick, wet flakes, and then it goes and then it comes again. But by Hallowe'en it has come to stay. It will not vanish until April.

The snow, in those first glamorous days of northern winter, is still wet enough to pack, which means that snowballs can be fashioned for battle or great mountains of snow can be rolled in ever-increasing balls down the little streets that lead to the grey, hissing river. But this is a brief interlude before winter truly sets in. As the thermometer drops, the snow becomes as dry as desert sand; in the clear, chill nights it squeaks eerily beneath one's moccasins, and when the moon is out you can see the pinpoints of light glittering on the cold crust that forms upon it.

I do not miss the northern winters, which are too long for human endurance, but I do miss the dry northern snow, which is far preferable to the slushy variety that comes and goes like an unwelcome guest here in southern Ontario.

Most of my childhood memories are bound up with snow: I remember once being told, at the age of nine, that in certain parts of Canada there was no snow at all at Christmastime, and that in

December in Victoria, B.C., flowers actually bloomed. I did not believe it—any more than I believed the legend that in the outside world a bottle of soda pop could be purchased for a nickel. I had never seen a nickel, since twenty-five cents was our smallest coin; and I had never seen a winter without deep and abiding snow.

Contrary to general belief, it does not snow heavily in the Yukon valley, which has a remarkably low precipitation. Indeed, the rainfall and the snowfall are so light that the great glaciers of the Ice Age, which covered all the rest of Canada and much of the United States thousands of years ago, never penetrated the Yukon interior. An ice age needs a long build-up of unmelting snow, year after year, and there simply wasn't enough in the interior Yukon valley.

I remember few real blizzards worthy of the name during my childhood. When I think of Yukon winters I think not of snow falling but of clear, cold days—the sky a thin grey-blue, the sun pale or absent entirely and the whole world still and white.

Yet, because the snow did not melt during a six-month period there was, as the winter progressed, a great deal of it. Dawson City is built on a swamp that has been drained by great ditches, and during the winter these ditches would fill with six feet of snow. A boy could pull his toque over his face for protection and dive headfirst into these snow-filled ditches, as in a swimming pool, without fear of hitting bottom.

Directly behind our own home, the wilderness began. It stretched in an unbroken series of forested hills without manmade hindrance directly to the Arctic Ocean. In this no man's land of conifers and willow thickets the snow lay so thick as to be all but impassable. The dark trees were burdened with it so that the branches were sometimes completely hidden. On the forest floor the snow lay in knee-deep drifts. Sometimes we boys invaded this white, silent world, our pockets stuffed with sandwiches frozen hard as shale. We felt like explorers entering an unknown and mysterious country where no man had trodden before.

Most of today's popular sports were unknown to us then. We did not skate and we did not ski. The river, when it finally froze in

November, resembled an unmade bed—far too lumpy for skating. Skiing, in my youth, had not attained its present popularity. But we had other diversions.

Bobsledding was a great community sport in those days and so was snowshoeing, which seems to have become a lost art. The Yukon snowshoe is a slender affair, and it is as long as the wearer is tall, being made for support on dry snow and thus quite different in its engineering from the racquet-shaped shoes that are common to eastern Canada. We snowshoed through the bush, sometimes, but more often on large fields where there was a great unbroken expanse of deep, crusted snow. As boys we trudged back and forth constructing snowshoe trails, which after a day or so would bear our weight. One of my most pleasant childhood memories is that of sliding effortlessly along these blue-white trails in the late afternoon, with the dusk already upon us and the lights of the little town winking on, one by one.

Another great sport was to slide off the tops of houses into the banks of snow made by countless winter shovellings. Northern houses, whether they be built of logs or frame, have steeply angled roofs, usually of corrugated iron, to make snow-shovelling easy. Unless a roof is shovelled after every snowfall it is liable to cave in from the crushing weight. That is why roofless log cabins are a common scene in the wilderness; left unattended, they crumble beneath the winter snows.

Around every house, then, a mountain of snow begins to pile up from the months of roof-shovelling. We boys used to clamber up on the roofs all over town and slide at breakneck speed down the steep, ice-sheathed sides, burying ourselves in the drifts below. I wonder if they do it still in the little towns of the Canadian north?

Occasionally, in the late afternoons when school was done, I used to hitch my husky dog to my small sled and take a ride for a couple of miles up the Klondike River valley. Neither the dog nor I cared much for this, and we went only at the coaxing of my parents, who felt it somehow a proper thing to do. I much preferred walking with my dog to being pulled by him, and, indeed, there was hardly a Sunday on which we did not walk through the snow *en famille* along the trails that twisted back and forth between the ice blocks of the frozen river or through the tunnel-like passes trodden in the drifts of the woods behind our home. Walking has ceased to be a sport, too; in the mud and slush of a Toronto winter it is not a rewarding recreation. Yet, when the air is crisp and the snow dry and you have three pairs of all-wool socks inside your felt boots, a brisk walk is as fine a tonic as I know.

Perhaps this year, by some miracle, we will have enough snow and enough cold weather to make winter walking a possible diversion. Is it too much to pray for?

The Anatomy of the Classic Con

From *The Big Sell*, 1963

1

JACOB THURSTON[1] DID NOT KNOW he was an Egg. Even after he had lost the $3,300, he did not know he was an Egg. But when he sat down in the Canadian National Station in Edmonton, Alberta, he was spotted immediately as an Egg and a very special kind of Egg at that—not a Bite Egg or a Match Egg or a Payoff Egg, but a Duke Egg.

The signs were all there if you could read them, and the thin-faced Steer man sauntering casually about the lobby read them at once. It was not only the tousled hair, the shrewd, small eyes, and the big, freckled hands; there was also an aura that said that Thurston was not above making a fast dollar, that he fancied himself a shrewd man in a deal, that he felt like a fish out of water in Edmonton, and that he did not have too much experience of the world.

The thin-faced man sat down beside Jacob Thurston, asked him for a match, and began a genial, casual conversation. It was not long before Thurston volunteered the information that he was from the little town of Stony Plain.

"Stony Plain?" asked the thin-faced man in surprise. "Did you say Stony Plain?" Thurston nodded.

"Now *there's* a coincidence!" said the thin-faced man. "How long have you lived there?" Thurston told him proudly that he was born and raised in Stony Plain. The thin-faced man caught him by the arm.

"Look," he said earnestly, "before I say anything more I would like you to give me your word of honour that you will never

---

[1] All the names in this chapter have been changed.

expose anything I'm going to tell you." Thurston nodded and leaned forward with interest.

"My name is Blake," said the thin-faced man. "I'm from back east, but the odd thing is that I'm on my way down to Stony Plain. I'm looking for a piece of property in that area. I was in town on other business, but I have to attend to this matter for my two brothers. Now, look: I don't want any of this to come to the attention of real-estate agents. I don't want any sharpshooters in the know. They'll put a bill of goods over on you if they can, and as I'm not familiar at all with this territory, I could easily be sold a lemon. Now you know the area and you know the farms. Do you know of any that are actually for sale? There could be a nice piece of change in it for you if you're willing to keep your mouth shut."

"I think so," said Thurston. "Will Osborne would sell if he got a decent offer."

And, as they began to discuss Will Osborne's farm, the man who called himself Blake could see the wheels turning in the other's head, and he knew from long observation of his fellows that Will Osborne's farm was a lemon and the Egg was planning to make a good thing out of it. "Look," he said. "What time does your train go out? Six? Well, you've got three hours to kill. I was just sitting here waiting. I don't know the city at all. Why don't we go over somewhere and have a bottle of beer together?" Jacob Thurston, mentally calculating the cut of the profit he would get from Will Osborne as well as from the gullible stranger, cheerfully agreed.

When Thurston suggested a second bottle of beer, Blake, the Steer man, knew that he was caught. He was looking quietly around for the Takeoff man, whose name that day was to be Billy Moore. He appeared, almost on cue, and seeing the Steer man, burst into a whoop of surprise:

"For God's sake. You're Jack Blake!"

"Billy Moore! Where on earth did you spring from?"

"Why, I been in town three months."

"Aren't you doing any work these days, Billy? Doesn't your old man get sick of feeding you money all the time?"

"He might get sick of it, but he's still giving it to me. He better not stop!"

The conversation continued, the Takeoff man still standing and the Steer man acting toward him with just a slight suggestion of disdain.

"Oh, come on—you better sit down and have a beer with us. God Almighty, you're blocking the aisle where you are," the Steer man finally said, and as he did so, he turned to Thurston and gave a slight shrug.

After some conversation, the Takeoff man excused himself and went to the men's room.

"I've known him all my life," Blake explained to Thurston. "He's all right, but he's a showoff. His father's money buys him out of everything. Actually, he's never done a tap of real work. He isn't like you. He's mooched off his father all his life. I don't know how he stands it. Personally, *I've* earned every dime I've ever got."

Thurston was warming to Blake. He saw that they had a good deal in common, including their disdain for Billy Moore, the prodigal son.

When Moore returned, he suggested they go up to his room, but Blake demurred. Moore said he had a letter from his sister, who had been asking about Blake. Blake allowed himself to be persuaded, and the three adjourned to Moore's hotel. There was some light conversation and a few jokes with a slight suggestion of sex to them. Blake showed a couple of tricks with matches. ("Can you spell Child's Restaurant with five matches? No? Here's how," and he formed the letters TIT.)

"Wait a minute, I got another one," he said. "Hey, Moore, have you got a pack of cards about?"

"Oh, I guess I've got a deck somewhere," Moore said. He found them, and Blake proceeded to show a few simple card tricks.

"Let's have a hand of rummy," Moore suggested, but Blake shook his head. "I can't stand that game," he said. "Fact is, I'm not much of a card player at all. I've never really bothered with cards in my life."

"Oh, come on," said Moore. "You must know some kind of a game to pass an hour. How about Spit-in-the-Ocean?"

"The only game I've ever played is English High Pair, and I'm no good at that," said Blake. He explained that in this card game a high pair usually won since straights and flushes had no value. After some further prodding by Moore, he agreed to play a hand or two, and it was decided that all bets would be a nickel, with raises limited to the size of the pot. It would serve to while away the time before the train left, said Blake, and the winner would have to buy the beer.

It sounded innocent enough. Thurston, the Egg, won the first pot—about eight dollars—and with it the deal. He pushed the pack over to Moore, on his right, who casually cut the cards. In doing so, Moore placed a "cap" of one dozen carefully arranged cards on the top of the pack. It was his habit to carry such a cap in his pocket for just such a purpose and to transfer it to his inner palm whenever a game began. For it was no simple card game these three were now engaged in; the game is known in the argot of the con fraternity as the Duke (so called because the Takeoff man's job at this point is to place his "dukes" on the deck). It can be a very expensive pastime.

In Vancouver, in 1929, an Egg was relieved of $50,000 playing the game that Jacob Thurston played.

Thurston dealt one card down and one card face up, and each player discovered he had a pair. Blake had deuces; Moore had jacks; and Thurston, to his elation, found himself with aces.

"Hey, you're pretty lucky!" his friend Blake told him. "You sure know what you're doing. Look, if you want to waive the size of the pot, that's okay by me. We'll make the winner buy a couple of bottles of whisky for the train."

Thurston eagerly agreed and bet a quarter. Blake called the bet and raised it half a dollar. Moore saw that bet and raised it two dollars, and the pot began to build.

"Hold on a minute," said Blake. "This is too steep for me. All I got is two deuces. You guys have me beat." He turned over his cards, pulled back his chair, and went over behind Thurston. From then on, he controlled Thurston's play as surely as a hypnotist controls his subject.

A whispered side conversation went on for the rest of the game between the Egg and his new friend, who appeared to have joined forces with him against the overly confident Moore. ("Look," Blake would say to Thurston, "this guy deserves a lesson. He thinks money will take him anywhere. Just because I know him don't hesitate to sock it to him. . . . Don't worry; that guy can afford to lose, and if you ask me, it's time he lost at something.")

Before the third game was played, Thurston and Moore, through raises and counter-raises, had put $50 in the pot.

The third card did not improve Moore's hand. Thurston, however, drew a king, and this increased his sense of elation. He found himself tossing fifty dollars into the pot and then, when Moore raised, two hundred dollars. By the time the fourth card was drawn, the pot had grown to several hundred dollars.

On the fourth card Thurston drew a second king, and the betting increased as the two men called and raised back and forth.

Thurston ran out of cash and asked if a cheque would be acceptable. Moore agreed, since he, too, was out of cash and wanted to use cheques, and the betting continued. Moore now appeared to be less cocky and more and more nervous. Finally he announced that as far as he was concerned the betting was over. He turned to Blake.

"You understand this game a lot better than I do," he said. "As far as I can see, he has me beat, and I'm sorry I got into it at all. What I want to know is this—is there anything at all that could beat two high pair? He's got two there. He must have. Is there anything that can beat them, or am I wasting my time? Should I give him the pot right now?"

"You might as well," said Blake, and then added casually, "well, theoretically I suppose you could win with three of a kind, but that's hopeless—it's a mathematical rarity."

"Well," said Moore, "what do you say we let the fifth card decide it?" This was agreeable to Thurston, who discovered that in the space of a minute he had put $3,000 in cash and cheques into the pot.

Before the fifth card was dealt, however, Blake insisted on protecting Thurston's interests: Moore would simply have to produce cash for the cheques he had written. After all, Blake pointed out, Thurston was from out of town; he didn't know Moore, and he might not see him again when the game was done. It was only fair, then, that he take his winnings in cash. Blake insinuated that Moore was just the type of man to stop the cheques before Thurston could get them cashed. He turned to get Thurston's assent, and the farmer agreed enthusiastically. Of course, he said, he was prepared to get cash for his cheques, too, as a token of good faith.[2]

A small ceremony followed. Each hand was sealed separately with Scotch tape. The pack itself was sealed. The cards, together with the money and the cheques, were placed in an envelope. The envelope was sealed, with the signatures of all three participants scrawled across the flap to prevent anyone's tampering with it.

The train was forgotten. Thurston and his new friend hired a taxi and drove the twenty miles to Stony Plain, where the farmer got his cash. Then they returned to the hotel room, where Moore was awaiting them.

The envelope was unsealed and the last card dealt. Moore drew a jack, face up. Thurston's hand did not improve.

When the cards were turned over, it was quickly revealed that Moore's three jacks beat Thurston's two pairs.

---

[2] Thus the confidence game known as the Duke was transformed into a variation known as the Payoff Duke. In the simpler version nobody goes for money. The Steer man, who always has a set of dummy cheques in his pocket, insists that the friendly little game has gone too far, that the cheques ought to be removed from the pot and the game confined to cash betting alone. He then pretends to tear up and burn the cheques in front of the Egg but, in fact, does nothing of the kind. When the game is ended, the Egg is kept occupied while the Takeoff man cashes the real cheques.

In this instance, however, the Steer man sensed that Thurston would be quite willing to go back to Stony Plain for the money. Since it is becoming increasingly difficult to cozen banks into cashing cheques of this size without inquiry, the alternative plan was better.

153

"My God!" said Blake to Moore in surprise. "Do you mean to tell me you went all that way with a pair of jacks? How lucky can you get on the last card?"

"I thought he was bluffing there at first," said Moore, raking in the cash. "I thought he was trying to buy the pot. Then I got cold feet, but now I'm glad I stayed."

For the first moment or two, Thurston's reaction was stunned silence. Then he broke out in a rage—not at Blake or Moore but at himself. He slammed his fist so heavily on the table he all but cracked it.

"It's my own fault!" he cried out. "My own fault! I should have known better."

He wheeled around and gave Blake a momentarily hostile look.

"Don't blame me," said Blake. "I told you three or four times that you shouldn't bluff, but you wouldn't pay any attention."

"You did?" asked Thurston in bewilderment.

"You didn't even hear me, I guess, in the excitement of the game," said Blake. "But now look. The last thing that you and I want to do is quarrel. I'm partly responsible for this—at least 50 percent. If you'd bet your cards properly, you wouldn't be in that last round, but never mind. It isn't much money—half of $3,300— and I'm going to make it good. I'll get on the phone and get it. You'll get twice that, anyway, when our deal is completed; I can promise you that. I won't deal with anybody else but you. I told you that at the beginning and that's the way it's going to be."

He went to the phone, made a call and then returned.

"I'm having the money sent right away," he said. "Now, meantime, they want more details on this Stony Plain property."

And so Thurston, still somewhat stunned but ever hopeful, returned to Stony Plain with Blake, who made a great show of being interested in the Will Osborne property. Off he went to Edmonton, promising to return immediately with Thurston's cash and close the deal. But he did not return, then or ever, and the bewildered Thurston still waits and wonders how he could have lost $3,300 on a single hand of cards in the space of less than an hour while waiting for a train.

2

Any student of the classic confidence games must be struck by the several parallels they present with some modern big-sell techniques. The confidence man sells nothing but himself, of course, while the salesman peddles more tangible merchandise; but the psychological techniques each employs are remarkably similar.

The classic con games preceded the big sell and have been polished and perfected over three-quarters of a century, ever since the days in Creede, Colorado, when Jefferson Randolph Smith earned his nickname of Soapy by convincing the customers there was a banknote concealed beneath every wrapper of shaving soap.

The dialogue of the con games is memorized almost to the exact phrase, so that a good Steer man or Spiel man or Tail man can walk into any city in the world, make contact with others of his craft, and begin to play the classic Duke, Match, Bite, Payoff or Rag. Except for the Bite, all these games are based on a shrewd observation of human nature: that there is a little bit of larceny in most of us. Having gained the confidence of the Egg, the Steer man must then convince him that he can make a large sum of money, usually at somebody else's expense.

The Egg, then, has three qualities. He is, first of all, a man who wants to be in on a sure thing. He is, second, a person who can be manipulated through the warmth of personal relationship and through subtle methods of flattery. He is, third, a man who is unsure of himself. In the classic con games, the Egg is always a traveller in a strange city. But in the legal games of the big sell, the Egg is simply someone seeking guidance: a newcomer from a foreign land, often enough, or a gullible housewife with no one to talk to, or a young spinster trying to achieve self-assurance through dancing lessons.

I have an acquaintance who happens to be one of the best con men on the continent. He is a master psychologist, a consummate actor and a highly educated expert in the ways of the world. He can slide easily into half a dozen dialects, and I know of no stage performer who can touch him. He not only has the accents down pat but he has also studied speech patterns and idioms so that he can take on the role of a Polish immigrant and suddenly *look* Polish. I once asked him to try to explain the psychology by which a stranger in a railway station can, in a few minutes, exert such a hold over another man that that man will trust him with his life savings. Here is the way it went onto the tape recorder:

"You never attempt to con a man in his own town. That is why you choose people who are travelling. In the first place, the Egg's mind is free; you must be able to capture his full attention to beat him. You see, he is not sure of himself and he's glad to talk to someone when he's alone and travelling.

"He's a different man altogether when he's not at home. At home he feels secure. No one can tell him anything that he doesn't have a preconceived idea about. At home he'd argue with you. Now, when he's being steered, you can tell him almost anything because he's on a trip and he's seen things he didn't know existed before. This shakes him. He's not so sure of the things he once thought he knew. There's doubt in his mind. Maybe there are other things he doesn't know about. Maybe the ideas and opinions he's held could be revised.

"A man away from home is like a fish out of water. If you're able to understand his psychology and think a step or two ahead of him, then you're filling a void that he needs filled. He's been among people all his life that he knows well. Now, suddenly, he's alone and out of his element.

"So a con man comes along who understands exactly how he feels. He knows the man is lonely and yet slightly suspicious. He knows he's slightly off balance psychologically. The con man reads all this in a few seconds. With a single look he can tell if the Egg is a Duke man or a Bite man or a Match man.

"Before the Egg realizes it he is saying to himself, 'Well, I know this stranger is all right.'

"Your Egg has to be a believer. Even a sophisticated man can be a believer. In this case he believes in *you*. Why he should place his confidence in a stranger is very difficult to explain. But what he does is to protect an image of himself that is accepted and reflected by the con man. When that happens, the Egg would do anything in the world rather than part from you.

"It's rather like a man in love. He projects an image of himself to the girl. She flatters him and raves about him so he begins to believe that the image is *really* himself. He'd do anything on earth rather than destroy that image of himself. That's why, when some romances break up, the people involved have difficulty in adjusting. When the girl finally refuses her man, the image is shattered and he can't put it back together again—and so his personality is shattered.

"Well, the Egg is the same way, and I've seen them shattered just as badly. The confidence man is like a seducer. The hold he has over the Egg isn't sexual, of course, but the parallel is there. You let the Egg see, through you, the flattering image he wants to project of himself. When he sees you are accepting that image, he will do absolutely anything you ask of him."

In salesmanship it is also the image that counts—and it matters little that the image is often phony.

Con games are not played for peanuts. Even in a simple game like the Match, which resembles the Duke but revolves around coin-tossing on the street, an Egg can lose a thousand dollars in the space of a few minutes. Yet Eggs seldom squawk to the police, partly because they are ashamed and embarrassed and partly because no good con game ever ends when the Egg parts with his money. An elaborate mechanism has been worked out to ensure that the Egg is never alone in the hours or days that follow; he is still under the influence of the Steer man, whose job is first to confuse him and then to convince him that he has been involved in a shady enterprise that can never be revealed.

The one major con game that does not play on the larceny of the Egg is the Bite, in which a good operator can single-handedly pick up one hundred dollars from a likely looking Egg in about seven minutes. The Bite is based entirely on trust.

"You got to size up your man," an expert in the game once told me. "Some are Match Eggs and some are Duke Eggs. A Bite Egg is a different kind of Egg. It's hard to put into words, but it is chiefly character, kindliness of expression, and general demeanour."

In the Bite, the only equipment needed is a ten-cent newspaper. The game, like most confidence games, is traditionally played at the railway station (and today, though less frequently, at airports). The con man shrewdly assesses the crowd, and when he spots a Bite Egg he falls into conversation with him, usually establishing himself by explaining that the two are travelling on the same train. He represents himself as a solid citizen from say, Saskatoon.

"You know," says the con man, "I'm on my way to my niece's wedding, and I've had a very difficult time regarding her gift. Now out home I knew what she wanted all right: it's a silverware set—a Rogers 1870 called Lilac Time."

("We always go into these details," a member of the fraternity told me, "because the reaction you get from a man helps you a lot. It gives you an idea of how you're going along with him and how he's taking hold. If he's interested, you know you've got him.")

"Well, to order the gift I had to go into Saskatoon from Pumphandle. I went to Birks Jewellers there. Now, of course, there are seventy-seven pieces, and I wanted her initials on each piece. That's considerable engraving, and they couldn't do it in time for me to pick it up and take it with me on the train. I was going to cancel; but they suggested they notify their Toronto store, and while I was travelling they could do the work in Toronto and I could pick it up on arrival. When I got off the train this morning I had some breakfast and then went into the store. Doggone it, it wasn't ready!

"You know, I've been back four times, and I was getting real discouraged. They took pity on me and told me just to come back here to the depot and relax and they'd bring it down when it was ready. It's supposed to be ready by eight o'clock."

The con man always sets the time a few minutes before the train is to leave. At this point he breaks off and looks at his watch.

"By George, it's three minutes to eight now and I have a bill to change. If he's not here now, he will be by the time I break it."

Now comes the key to the wicked little game called the Bite. The con man has a newspaper folded under his arm.

"Just hold this for me, will you please?" he says, handing the paper to the Egg. "I always make a hobby whenever I go on a trip of saving a newspaper from each place I've ever visited."

This simple action is called "conditioning." It establishes a bond of trust between the con man and the Egg.

"I'll be right back," says the con man. "Be sure to look after that paper." In about one minute he is back again.

"Well," he says in slight exasperation, taking the folded newspaper back from the Egg. "This is a new experience for me. I never had this happen before. It certainly couldn't happen out West."

"What's wrong?" asks the Egg. "Did you get it?"

"No. The messenger was there all right, but he didn't have the change and do you know?—these people here at the CNR refund and all those wickets won't change it! They just wouldn't accommodate me."

At this point the Egg usually offers to change the bill. If he doesn't, the con man says, "This poor old messenger must be about eighty-four. He really looks beat. I feel bad holding him up—he's been working overtime and I hate to keep him waiting. By George! It never struck me before, Mr. Smith, but would you happen to have change for a hundred-dollar bill?"

The Egg has.

"I should have thought of this before," says the con man, much relieved.

The Egg is now busily counting out tens and fives or five twenties. "This is very good of you," says the con man. And he takes all the money.

At this point—and this is the key moment in the game—*he hands the newspaper back to the Egg.*

The psychologists, no doubt, will know exactly what transpires in the Egg's subconscious. Confidence men have had no professional psychological training, but they are masters of the practice. They have learned that this transfer of a ten-cent newspaper somehow gives the Egg confidence that the stranger will return.

As the con man hands over the newspaper, he says, "This is very decent of you, Mr. Smith. The messenger has the bill, and the poor fellow is trying to get the change. I'll just intercept him and be right back. You just wait here, the same as before."

The con man, of course, has not revealed to the Egg that he himself does not have the hundred-dollar bill until he gets the Egg's money in his hand. Then, instead of handing him the mythical hundred-dollar bill he hands him the newspaper, which becomes a sort of substitute.

One con man told me that some Eggs think they are getting the bill with the newspaper, and he has to spell it out for them. "No! No! I told you the messenger has the bill. I'll get it from him and be right back. Just wait there."

It is difficult to believe that anybody would give an utter stranger one hundred dollars in return for a ten-cent newspaper, but it has happened in thousands of cases. Once a man is sized up as a Bite Egg, the con fraternity seldom has any trouble with him.

The Egg rarely calls the police because he has a train to catch. He waits patiently as long as he dares and then climbs on board wondering what happened. So skilful are some con men that there have been Eggs who never realized they were cheated. They have abided forever in the belief that the nice stranger was somehow lost or delayed and—were there only a little more time—would have returned with all that money to reclaim his valuable newspaper.

3

Except that the names and occasional small details have had to be changed, the following strange story happened exactly as I relate it in the city of Toronto, about ten years ago. It began when Julius Steirhouse, a retired Montreal furrier, paid his first visit to the

Queen City to investigate some stocks in which he was planning to invest his savings of $35,000.

Steirhouse booked into the King Edward Hotel and then walked west on King Street, looking for the financial district. At the corner of Yonge he paused to get his bearings; an amiable stranger strolled up, asked if he could help, and directed him toward Bay Street. By coincidence, the stranger was going in the same direction, and so the two men walked along together chatting as they went, stopping occasionally at the stranger's suggestion to look into the store windows and talk.

The stranger, whose name was Reg Johnstone, was cheerfully talkative. He told Steirhouse that he had just come into a bit of money through the sale of the family business. By another coincidence he was interested in some of the same stocks that Steirhouse was looking at; indeed, he showed considerable knowledge of the market.

Alone in a strange city, Steirhouse warmed to him. Mr. Johnstone told him small, intimate secrets of his life, and the furrier soon found himself exchanging confidences—including the intelligence that he had $35,000 in negotiable securities in a safety-deposit box in Montreal. He was not to have it long.

Steirhouse could not know that he was about to be set up for the most ingenious and complicated of all modern confidence games, the Payoff. In North America, millions of dollars have been mulcted from gullible people through this one game. Though con men have gone to jail for playing it, this swindle is so carefully planned and executed that in case after case the culprits have never been apprehended.

Honed to a fine edge by generations of con men, the Payoff is as carefully rehearsed as a stage play. Since the rules and *modus operandi* are always the same, a good Payoff man can work anywhere in the world; and Reg Johnstone was a good Payoff man: he had once taken $100,000 from a victim in less than a week.

There is a saying in the half-world of the con fraternity that if you do not find an Egg, the Egg will find you, and Johnstone had been idling at the corner of King and Yonge, certain that one would soon come along. It had been his observation that one third of humanity was composed of Eggs. Johnstone was looking for an elderly, affluent stranger, and his shrewd eye, trained from twenty-five years' experience, easily picked out Julius Steirhouse.

The two new-found friends visited the stock exchange together, dined together that evening, and took in a movie. The following day they went sightseeing around town, and during the next three days they became inseparable. Mr. Johnstone, who was also from Montreal, said he was staying at a small, private hotel—he didn't reveal the address—and said he would try to get his new friend settled there, too.

There is a bench on the pedestrian island on University Avenue at Dundas and, as the two crossed the street one noon hour, Johnstone suggested they sit down to rest and have a smoke.

"Excuse me," he said, after they were seated. "I stepped on your foot!"

"No, you didn't," replied Steirhouse.

"Well, I stepped on *something*," said Johnstone, reaching down below him. "Hullo! What's this?"

He picked up a large and very expensive wallet. The two men examined it curiously, opened it, and found a thousand dollars inside.

"Better see who it belongs to," said Johnstone, pulling out several credit cards, some betting slips and a membership card to a club called the Turf Exchange on Bay Street. He delved further and produced a folded clipping from a Chicago newspaper with a three-column headline and a photograph of a man named Webster.

The two read the clipping together. N.R. Webster, it developed, was something of a mystery man—a big plunger and horse bettor believed to be a key man in a large New York gambling syndicate warring with certain bookmakers. Webster was suspected of the practice known as "past posting," i.e., betting on a horse race after it was won. He had left Chicago, the clipping said, and appeared to be in trouble with the syndicate.

Johnstone, dipping once again into the wallet, pulled out a letter, on expensive stationery, from a man in New York. It was addressed to N.R. Webster.

"If it were not for my close friendship with your late father," the letter read, "I should never have interceded for you at the top. But you must not put me on the spot again. I must warn you that this Toronto posting represents your final chance with us and that, should you ever again use confidential information for your own financial gain, that will be the end of it. Surely you ought to be satisfied with a salary and commission position that equals that of the U.S. President. . . ."

"My God!" said the awed Johnstone. "We're on to something big!"

He was, but not in the way that poor Julius Steirhouse understood him to mean.

The Payoff has its own vernacular. The letter the two men had just read is known as the "bawl-out" letter, and it, together with the phony newspaper clipping and the other paraphernalia, had been printed the previous day by a four-man confidence ring in Toronto. Johnstone was known as the Steerer, and it was his job to steer the Egg—Steirhouse—into the arms of the Player, Webster.

Across the street was a third member of the ring known as the Tail man. For the past fifteen minutes he had been examining the Egg closely. From this moment on, the Tail man, in various disguises, would never be far from Julius Steirhouse's side; it was important that the Egg should not slip through the gang's fingers. A fourth man would enter the elaborate play later in the day. All four would eventually split Mr. Steirhouse's $35,000.

The last item that Johnstone pulled from the mysterious wallet was a business card bearing the name of N.R. Webster, Esq., and giving, as an address, a suite at the Royal York Hotel. Johnstone steered his quarry to a phone booth and put in a call to Webster, the mystery man. Webster, told that the wallet had been found, sounded grateful but also suspicious. They weren't newspapermen, were they? Thank God! The press had almost ruined him in

Chicago. Well, then, they must take a taxi to the hotel at once. But remember—no publicity! They must not even discuss the matter in front of the taxi driver!

In his Royal York suite, N.R. Webster, dripping affluence, was beside himself with gratitude.

"You'll have to forgive us for reading your personal papers," said Johnstone, repeating a phrase that he had used in dozens of previous Payoff games, "but we had to do it in order to identify you."

"That's perfectly all right, boys," Webster replied. "But for God's sake now, give me your promise you'll never mention any of this to a living soul. Now here—I want you to take a thousand dollars for your trouble."

"No! No!" cried Johnstone. "Honesty is a way of life with me. I don't do these things for reward. I wouldn't dream of taking your money, and I'm sure Mr. Steirhouse wouldn't either."

Steirhouse, flattered, nodded agreement. A good-humoured argument followed.

"Well, look," said Johnstone finally, laughing. "If you really insist on doing something—put some money for us on the next horse you bet."

"I'll be happy to!" boomed Webster. "Mind you, I've never involved anyone else in this business before. I'm taking a big enough chance when I do it for my own benefit."

He paused and looked about, then dropped his voice. "You know, we're betting these horses after they win. We have a situation here where we can get a delay in the wired results to the bookies of five or ten minutes, depending on how much we want to pay. It costs us a thousand dollars a day for each minute of delay. Of course, the money comes from big Wall Street bankers. It's the principle of the thing they're interested in, not profits. They want to break the hold of these bookmakers who are bleeding the working man white—put them right out of business. But I don't mind telling you I've made a good thing out this personally."

As he was speaking, Webster opened a window as if to get air. This was a signal for the Tail man to phone the room.

"Now I can't tell when there'll be another big one," Webster was saying as he raised the window. "But when it comes up, you can bet I'll let you boys in on it." The phone rang, and he made a signal of dismissal as he moved to answer it. The Steer man began to edge the Egg from the room.

"Bye, now!" waved Webster, picking up the phone. "I'll be in touch."

"Don't worry," whispered the Steer man as the two reached the door. "He's obviously a man of his word."

"Hold on a minute," Webster called as they were about to close the door. "We're in luck. A good one's just come up. Here, Johnstone. I want you to take this thousand dollars and these credit slips and get right over to the Turf Exchange."

He pulled three small cards from his wallet. "I'm placing one thousand dollars for each of you to win on the next race and a couple of thousand for myself," Webster said. "I'll just get your names down here. Let me have your initials, will you, Johnstone: R.G.? Right. And yours, Steirhouse? J.S.? Fine."

But on the credit slip Webster reversed Steirhouse's initials to S.J. It is the kind of simple slip that many people make, but in the Payoff it is no mistake; it is in the script, and it is the key to a colossal swindle.

"This admission card will get you into the Exchange," Webster said. "I'll call my chauffeur in the lobby and he'll take you over in the Cadillac. He'll be the man at the side door with the black uniform."

And so, after some further play-acting, the Steer man left the suite, to return presently, his eyes shining.

"You ought to see that place," he told the wide-eyed Steirhouse, referring to the fictional Turf Exchange. "It's absolutely fabulous. Why, they're betting hundreds of thousands. . ."

The phone rang to inform Webster that his horse had won.

"Look, boys," Webster said. "There's another good one coming up. What do you say we bet our winnings?"

The three men bet twice more, and won each time. Finally Webster called a halt.

"That's all today, gentlemen. Not bad; we've won $140,000 between us. That's $70,000 for me and $35,000 apiece for you two. I'll have them deliver the cash right away."

He picked up the phone. "Hello, this is Webster. Yes, that's right. Will you bring it over, please? You know my suite. How long? Yes, I know it takes time, but no more than forty minutes, now. I have an engagement for the evening."

Half an hour later there was a rap on the door, and the fourth member of the confidence ring, in the role of the bookmaker's messenger, arrived with a satchel that appeared to be loaded with money.

"Let's count it out," Webster was saying when the phone rang again. "Yes—he's just arrived. I'll let you speak to him"—and he turned the phone over to the messenger, who spoke briefly and hung up.

"I'm sorry, gentlemen," the fake messenger said, closing the satchel. "That was the manager of the Exchange. He's just learned that the major portion of this was a credit bet, and he's instructed me not to issue the money until you can show evidence that you were financially able to pay in case of a loss."

"What do we have to do?" Webster asked.

"You'll have to show that you could have paid $140,000 in order to win that much. It's a strict rule at the Exchange."

"How long have we got?"

The messenger made another call: "Forty-eight hours—no more," he said.

Then he left.

"Oh, well," said Webster, with relief. "That's no trouble, really. I haven't got that much cash here, but I certainly can get $70,000 within a day. I have to be very careful, you know, not to excite suspicion, but I'll have my brother wire it to my bank here. He's in Mexico."

He turned to Johnstone. "What's the most you can raise without discussing it with anybody?—and I mean *anybody:* not even your wife!"

"Well, I've got $35,000 in cash in a safety-deposit box in Montreal," the Steer man replied.

"Let's see: that gives us $105,000. We're still short. Well, it's no use, I just can't lay my hands on any more without causing suspicion. I guess we'll have to forget it."

"Wait!" said Steirhouse, coming in on cue. "I could get the rest, I think."

"That's right," said Johnstone. "Mr. Steirhouse is no bum, you know, Mr. Webster. He's a man of substantial means."

"How can you get it?" Webster wanted to know, suspicion in his voice. "You can't go to anybody you know."

"I can cash my securities in Montreal and transfer the funds to the bank here," Steirhouse told him eagerly.

"Well, all we've got to do is show that the money's on account here in town and we'll be paid," said Webster. "It's just a formality with the Turf Exchange. They'll be quite happy to pay if we can each show substantial accounts."

It is important to note here that Steirhouse had no reason to believe his money was in jeopardy since he would not be required to draw it from the bank but only to show a slip confirming that it was on deposit. It is also significant that with a fortune apparently in his grasp he did not question the arithmetic or the logic of this preposterous proposition. He was, in short, acting like all Eggs at this stage of the Payoff game. (I have been assured by con artists that by the time this act in the play is reached, no Egg ever backs down, questions the set-up, or calls his new-found friends liars, swindlers or cheats. He has put his confidence in the Steer man, and he acts like a lover who believes his beloved is ever true. He is, in short, mesmerized.)

Off went Julius Steirhouse to Montreal with the ever-present Johnstone, who also was supposed to be raising $35,000 but whose real purpose was to keep the Egg warmed up and in a relaxed frame of mind.

Two days later, the charade was resumed in Webster's Royal York suite. Back came the messenger with his satchel full of bills.

But now a second hitch developed. Steirhouse's credit slip, it turned out, bore the wrong name.

"I'm sorry," said the messenger. "My instructions are to pay S.J. Steirhouse. The name on the bank slip is J.S. Steirhouse. I just can't pay you."

"Well, there's only one thing to do, then," said Webster briskly, standing up. "We've only a very short time left and we're going to have to move quickly. We'll have to draw our cash from the bank and bring it back here to show our good faith." With that, he hustled the other two from the room before the Egg had time to think.

And that is how Julius Steirhouse came to draw $35,000 in cash from the bank in Montreal and take it in a neat bundle to the Royal York—with a Tail man walking carefully in his wake every step of the way.

Back in the suite the two con men also produced neat packages of what appeared to be money. Each placed his money in a briefcase and then Webster, always in complete charge, gave Johnstone orders to go to the mythical Turf Exchange for the cash.

"They'll have no out this time," he said. Then, as an afterthought, "Oh, Johnstone—just before you go. Here's a betting slip for my share. Place my money here, will you?"—and he indicated the betting slip.

Reg Johnstone, Steer man extraordinary, was a consummate actor, as all good con men must be. When he returned, forty minutes later, he gave one of his finest performances, using only two props—the betting slip and the briefcase, now empty of cash.

He entered the room, almost in tears, and Webster in dismay asked what was wrong.

"Oh, my God, I could kill myself!" Johnstone cried. "I don't know what happened. I was only trying to do the best for everybody. You told me we were betting on sure winners. I can't understand what went wrong."

"What are you talking about?" cried Webster, seizing him by the lapels. "What have you done?"

"Well, I put your share on this horse, like you told me, and then . . . I put ours on, too, thinking the horse had won. Why didn't it win?"

"You idiot!" cried Webster, seizing the betting slip. "I told you to *place* that bet! Here it is, plain as day. Don't you know what 'place' means? There's a win, a place and a show—first, second and third. Of course we can't keep betting on winners; the Exchange wouldn't accept it. We have to take the occasional place and show horse. I thought you had normal intelligence, but you turn out to be an utter idiot. By God, Johnstone, I could kill you. Here, Steirhouse—open that window—"

"Please! Please!" cried Steirhouse, fearing trouble. Webster pretended to calm down.

"Now, look, Steirhouse—none of this is your fault, and as far as I'm concerned you haven't lost a thing. We'll fix that up. But this man has got to go. I suppose he made an honest mistake, but I won't suffer fools around me. I only wish I'd sent you over, Steirhouse, and not this idiot. Johnstone, I want you to get out before I really get angry. Don't ever bother me again. And if I ever hear that you've breathed a word of this I'll see you're taken care of—and I don't mean the police; I have other connections."

Johnstone by this time was crying real tears. (It wasn't difficult. He had put in a tense five days to get that $35,000, and the excitement of the game had kept his emotions on edge.) Steirhouse felt so badly for his friend that he actually put his arms around him and promised that he'd split anything they made with him.

"Don't worry—I know you meant the best for us," Steirhouse said as Johnstone left, and Johnstone, hearing this, realized that this Egg would not be difficult to cool out.

The most important part of the Payoff game now followed: the process of cooling Steirhouse out so that he would not suspect anything crooked and go to the police.

"Don't worry," said Webster, after Johnstone left. "I'm going to look after you. In fact, you may be very useful to me as a front man. Here's the name of a hotel in Boston. Go there immediately and check in under the name of Monroe. I'll be in touch with you there."

Steirhouse, trailed to the train by the Tail man, did exactly what he was told. After a day in the Boston hotel, he received a long-distance call from Webster telling him to go to New York to another hotel and register under another name. In New York, Steirhouse was sent to Chicago. From Chicago he was sent to Minneapolis. The purpose of this was twofold: first, to tire Steirhouse out, second, to make any story to the police sound highly suspicious.

By the time he reached Minneapolis, the weary Steirhouse was pleading to be allowed to go home. When the gang decided he was sufficiently cool, Webster phoned him again. "The heat's on me," he said. "The syndicate has caught on to what I've been doing, and I'm in trouble. We'll have to wait until this thing blows over, but don't worry—I'll be in touch with you. You'd better go back to Montreal. I should be able to get things going again in ninety days."

And so Julius Steirhouse, $35,000 poorer, returned to Montreal and never again heard from Mr. Webster or Mr. Johnstone. For the rest of his life he believed all the hokum he had been told. He died a short time ago without ever suspecting that he had been the victim of one of the cleverest swindles in the world.

Why I Left the Anglican Church

From *The Comfortable Pew*, 1965

HERE IS AN OLD ANGLICAN hymn of which I am very fond called "The Day Thou Gavest, Lord, Is Ended." I like it above all others—above, even, the Easter hymns of jubilation and the familiar carols of Christmas—because it takes me back to my childhood Sundays and Evensong in the little Anglican pro-cathedral of St. Paul's in Dawson City. Here, after a summer's day spent picnicking in the blue Yukon hills or drifting on the tawny breast of the restless river, a child could really feel that the gracefully dying day had been a gift to him from an all-wise, all-powerful and all-embracing deity. Surrounded by family and neighbours, each of whom was an old and intimate friend, listening to the anthems of a choir that included his own mother, insulated by the softly comforting sermons of a man who was a frequent dinner guest, untouched by the dilemmas and perils of that real world beyond the hills, this child could feel at peace with his religion and his God.

For the white-bearded, white-robed God of my childhood was a very real person. Lost momentarily in the mysterious woods behind the town, one babbled almost incoherently to God to keep the bears away. Caught red-handed in some minor childhood crime (such as "talking dirty" or "telling fibs"), one pleaded with God to overlook the sin and keep the gates of Heaven open at least a crack.

I am not sure when this picture of an anthropomorphic God and a finite Heaven began to lose its shape, but I think it probably began on the morning when my Sunday School teacher, an Anglican spinster missionary who worked in the hostel for mixed-blood children during the week and taught us about Heaven and Hell on Sunday, explained (not without a note of contempt that I should even bring the matter up) that dogs certainly did *not* go to Heaven because they had no souls. I was quite shaken by this revelation;

an afterworld that deprived me of my dog seemed to me less than heavenly.

I was more shaken by the three discoveries that followed. First, I learned that Santa Claus, the other supranormal figure in my life, was nothing more than the figment of a pleasant adult conspiracy. Second, I learned that the stork did not bring babies; they were the product of a more interesting process that by all the evidence it had chosen to give me my church considered sinful and wicked. The third discovery was even more shattering. For months my Sunday School teachers had been impressing me with the power of prayer. "If you pray hard enough," they had said, "God will answer you." One night I prayed very hard to God to give me and my sister two small, self-propelled automobiles. It never crossed my mind that when I hurried out of the house early the next morning they would not be there. The discovery shook me. And from this point on, I began to be sceptical of everything that was told to me by the adult world in general and by my church in particular.

But I did not reject the Church. God remained a real, if a somewhat less effective, figure. I attended church and Sunday School regularly, though as I grew older I found myself fidgeting through a service grown monotonous with familiarity. In addition, I respected some of the great figures of the church in my town. Chief among these was the Bishop of the Yukon, Isaac O. Stringer, a walking sermon who in the service of his God and his fellow man paddled a canoe untold miles, trudged, pack on back, across some of the harshest country known to man, and even on one memorable occasion cooked and ate his boots to stave off starvation. Indians and whites, children and adults respected him for these rugged qualities and loved him for his genuine saintliness.

The second great figure of my middle boyhood was the rector, Mr. Bryne. More than any of the others who came before or followed after, this man devoted himself to the youth of the town. Of all the many clerics whom I was to encounter in my twenty-odd years in the bosom of the Anglican Church, Mr. Bryne was the only one from whom I did not feel, in some sense, remote. He was genuinely interested in boys. He formed us into Cub and Scout groups. He took us on long hikes into the woods, on wiener roasts in the bright summer nights and on week-long camps in the summer. He talked to us frankly about things that counted. Though he never preached, he always had something to say, and when he used parables (as I now realize he did), they were modern ones, based on people and events we all recognized.

The church elders were suspicious and mistrustful of him. For one thing, he was disturbingly cheerful at all times. The comfortable aura of pious sanctity sat ill upon him. The congregation lived in terror that he might commit the unspeakable crime of telling a joke in church, though he never did. Worse, he was an innovator. He wanted to change things around in the service so that the congregation would take a more active part. He wanted some of the boys in the Wolf Cub pack to read the lesson, for instance. This raw radicalism was promptly squashed. Mr. Bryne disturbed people; when it came to the ears of some parents that he had actually discussed the facts of life with the older Scouts, there were shocked whispers. In the end, Mr. Bryne departed and, even to a small boy, the sigh of relief in the adult world was apparent. And, to a small boy, things were never quite the same again without him. Years later I learned that he had left the ministry to become a high-school teacher.

When my family left the Yukon and settled in Victoria, B.C. (I was twelve at the time), I continued to be a regular churchgoer and Sunday School attendant. My recollections of that particular Sunday School are among the most colourful of my teens. It was simple mayhem. In retrospect, it seems to me that from the moment I entered the Sunday School hall until the moment I left I was subjected to a hair-raising barrage of horse chestnuts, B-BS, elastic bands, paper darts, spit balls, gum wads and the occasional Bible, all of which I returned in kind. There must have been hymns, prayers and Biblical instruction of a sort, but I cannot recall them. All I can recall is a state of utter anarchy.

After the hurly-burly of Sunday School, the cool church provided a kind of quiet refuge. It was also, for a youth rapidly moving into puberty, a colossal bore. One went because one's parents insisted on it, because the girls in their Sunday best were becoming unaccountably attractive, and because one still harboured the definite belief that somewhere Up There a somewhat less anthropomorphic but still-believable God was writing down one's attendance record in a giant ledger against a day of ultimate reckoning. But one did not listen to the prayers, which were babbled by rote, or the lessons, which though beautifully phrased and intoned might as well have been in a foreign tongue, or the sermons that had nothing to say.

Yet I took my confirmation instruction seriously, examining the sacraments with awe and piety. I remember being genuinely shocked when some of the other boys spoke flippantly of the use of wine in the communion. During this period I was both pious, God-fearing and fully aware that I was a sinner, probably incapable of salvation. Certain questions nibbled at the fringes of my rationale, but I preferred to put them aside. Where, for instance, did myth end and reality begin? The rector explained that the seven days of Genesis were symbolic—a tale invented for primitive people who could not comprehend modern geological findings. So, too, with Jonah and Noah and the other Biblical figures of the Old Testament. On matters equally miraculous, such as the raising of corpses from the dead and the puzzling business of the virgin birth, he was less explicit. Though something deep down inside me was beginning to ask questions, these questions were never properly formed in my own mind or voiced in class. Nor were they ever answered. We did not think then about the unthinkable.

A few days before my confirmation, I received a baffling house call from the rector. He said he wished to speak to me alone on the eve of this important step. My family withdrew, leaving the two of us shifting about uncomfortably in the dining room. He engaged in some unimportant small talk, made a few remarks about the seriousness of the move I was making and explained that I could never be the same man again after my confirmation. While I was puzzling over that intelligence, and after one of those awkward little silences that always presage a profound but embarrassing statement, the rector coughed, looked me in the eye and stated that I should never act with another woman in any manner save that in which I would wish my own sister to be treated. The significance of this remark totally escaped me, and I was left confused and uncertain. Why had the rector travelled all the way to my house and drawn me aside to say that? What was the meaning of it? Did he know I had been fighting with my sister? But didn't everybody? And if I didn't treat other women as I treated my sister, how was I expected to treat them? I could make little sense out of it, but this was obviously the key matter on the rector's mind—that all women should be treated the way I treated my sister. Having said his piece, he took his leave, and shortly after that I joined the church and received, with trembling hands, the chalice of my first communion.

I was a dutiful communicant. Each Sunday I rose before seven, faithfully eschewed breakfast, trudged the mile to church and, a little weak from hunger, took the sacrament. It was never clear to me why I should eat nothing until the bread and wine had passed my lips, or how that kind of denial on the part of a growing and half-famished youth would somehow make him a better man. But I accepted it as part of the Mystery. And it was the Mystery that gripped me in these formative years. Not the words of Christ on the Sea of Galilee; not the moving tales of sacrifice and unselfishness that had long since lost their meaning through singsong repetition; not even those effectively simple parables that in another place and at another time had torn at men's souls with all the relevance of a newspaper headline. It was the packaging that intrigued me, not the content, for the packaging obscured the content or at least that was my experience.

Ritual, alas, cannot long remain exotic when it becomes a weekly commonplace. It may become as comfortable and as reassuring as an old slipper, or it may become a drag. For myself, and for most of my contemporaries, it became a drag.

Now in the eerie morning silence of the church, broken only by the low mumblings of the supplicants, I began to listen for the first time, out of boredom and curiosity, to what was really being said: "*We are not worthy so much as to gather up the crumbs under Thy table.*" That sentence had always bothered me. Most of the businessmen who heard it did not look as if they would stoop to gather up anybody's crumbs. A few moments before, the entire congregation had muttered in unison that the burden of their misdeeds was "intolerable." Was it, really? Or was this just something that was said because it had been said a thousand times before, because it was a conventional and even a comfortable thing to say—a hollow phrase without real meaning? What *were* these misdeeds that were so intolerable?

The ministers in the pulpit talked about wickedness in a vague way, but I cannot recall that this wickedness was ever linked with human action, save in the very narrow personal sphere. The grave injustices and oppressions that were then plaguing the nation, the inhumanity of man in the mass to man the individual—matters that were just beginning to concern me at the dawn of adulthood— were never mentioned. When one entered that church—or, indeed, most of the other churches that we visited from time to time—one fled the contemporary world; most of what was said could just as easily have been said during the previous century.

Thus began a slow drift away from the Church, unmarked by any really violent, anti-religious convictions. Mine was a rebellion born of apathy. More compelling interests entered my life: summers spent in mining camps, winters spent at college. On the campus and in the bunkhouse, there were the inevitable religious discussions. I cannot remember which side I was on.

And then, when I was graduated, I joined the staff of a Vancouver daily newspaper and was appointed, of all things, church editor. Thus was I exposed almost daily to the Christian Church in all its curious and disparate manifestations.

From a newspaperman's point of view, the brief contacts I had with the Roman Catholic clergy were generally the most satisfactory.

The Romans did not come pounding on my door asking for publicity, nor did they complain if I got things wrong. But whenever I asked for information or help, they were unfailingly courteous and polite. Only occasionally would their sermons make news.

The Anglicans I found to be snobbish and often testy about giving me help; they felt I should come to church to get information. I tried to explain that I could not attend every service in town and that by giving me the theme of the sermon in advance for publication on Monday morning, they might widen the circle of their congregation. But I was not always successful. The Anglican sermons were rarely newsworthy anyway.

The United Church people tended to be either very crusty or very eager with the press. Certainly they were worth cultivating, for they often had something to say, at least from a newspaperman's point of view, especially in the fields of drink and morals. If not, they would sometimes ask *me* what they should say, or even make up something on the spot if they thought it would be effective.

The fundamentalists, the evangelists and the smaller, exotic sects continued to distress me as a human being, just as they intrigued me as a reporter. The most successful leader of all, who attracted the largest congregations and made the most news, told the newspapermen quite frankly (off the record, of course), "I went into this God racket, boys, because I found it was the easiest way to make money."

In my months as a church editor, I met a few unselfish and genuinely stimulating men among the clergy, and also a few rogues and charlatans. What really concerned me was the discovery that the vast mass of ecclesiastics differed in no real sense from the vast mass of laymen. They conformed.

Regular contact with the various Christian denominations bred in me a feeling of dismay. Apart from everything else, I was to discover firsthand how hopelessly fragmented the Christian Church appeared to be. The message that was delivered from one pulpit was at odds with the message delivered from another; yet in each instance I was given to understand that this was the only true message—others were false. By this time I was seriously examining the possibility that all were false, for I had rarely seen such a display of mass arrogance on the part of men who proclaimed, always in general terms, their own humility. When I was promoted from church editor, I ceased all church attendance. I had had enough.

In this frame of mind I joined the army and was at once subjected to that peculiar form of military torture, the compulsory church parade. I have often wondered from where the impetus came to make weekly attendance at church compulsory. My experience as a private soldier, a non-commissioned officer and a commissioned officer suggests that it was compulsory because the weight of the religious establishment insisted that it be so. Certainly the vast majority of the officers and men I trained with considered it a nuisance that they would gladly have dispensed with. From the point of view of the Christian Church, it was surely a disaster.

Simply because it was compulsory, the church parade did more to drive men away from the Church than did any other aspect of the religious establishment. Some men were driven into a white fury by it. I was one. This was because the first chaplain I encountered happened to be a British Israelite who insisted on preaching idiocies to the captive audience that wartime expediency had delivered up to him. Some of us regularly risked detention by arranging for friends to call out our names on parade while we headed, literally, for the hills.

Here, bathed in the spring sunlight, overlooking the misty Okanagan Valley, we would discuss the whole business of religion. Why did the Church *need* a captive audience, if the message was as exciting as it claimed? After all, in the beginning the Church did not have to exercise compulsion. Didn't this very compulsion—not only the overt compulsion of the military, but also the subtle compulsion of society—really militate against the Church? Wasn't it possible that by virtue of its various captive audiences the Church in modern society had grown lazy, had ceased to try hard enough to get its message across? And how effective was a Church that seemed to believe it could effectively proselytize men who were dragged unwillingly from their beds and marched, grumbling, to a cavernous drill hall on the one day the army required no other regular duties? Wasn't the Church kidding itself?

"There are no atheists in the foxholes," somebody said with a bitter laugh, and we all joined in the merriment. Of all the nonsense uttered by the pious during World War II, this one sentence was surely the most inane. I did not see a foxhole during World War II, but those of my friends who did and who entered as atheists also emerged as atheists. The churches offended many of us during the war by subtly encouraging that phrase: it suggested that men could be (and perhaps should be) blackmailed into a form of religion by the imminence of death. No doubt some were, but it has never seemed to me to be a very effective way of getting converts. Dietrich Bonhoeffer, the German Christian martyr who was hanged by the Nazis and whose influence on modern theological thought has been considerable, shunned this cheap method of boosting religious statistics. Lying flat on his prison floor during a bombing raid, he heard the man next to him, "normally a frivolous sort of chap," mutter the words, "Oh, God, oh, God!" Bonhoeffer wrote to a friend that he could not bring himself to proselytize. "All I did was glance at my watch and say: 'It won't last any more than ten minutes now.' There was nothing premeditated about it; it came quite automatically though perhaps I had a feeling that it was wrong to force religion down his throat just then." Bonhoeffer added that Christ himself did not try to convert the two thieves on the cross; one of them turned to him.

One Sunday immediately after my discharge, my mother urged me to accompany her to Matins at the local Anglican church. I went along readily, but when we came out I told her that I could not bring myself to return. We had just come through a long depression and a long war, and the world was topsy-turvy. I had been to Europe and back and had seen some of the real problems that distress the human animal. My head was crowded with questions, ideas, vague longings, half-formed resolves and some small troubles. Whatever it was I was seeking, I did not find it in that church. Instead, I was subjected to a string of religious clichés, which while doubtless comforting to those who seek solace in the repetition of old, familiar phrases was maddening to me. We were all about to enter a New Age; yet there was nothing in that service to indicate that the world was different, that the language was different, that communication was different, that men were different. Sermon and all, it was a carbon copy of those Sunday rituals in the pro-cathedral in Dawson City in the 1920s.

I was married in the United Church, not for any special reason save that it was my wife's church. It was of little consequence to me who officiated. But when the first child arrived, I had to make some decisions. I felt it proper that my children should be exposed to whatever message the Church had for them and that they should then make up their own minds, on the basis of this teaching and their own observations, as to whether or not they wished to continue into adulthood as active churchgoers.

Accordingly, I made plans to have my daughter christened an Anglican. In preparation, I read the Anglican order of service for the Publick Baptism of Infants. I found I could not, without hypocrisy, take part in it. The very first phrase that "all men are conceived and born in sin" stuck in my craw, for I simply did not believe it.

First, I do not believe that any newborn baby is either sinful or angelic. She inherits certain characteristics that I would under no circumstances consider sins; apart from that, she is as an empty slate, waiting to be written upon. She may acquire sin, but at the time of christening she is innocent.

Second, and this is perhaps the crux of the matter, I refuse to believe that the act of procreation, which is at once the most sublime and mysterious and ennobling of all acts, can be designated as sinful. This is the clear implication of the passage in the Publick Baptism of Infants. It is also implicit in a good deal of the Church's teachings down through the ages.

Since that experience, a variety of enlightened priests have indicated to me that this passage does not really mean what it seems to mean. I have heard various rationalizations: the Church does not really consider the act of procreation sinful (though it perhaps once did); babies are no longer thought to be inherently wicked (though they once were). All the passage is said to have meant is that we are all imperfect in the sight of God.

Perhaps that is so. But if it *was* so, if that was what the Church really believed, if the passage that I was required to attest to in this most sacred moment meant something other than what it seemed to mean, why—in the name of that God who was being invoked—why was not all this stated in the clearest possible English? If the priests of the Church themselves did not believe the literal truth of what they were saying, why were they required to say it?

I called a friend in the United Church ministry who had been a classmate of my wife and myself at college and asked him to go over his order of baptism with me. It was simple, clear and to the point. My daughter and the five other children who followed were baptised members of the United Church.

Twelve years after this incident, the Anglican Church finally published a revised prayer book. In addition to spelling English words like "publick" in the modern manner, there were some other notable changes and omissions. The phrase "conceived and born in sin" is gone forever. That and certain other significant events and portents suggest that the Church may be struggling to make a genuine and honest effort to join the twentieth century, that, indeed, it may be on the verge of a fundamental revolution as earth-shaking as the Lutheran Reformation.

But I wonder if that revolution will come in time?

Dialogue with Myself

From *The Restless Church*, 1966

SELF: Well, the tumult and the shouting have died and the name-calling is almost at an end. The adjectives have all been used up: shallow, superficial, profound, prophetic, hasty, ill-advised, accurate, pretentious, insufferable, powerful, incisive, pompous, ignorant, atheistic, Christian. So what do you think about it all?

ME: You know, I find myself agreeing with almost everything that's been said, even when it's contradictory, because, you see, I think a pretty good case can be made *against The Comfortable Pew*, just as I think a pretty good case can be made for it. When I read some of the pieces in this book I was nagged by the usual self-doubts that assail any author who suffers from the fear that he may have been too glib. I could make an excellent case against my own book.

SELF: What would you say?

ME: I'd say, in a nutshell, that it bore the signs of being hastily written, that it left out vast areas of Christian concern, that it wasn't nearly trenchant enough in certain areas and that in places it was superficial, contradictory and confused. How's that for a start?

SELF: So you agree that it could have been a better book. If you'd given it more time, study and thought you might have produced a lasting work of real literary quality.

ME: Perhaps. But then I didn't set out to write a "good" book. I set out to write an *effective* book and that's a different thing. *The Comfortable Pew* comes closer to propaganda than it does to literature, and this was the intention of sponsor and author alike. I'll tell you a secret: at one time I thought of asking the church people to give me another year, but I decided against it. The book was designed as an instrument for action. If it has been effective, much of its value lies in its timing. If I *had* taken another year and produced a "better" book, I do not believe it would have been as useful. It seemed to me that the book had to be published as soon as possible, and I think the results have borne me out. It may be that its content wasn't as important as the *event* of its publication.

SELF: The critics are right, you know. The book is full of generalities and oversimplifications, and there are great areas of legitimate criticism that you've ignored.

ME: The same thing can be said of most sermons, including the good ones. There's nothing wrong with generalities providing you label them as such. The book *could* have been hedged with qualifications; it *could* have been three times as long; it *could* have been more profound—more "literary," if you like. But under those conditions I think it would have been much harder going for the people I wanted to reach. It was designed to pack a wallop.

SELF: So! You admit you set out deliberately to be as controversial as possible. Doesn't it make you cringe to be called a professional controversialist?

ME: It makes me cringe only because I admit nothing of the sort. I was asked to launch what the Church calls "a dialogue" and to take a position in that dialogue. I did what any good debater does when he wants to provoke rebuttal. But if the dialogue has been effectively launched, it is because the views I expressed were honestly held.

SELF: Oh, *come* now! Surely you expected a controversy and surely you revelled in it.

ME: I expected to be attacked, but none of us really expected a controversy of the proportions this one achieved. I revel in the fact that the book was more effective than I thought it would be. I thought most of what I said was self-evident, and I was astonished that things that seemed self-evident to me should have provoked such a reaction.

SELF: But that's what many of your critics said—that there was nothing new in the book, nothing fresh, just "a pretty collection of anti-Christian clichés that have been kicking around high school and university student cafés for half a century or more."

ME: Well, *that* irritates me. In my original preface I wrote: "I would not pretend that there is much in this book that is new. Most of what I have to say has been said before in various ways, and often more eloquently, by others. Many of these have been practising Christians and clergymen. . . ." A raft of critics act as if they had made this discovery independently.

Of course the ideas in the book weren't new. I've held many of them for more than twenty years. After all, that's why I left the Church. Still, you know, an opinion doesn't have to be new to be valid or effective. The Church holds some that are two thousand years old.

New or old, a great deal of what I said has either angered or stimulated or goaded some tens of thousands of readers and clerics, perhaps because it was, in one reviewer's phrase, "the expression of thoughts the reader has had in the back of his mind for some time but has never expressed." It's interesting, but not surprising, that some of the most favourable reviews of the book have come from the clergy and some of the angriest from critics who are atheists, agnostics or nothings. To these latter critics much of the book is, indeed, old stuff, and they rightly ask from their point of view, "What's all the fuss about? We've been saying this for years." But the book was not written for atheists; it was written for Anglican churchgoers. The letters I've received from these people suggest that though the ideas in the book aren't really very new, they are new to these people in the sense that they haven't been exposed to them in straightforward print before. I saw it as part of my task to express in simple terms certain critiques of organized religion that had heretofore been expressed more obscurely, if more profoundly. So, when a lady in Saskatchewan writes to say she needed to look up only one word in the dictionary, I take it as high praise.

SELF: So then you're not much more than a popularizer—a kind of ecclesiastical rewrite man?

ME: Perhaps more. A synthesizer, too, and maybe a catalyst. And, you know, there *are* one or two things in the book that might be described as fairly new—much *too* new for some people. I hesitate to bring up the matter of sex and the Church's attitude to it again because to do so is to rub a fingernail against the blackboard of conventional morality, but that passage is only a couple of years old. When the critics say there's nothing new in the book, they sometimes mean that the parts they agree with are "old stuff"; they ignore the rest.

SELF: All the same, you've got to admit the truth of such remarks as Ruth Taylor's in *The Churchman*, that many of the criticisms you make "aren't so true today as they were ten years ago" and that you really didn't take into account the enormous revolution that's been going on inside the Church.

ME: I suppose I should have paid more attention to it. Certainly I was exposed to it. After all, the commissioning of the book was part of the revolution. But the Church has yet to live down its past. And, to be brutally frank about it, I'm not convinced that the revolution is nearly as extensive as the insiders seem to believe it is. Part of this, perhaps, has to do with the Church's inability to communicate with the world. When I started on the book I had only the vaguest idea of the ferment within the Anglican community. The event of the book's publication has helped to change that—and there's a paradox. The public has now been *told*, in this way, that something has happened. I wonder if it has also been *shown*.

SELF: Oh, come off it! How about the thousands of clergymen who were involved last year in demonstrations, such as Selma? How about the Vietnam protests, the switch of position by the Anglicans on divorce, the change in the Sunday

School curriculum? The examples are legion. Surely there *is* a fresh breeze blowing through the Church, and surely the evidence of that clean wind is everywhere.

ME: Yes, but I'm not at all certain that this constitutes revolution. It seems to me that a lot of it is just the Church catching up on issues that were once too hot to handle and are now safely respectable. The Church sometimes confuses this catching-up-with-the-past with progress.

In *The Comfortable Pew* I made reference to a nineteenth-century missionary practice that several of my church critics have, I think, purposely chosen to misread in their zeal to prove things have changed. They keep saying that I am way behind the times because missionary work in Africa and Asia has undergone a revolution. I'm well aware of that and tried to make it clear in my book. For I was using the old missionary image to make a point about the Church's role in Canada. I wrote that "the same kind of refusal to adapt to native conditions operates in the latter half of the twentieth century in Western society." By native conditions I meant, of course, conditions in Canadian suburban parishes, not Congo villages.

The question is this: A generation from now will another writer in another critical book be able to say that the Church in the 1960s continued to cater to the comfortable pew by ignoring the uncomfortable issues that lay just below the surface? After all, most of the causes I outlined already belong to the past. Mopping-up operations may continue, but the real battles have been won. Birth control may seem a lively controversy today, but in the Protestant world at least it is no longer an uncomfortable one. Back in 1912 it was uncomfortable, just as the racial issue was uncomfortable in the twenties and thirties and the nuclear issue uncomfortable in the forties and early fifties. The Church must continue to take a position on these matters, but it must also try to understand and come to grips with the problems of present and future. Some of these problems, and the Church's general inattention to them, have been outlined by William Stringfellow in his excellent essay in this book.

SELF: But isn't it the most difficult thing in the world to sense what the real problems are, as opposed to the pretend problems?

ME: Agreed. Certainly we are groping in at least two areas: the sexual area and the area of work and leisure—not that we all necessarily hold old-fashioned attitudes in these areas but simply that we don't know how to cope with new social patterns.

But there's one uncomfortable issue that is fairly obvious. That is what I would call the New Racial Problem as opposed to the Old Racial Problem. The Old Racial Problem had to do with the unequal treatment of minority racial groups within the bounds of our own country—with job opportunities, housing, public attitudes and so on. The New Racial Problem has to do with the same inequalities on a world scale: the presence of overly rich white nations living within a jet-plane ride of undeveloped coloured nations. These white nations, two of which inhabit the mansion of North America, give alms to the poor, but they are not so Christian that they will let the poor into the mansion.

I made some passing reference to this in a passage in *The Comfortable Pew*, which several critics have chosen to misread. I compared the poor of our time—the masses of India, Asia and Africa—to the poor of an earlier period pressing their faces against the windows of the château. The château is not a continent, and the window is symbolic; but the faces continue to press against it pleading for admittance. I was astonished to discover several critics taking my imagery literally and upbraiding me for failing to realize that the Church has always helped the poor. I think one man even used the Fred Victor Mission in Toronto as an example!

SELF: But are these political matters properly the concern of the Church? Can the Church really take a unified stand as an institution on this sort of thing? One of the criticisms of your book, and a fairly widely held one, was that this sort of matter is really outside the Church's province, that there are many varying stands a Christian can take—

ME: I want to go into that in detail later. But really, you know, a very large section of the Christian Church *has* now made up its mind on the subject of racial brotherhood, otherwise we wouldn't have had so many ministers in the Selma parades. Some issues are complex and difficult, but as Rabbi Fackenheim points out in his perceptive piece in this volume, "With racial justice, the required stand is straightforward." And what we are talking about is racial injustice as we see it selfishly reflected in the immigration policies we tacitly support.

Recently I attended a discussion on *The Comfortable Pew* at an Anglican church, and we got onto this subject. I suggested that the Church either meant what it said or else it was being hypocritical. Unless my hearing is faulty, the scriptures tell us in a variety of ways that we are our brother's keeper. I suggested, therefore, that if the Church wanted to demonstrate that it meant on Monday what it said from the altar and pulpit on Sunday, it had no other course than to press for wide-open immigration policy, regardless of race, creed, colour, or training. This remark produced some interesting reactions. A leading layman stood up and said bluntly that such a policy was impractical. It would cause us all (we whites) to lose jobs. It would force us to adopt a lower standard of living. The country would be flooded with unskilled workers, and we'd have to spend money training them. We'd suffer from unheard-of racial problems. Again it may be that my perception is faulty and that, as some critics insist, I do not understand what the Church's leaders have been saying over the years and that I misread the implications of the gospels; yet I must persist in my belief that everything this layman was saying, while undeniably true, was also undeniably un-Christian. A cry for a wide-open immigration policy is perhaps impractical, but when did practicality ever enter into the basic teachings of the Christian Church? "Take all thou hast and give to the poor" appears to some to be manifestly impractical. "Consider the lilies of the field; they toil not, neither do they spin" is at odds with the practicality of a work-oriented society. "Turn the other cheek" is scarcely practical given the necessities of modern advertising. The Church has for years been preaching the virtues of impracticality without ever being prepared to accept the sacrifices of its consequences. This is why so many people see it as a hypocritical institution. I say the time has come for the Church to put up or shut up. Let it show that it believes what it says, and what its Messiah said, or let it rewrite the Scriptures.

The reaction of the minister of that particular church was as interesting as that of his laymen. He announced that he would be prepared to set up a committee to look into the matter. I really believe he thought he was on my side of the dialogue. But what he was really doing, with the best of intentions, was squirming out of an uncomfortable situation. Is a committee needed to dig out the unappetizing facts? They are simple and widely understood: We live in the richest and emptiest continent in the world. Just across the water from this roomy continental palace, black and yellow people exist in grinding poverty, crowded together amid filth, disease, despair and death. What is the Christian attitude to these people? To keep them in the ghetto and send them tracts, missionaries and the occasional crust? Or to let them into the mansion? Yet anyone who advocates such a policy will be attacked first as naïve and impractical and later as dangerous and demented—adjectives, I suppose, that were in use some two thousand years ago in Jerusalem. He will encounter the bitterest and most violent opposition from organized capital and organized labour. It will be pointed out that such a policy will not work, since it would quickly cause hardship, hunger, unemployment, loss of income and property rights—meaning, of course, that it would cause these ills among white Christian Canadians. All this is no doubt true. Our standard of living would certainly drop. But what has one's standard of living got to do with Christianity? The causes of an unfettered, or even of a limited, immigration policy from the underdeveloped countries are awesome to contemplate: for the first time millions of people who pay lip service to the Christian ideals of the brotherhood of man and universal voluntary love would actually be forced to do some of the same things their Christ did: to move on the same level as the halt, the sick, the afflicted, the lonely, the hungry, and the cast-offs of this world—and not as observers but as part of the motley, anguished throng.

SELF: I suspect you've got your tongue in your cheek. You don't really believe in a policy of unlimited immigration any more than you believe in a policy of total disarmament. You know very well that it's impractical and foolish.

ME: Yes, I probably do. But when I tell my friends in the clergy that much of Christianity seems to me impossible to attain, and for many of the same reasons, they tell me that Christianity is itself an ideal and that even though we can't achieve it perfectly, we ought to strive for it. If this is so, then again I say the Church's anointed ought to be advocating the impossible, impractical, but very Christian idea of unlimited immigration.

SELF: And you? It's all very well to say these things from your own comfortable pew. Would you personally be willing to accept the consequences of the action you say the Church should press for? Are you prepared to divide your acreage into small parcels to accommodate the overpopulation that would result? Are you prepared to see your income dwindle to the point where you and your family might go hungry? In a pig's eye you are!

ME: I don't view it with any particular relish. It would all be very uncomfortable and distressing—almost as distressing as living in Calcutta as an untouchable. If you ask me if I intend today to parcel up my land, home, and income, I'd say no. I'm not strong enough to do it by myself, I guess. But if all of us—neighbours, friends, strangers, chance acquaintances—were in the same boat, as one is in wartime, say, it might be possible to bear. It might even be exciting, as war often is, and not really as dangerous in the end, if you want to be practical, since it might remove the chief cause of wars and thus, uncomfortable or not, be somewhat preferable to the inevitable alternative of out-and-out destruction. But these are not really Christian considerations. My real point is, in my own naïveté, I cannot, after reading the Gospels and listening to my clerical friends, see any other stand for the Church to take.

SELF: Oh you can't, can't you? Isn't that one of the most telling criticisms of your book? That you, of all people, who criticize the Church in the sexual area, for instance, because it insists on a code of absolutes—you, yourself, are laying down rules of absolute conduct for the Church, and these absolutes very often tend to be little more than a reflection of your own small "l" liberal views. Aren't you, too, suffering "pretensions to absolute rightness"?

ME: I suppose I am. The dilemma I suffer from is the same as the one that afflicts the Church. The only difference is that we are on opposite sides of the same coin. What I was trying to say was this: If the Church insists on taking absolute positions in such fields as that of sexual morality then it must be prepared to be criticized for not taking absolute positions in such fields as business ethics, war, racial injustice and so on. It can't have things both ways.

SELF: But that doesn't let you off the hook, does it? You advocate a flexible position in the area of sexual morality—something like the views of some British Quakers—but an absolute

191

position on, for instance, warfare. Surely that's inconsistent.

ME: I said we were on two sides of the same coin. But what I did not make clear in the book is that there is a considerable difference between what I personally think and what I believe the Church has to do if it is to act in accordance with its own words. I am not, for instance, an out-and-out pacifist in the sense that some Christians are pacifist. I would not advocate unilateral disarmament. I would not have opposed and did not oppose World War II. There are conditions, I think, under which I might still advocate armed revolution, though such things are much more difficult to advocate in a nuclear age. But then, I do not call myself a Christian. The churchmen around me, however, continue to talk of peace . . . peace . . . peace. The word is dragged out at Christmas time and made synonymous with Christianity. Yet some of the very men who talk so glibly of the Prince of Peace are to be found symbolically or literally blessing weapons and passively accepting in the name of wartime expediency every kind of human villainy from the indiscriminate bombing of civilians to the torture of Vietcong prisoners.

It is not that I have attacked the Church because it sometimes fails to share my personal social and political convictions. It is because it appears to be failing to follow its *own* convictions. The Church of England, as I pointed out, *has* come to a conclusion about the use of nuclear weapons. But it took fourteen years for it to make up its mind. Surely what turned out to be an offence against God in 1964 was also an offence against God at the time of Hiroshima.

One area of social concern that I did not deal with may serve to make my point. Though some of the clergy still argue that hanging is necessary to the safety of a civilized society, I doubt that any now believe, as many once believed, that seven-year-olds should be strung up for pilfering spoons or traitors publicly disembowelled. In that sense, the whole body of the Christian Church has come to a definite and absolute conclusion. But it ought to be remembered that the English bishops were among the last to change their minds on these points.

SELF: But really now, can any large Protestant denomination with its emphasis on individual conscience and its absence of totalitarian authority—can it ever take a consistently strong position on such issues?

ME: Perhaps not, though, as I have pointed out, it eventually does. But it can change the climate to allow, nay, even encourage, more radicals in its midst and to allow these radicals more expression.

SELF: But don't you think it does that? Look, for instance, at Bishop Pike in the States or Bishop Robinson in Britain. Look at the Red Dean. Look at some of the men who commissioned *The Comfortable Pew*.

ME: Right! But such men still seem to me to be in the minority.

SELF: Won't they always be? Haven't they always been?

ME: If the church is to survive and grow, their number will have to increase.

SELF: But what's stopping that increase? Surely not the hierarchy of the Church?

ME: To some extent the hierarchy. To some extent the system— the institutionalism that flourishes only when the status quo is maintained. To some extent the large mass of the laity who continue to prefer their pews comfortable.

SELF: *So!* You blame the laymen, do you? You virtually ignored the large mass of the laity in your book. You airily defined "the Church" as the hierarchy and leadership when the real Church is the whole body of Christ—worshippers and priests combined. They ticked you off for that, didn't they?

ME: Oh, yes; though why a man should be blamed for explicitly defining his terms of reference at the outset, I don't know.

SELF: Surely those terms of reference were too narrow.

ME: If they were any wider I should not have been writing a critique of the Church but a critique of Canadian society. By "leadership," of course, I meant to include leading laymen—but certainly not the followers to whose comfort, I still insist, the leadership often caters. I cannot agree that my definition of the Church was too far away from what both clergy and laymen mean when they commonly use that phrase—or from what some of the writers in this book mean when they use it. After all, when people criticize General Motors they mean the management and board of directors; they certainly aren't including all the widows who happen to own a few shares of voting stock. I suggest that analogy isn't too far out.

SELF: But in a sense weren't you attacking Canadian society in spite of your narrower terms of reference? One critic said that you set up "a woozy straw man—the Church" and that you then used that term as an omnibus clause into which you lumped all that you found wrong with modern society.

ME: Well, perhaps. That's probably the sort of thing I myself would write if I were given the job of reviewing *The Comfortable Pew*. But then, one of the points I made was that the institution of the Church is sometimes indistinguishable from the institution of society as a whole.

SELF: Is that necessarily bad?

ME: If you believe that a kinetic social institution should be more than a mere reflection of the world around it, then it's bad. Remember, I was asked to point out what I personally thought was wrong with the Church. I said that I thought the Church would have to lead, not follow, if it was to survive and be respected. Thus it has to be in tension with society. I say it isn't.

SELF: But haven't you made the very serious error of equating Christianity with liberalism? Rabbi Fackenheim makes this point pretty tellingly in this book.

ME: I don't mean to suggest that Christianity and liberalism are the same thing, but I do think that liberalism—certainly my kind—is a reflection of the Christian concern for the individual. I suppose we can argue forever about the liberal tradition and where it springs from, but I would say that part of it springs out of the Christian tradition. It occurs to me that it is very difficult for the churchman to follow certain of the precepts of Christ and not find himself, from time to time, sharing the same highway with the liberal. Liberalism and Christianity often do meet on common ground, and it is on this ground, in my opinion, that the Church has sometimes been found wanting.

SELF: But once again I think you can't slither off the hook as easily as all that. You've got to admit that William Stringfellow has got you neatly trapped when he says that you admit your conviction that God *does* prefer Western democracy to all others. How do you equate that with your earlier message about God not being on *anyone's* side?

ME: I can't; and on the evidence of my own words, he's got me. I've read that passage again and I'm appalled by it. All I can say—and it sounds pretty weak—is that I didn't mean it the way it sounds. I said, correctly, I think, that Christian concepts are part of our heritage, that they form the basis of many Western attitudes, and that our national conscience, springing from this heritage, can when aroused shape the course of history for the betterment of mankind. I didn't mean to suggest that Western democracy has an exclusive lien on Christian concepts, and I hope the rest of the book makes that clear. I think the United Church was correct to call Communism a Christian heresy, and it is possible that (distressing as this will sound to some) this Christian heresy may have more to do with bettering mankind than our Christian Western society. I would further agree with Mr. Stringfellow that from the Christian point of view all idolatry of nation and worship of national ideology ought to be protested and exposed.

SELF: Which brings us, in a roundabout way, to the question that has really been eating at you. Is Christianity an instrument of political action or of personal reconciliation? What have the

195

Gospels to do, really, with any system of morals or ethics? And don't you, as Stringfellow charges, fail to distinguish between radical ethical idealism and voluntary love?

ME: If I fail to make that distinction so does the Church. Stringfellow writes that the Churches are content "merely to echo the secular ethics of humanism." I would agree, and to me the damaging word is "echo." If the Church is merely the echo of a secular society, then there is no real reason for the Church to exist at all. I think I have had something to say about Christian love in my book, and if, on occasion, I have equated the requirements of human love with the demands of a radical ethical system, I make no apology for it.

Furthermore, there is no reason why churchmen, in preaching about voluntary love, grace, sacramental action, and personal reconciliation (Stringfellow's words) cannot make use of some sound examples rooted in the contemporary situation to underline their message. Indeed, in those contemporary areas where love is denied, where the Devil is dominant, where Christ is blasphemed, and where the Gospel is profaned, then surely it is the duty of the Church to speak out—not on humanist terms, necessarily, but on its own.

Let me take one aspect of the conflict in South Vietnam as an example. There is an honest argument, I suppose, on which Christians may differ regarding the practical as well as the moral pros and cons of that war. But can any Christian or any humanist condone for an instant the torture of enemy prisoners as a means of getting information about the other side? The newspapers tend to cover these horror tales in much the same way that they cover a fracas in Maple Leaf Gardens, "objectively," with impersonal stories and deadpan captions. We are shown one prisoner with a knife placed against his belly, another with his head submerged in a tub of water, a third being flailed with clubs. We are told of terrified prisoners forced to watch one of their number tossed from a helicopter in flight as an object lesson in the dangers of not "co-operating," i.e., not betraying one's comrades. The ultimate horror of all this is the callous ease with which these matters have been accepted by the vast majority of newspaper readers and, it seems, newspaper writers, most of them at least nominally Christian. One might have expected a massive, continental wail of anguish. Instead, though there have been some notable individual protests, there has been much more official and unofficial justification, some of it implied, some of it direct.

As far as I can determine, the justification for this monstrous offence against humanity in South Vietnam (and surely, from the Church's point of view, against Christ) can be summed up as follows:

1 "Everybody's doing it." The other side is far worse than we are. It's a rough war, after all, and we've got to fight fire with fire—use the enemy's own tactics if we want to win.

2 We're *forced* to do it. It's the only way we can win. Sure, it's horrible, but it's better that a few individuals suffer pain than that thousands die—especially American boys.

3 It's not really our doing. White Westerners don't actually engage in torture. It's the Vietnamese that do these awful things. Our people are only observers. It's an internal matter in which we can't interfere.

4 After all, they're only Asians and they're used to it. Physical torture is almost a way of life with them.

Perhaps I misread my scriptures, but it seems to me that all of this is blasphemous. The Christian may attack it on different grounds than the humanists, but attack it he must. If I'm wrong, if I *do* misread my scriptures, if this sort of horror is *not* a matter of insistent Christian concern, if it is generally held that the Church should not cry out in protest when human beings are mangled in the name of expediency, then all I can say is that I lose all vestige of interest in the Church and in Christianity. It is not for me; if it fades and dies tomorrow, I shall not mourn.

SELF: But there you go again, talking in terms of principles and not in terms of individuals. You know very well that churchmen have always protested this kind of thing and will continue to do so, but you also know that the Church has another role, which you have largely ignored. That is to reach out to the suffering—not just the physical sufferers in a remote corner of the globe at a specific moment in history but those who come heavy-laden and in anguish to its doors at all times and in all places, tortured not by knives and clubs but by an inner ferment compounded of loneliness or self-hate or fear or guilt or any of those other ills of the spirit. It is to these people that ministers minister—yes, and sometimes, as you sneeringly put it, while balancing teacups on their knees—and this kind of traditional ministration and the need for it is glossed over in your book.

ME: I have no real answer to that charge except to say that *The Comfortable Pew* is a personal book and in no sense definitive. I was asked to write what I personally found wrong with the Church, not what I found right with it. I suppose when I wrote the book I felt that in this area of individual ministry the Church was less open to criticism than in some of the other areas I outlined.

SELF: Did you, really? Or did you simply feel that it didn't matter?

ME: Perhaps I did. Certainly by ignoring it I indicated that I did. But if I thought it unimportant, I erred, for I no longer think so.

SELF: But why did you think it unimportant? Why did you dismiss it? Come on—face me.

ME: I suspect it was because I knew, deep within myself, that if I were suffering from a kind of personal anguish, which

Mrs. Kilbourn describes in this book I would not turn to the Church for solace.

SELF: And why not?

ME: Because for me, and I think for many thousands of others like me, the Church by its failure in those other fields that matter to me has rendered itself impotent to help me as an individual. I simply cannot respect it.

SELF: But surely you are confused here. Surely a sufferer does not seek solace from *something* but from *someone*. Your critics have pointed out that you sometimes seem to ignore the fact that the Church is composed of individuals. And surely it is an individual clergyman or priest, whom they have come to respect, that the poor, the bruised and the blind seek out when their burdens become intolerable. You may be disillusioned with the institutional garment of the Church, you may be embarrassed and sickened by its postures, but can you say that within the framework of that amazing institution there are not individuals whom you respect and to whom you might easily turn, if, as may someday happen, you can no longer cope with the cares and complexities of this world?

ME: It's quite possible. It's equally possible that I might turn to a friend or acquaintance whom I admire and who is outside the Church.

SELF: The Church would say, in that case, that Christ was working in that person and thus you *were* turning to Christ.

ME: No doubt, and perhaps the Church would be right, though I often think it uses that device to get itself off the hook. It doesn't alter my original point, that whenever the Church bankrupts itself in one area of concern, it tends to bankrupt itself in others. By its own failure to come to grips with this world it loses its power to make *me* come to grips with the next.

SELF: Aha! You talk of the "next world" do you? And you call yourself an agnostic.

ME: I use it symbolically to mean the world that is not Caesar's. For want of a better phrase I don't mind calling it the "spiritual world." It exists within each of us. Whether or not it continues after we die, I don't know. I would doubt it.

SELF: It's strange to hear you using that word "spiritual." You certainly kept away from spiritual matters in your book. You rarely mentioned the Bible.

ME: If the Church had wanted a theological critique it would undoubtedly have commissioned a theologian to write *The Comfortable Pew.* As for the Bible, no, I didn't quote extensively from it. I assumed my readers had read it. Certainly a knowledge of the New Testament is by implication requisite to an understanding of the book.

SELF: You obviously agree with a good deal that's in the New Testament, especially the Sermon on the Mount. Many churchmen have said that your book shows a real concern for the survival of Christian faith. If so, then why don't you get in there and pitch? Why don't you join the Church? It's all very well to throw stones from the sidelines, but wouldn't you be more effective working from within?

ME: When I was writing a daily column, often critical of various social institutions to which I did not specifically belong, I was continually faced with this question. I suppose every social critic meets the same challenge. Perhaps by our very natures we are not joiners; certainly we cannot join everything. I *am* concerned about the survival of the Christian faith but not necessarily of the Christian Church.

SELF: But if the faith is to live, surely the Church in some form must continue.

ME: I hope not in its present form. Let me make a not entirely frivolous parallel. I happen to agree with and applaud several of the service aims of the Kiwanis Club. I think the Kiwanians do a great deal of good in this world, and I would like to see this attitude of service prevail. But to me, the idea of attending a Kiwanis luncheon every week is so appalling that I would move to Zanzibar before I would become an active member.

SELF: Are you really telling me that you equate the Christian Church with a mere service club?

ME: In a sense, I suppose, I do. And maybe that's the most searing indictment I can make of the Church. What I'm saying is this: I consider the Church an important institution in society, but it's not, for me, the *only* institution. The really important institution is society itself. Of that I am a member and I hope a reasonably active one.

SELF: But there's more to it than that, now isn't there?

ME: Yes. There's more to it. The other reason I don't belong is simply that the Church asks me to recite regularly a series of statements that I cannot take on faith. Specifically it asks me to believe, and to say aloud that I believe, in life after death, in the divinity of Christ, in the resurrection of the body and in certain other matters. I think thousands like me face this dilemma and are troubled by it. I might like to believe in these things; I might be more comfortable holding such beliefs; but, in point of fact, I do *not* believe such things, and I'm damned if I'm going to say I do when I don't. Moreover, I don't even think it is necessary to believe in such things to be a decent human being, to live a good, worthwhile and rewarding life, and even to be a "Christian," though that is a matter of semantics.

SELF: But aren't you aware that there are many churchmen—and some very important ones—who don't take these things literally, either? If they work within the institutional framework of the Church, why can't you?

ME: Maybe they have a different temperament—I don't know. Maybe they've stopped listening to what it is they say aloud every Sunday. Maybe they treat the prayers and hymns and even parts of the Gospels as we treat folk songs. Maybe they feel they're more effective as human beings inside the Church. That's their business. All I can say is I can't do it.

And personally, I think I've been more effective on the outside.

SELF: All of this sounds a bit odd in the light of the last few pages of your book in which you seem to predict and to welcome a Second Coming. . .

ME: That, it turns out, is the most controversial section of *The Comfortable Pew*, and I find *that* a bit odd. Several critics whom I admire have written that I am "beseeching" a new Christ to come down to earth or that I am "yearning" nostalgically for another Messiah or that I am "calling" for a Second Coming. I'm afraid, however, that these final pages are rooted in a deeper pessimism than seems apparent. I happen to be in agreement with Jim Lotz, who wrote in the University of British Columbia's student paper that "it is not to actions or to the promise of a single man that mankind must look. It is to themselves." If man is ultimately to be free of all dependencies, if he is to throw away his crutches, then that is certainly true. Alas, I see no prospect of such unfettered liberty. When I wrote at the conclusion of *The Comfortable Pew* that revolution, *real* revolution within the Church—would most probably come (if, indeed, it comes at all) through the actions of a single man, a traditional Suffering Servant, I wasn't advocating anything or even yearning for anything but simply outlining the most likely of several roads to change. I hold to this. The state of the Church being what it is, I still suspect that violent change is likelier to come as the result of the emergence of a single, passionate, selfless leader than by any spontaneous mass action.

SELF: What you are really underlining is your lack of faith in the adulthood of man—something you insisted had arrived.

ME: No, in the adulthood of the Church—something I've insisted hasn't arrived.

SELF: Don't you think it's possible that the change may come, not from a single leader and not from spontaneous mass action, as you put it, but from the emergence of a small but significant minority within the institution, each of whom may have, to some extent, those qualities that were Christ's and each of whom will make his witness and suffer his sacrifice?

ME: This is possible and even probable. There are signs that such a group is appearing now. How effective it can be is another matter. If it is effective, then I suspect that one man will stand out from this group. This has generally been the case. In the Negro revolution, which certainly has had its growing band of dedicated men and martyrs, one Messiah emerged, in the person of Martin Luther King, to electrify the movement into action. In India, there were many disciples, but only one Mahatma. I'm not sure this is necessarily a bad thing, and I'm not sure that if the Church is worth saving it isn't inevitable.

SELF: How do you mean "if the Church is worth saving"?

ME: You and I have been wrestling over that question all along, haven't we? And, paradoxical though it may sound, I think we've come to a conclusion: If revolution doesn't come, then the Church isn't worth saving. But if the Church *is* worth saving, then revolution is as inevitable as it was in Mississippi or Bombay.

Marguerite Oswald—Mom and Apple Pie

From *Voices from the Sixties,* 1966

*I*N OCTOBER *1964, Mrs. Marguerite Oswald came to Toronto for a television appearance on the controversial* CBC *program* This Hour Has Seven Days. *It did not seem to me that her appearance was very effective because she was asked to discuss a subject on which she was not an expert and had no firsthand knowledge: the assassination of John Kennedy and her son's role in that crime. She said she had circumstantial evidence, including documents, that suggested there were people in the United States State Department "who wanted Mr. Kennedy out of the way," but these remarks remained vague and unsubstantiated. She hinted that witnesses who might have appeared before the Warren Commission and might have cleared her boy were not called, but she did not name them or say what their evidence was. Accordingly, when she phoned me at home the following day and offered to appear on my program, I was disinclined to go over old and infertile ground.*

But then it occurred to me that although Mrs. Oswald was in no sense an expert on the assassination, she was an expert on the assassin. On the subject of his family background and upbringing she did *have firsthand knowledge. She had repeatedly indicated to the Warren Commission that Lee Harvey Oswald had enjoyed a normal upbringing and that his background was that of a typical American boy. How normal? I wondered. How typical? I invited Mrs. Oswald to appear on the program to discuss this subject and this subject only. She agreed.*

On first acquaintance, Marguerite Oswald is a disarming person. Walking into the television make-up room, she might have stepped directly out of one of those Florists' Telegraph Delivery ads that appear around Mother's Day. She projects the kind of image one generally associates with apple pie—a plump, homey-looking matron in a black wool suit and a black velvet hat, quiet-spoken, pleasant, just a little sad. Make no mistake about it—this was Mom herself, and it was as Mom that I interviewed her. I began by establishing the fact that Lee Harvey Oswald was born without a father.

MRS. OSWALD: Yes, that is correct. Lee was born two months after the death of his father.

PIERRE: So in his early years, before you were married again, he was literally fatherless?

MRS. OSWALD: Yes, he was.

PIERRE: How did this affect him, not having a father? This would make you have to work a little harder at being a parent, I guess.

MRS. OSWALD: Yes, I was the one parent, the only parent of three boys; but you must understand Lee had two brothers, so he wasn't actually raised by a woman alone. He had a brother who was seven years old and another brother who was five, at the time that he was born.

PIERRE: Your husband left you without very much money, and you had to go out and work at this time. Is that correct?

MRS. OSWALD: That is correct. I stayed home approximately two years with the children because I believe that a mother should be with the children as much as possible, and then, naturally, I had to go out to work in order to support them.

PIERRE: What were you working at in those days?

MRS. OSWALD: Oh, I have always been in retail merchandise.

PIERRE: You were in real estate, too, I believe, were you not?

MRS. OSWALD: No, no, insurance.

PIERRE: I thought you were also selling—at least, your own house and property.

MRS. OSWALD: Well, you might say, if you want to say real estate, but I had no agents or anything. I did it all on my own, in order to supplement my salary, which was very, very small. I would buy a piece of property, near a school always, because I was told you could always resell, and we would live in it for a year or two, and maybe I'd make fifteen hundred dollars, and that fifteen hundred dollars, supplemented to the salary I was earning, helped the four of us to survive.

PIERRE: You therefore moved from neighbourhood to neighbourhood?

MRS. OSWALD: Well, not in any short length of time. Sometimes we would stay two years or three years, which really isn't a home which, like, you know, you buy and stay in. But I think this was very good, because it did give us a sort of a decent living, where if I had to depend just on my salary for four, we would really have been poverty-stricken from the very beginning.

PIERRE: As it was, you didn't have a great deal of money.

MRS. OSWALD: No, and you must understand when my husband died that the Social Security law was not in effect. He died in August 1939, and it didn't become effective until January 1940. So I had no support for myself and three children like the women have today.

PIERRE: So who looked after the boys when you went out to work?

MRS. OSWALD: Well, it was during the war years. Now we're coming to about 1942, you see, where it's awfully hard to get help. And many, many a job I had to leave in order to stay home and mind my children, because the maids wouldn't show up. I was a church member—I am a Lutheran—so it was decided that we would place the two older boys in a Lutheran Church Home. Lee was not eligible. He had to be three years old in order to go to the church home.

PIERRE: The two older boys left, leaving you with one child. Who looked after him?

MRS. OSWALD: Well . . . babysitters and people I had living in the home with me, just like the women today when—well—we have many women today who have husbands who go out and work and leave their children home with babysitters. But as I explained before now, we're getting into the war years where it was awfully, awfully hard to get help. My sister helped to take care of Lee when the maids wouldn't show up, and many a job I had to quit. This was a very sad thing. I needed the money in order for our support, yet I was obligated to quit a job in order to stay home and mind my child. Then when Lee was three years old I put him in the Lutheran Church Home with his brothers.

PIERRE: How long was he in that home?

MRS. OSWALD: He was only there a year when I contemplated marriage. I remarried.

PIERRE: So when you remarried he had a stepfather?

MRS. OSWALD: Yes.

PIERRE: Would you say that he was close to that stepfather?

MRS. OSWALD: No, I really wouldn't say so. He was an electrical engineer, and he travelled, and Lee and I travelled with him. And, of course, I was the mother of the boy, and this was the stepfather, and the three of us were together, but travelling and living in hotels. Lee was more with me because the father was working and in conference, and so on and so forth. But he did have a father, if you want to put it this way. Now he had a father.

PIERRE: Was this your second husband?

MRS. OSWALD: Yes.

PIERRE: And you've been married again since? You've had three husbands. Would you say that he was a real father to Lee?

MRS. OSWALD: No. No, he wasn't a real father to Lee. This man that I married had a woman before he married me. And he also had the same woman while he was married to me. I left him. Of course I didn't know about the woman when I left him the first time. I left him because I really wasn't his wife. I will say it this way: I didn't share his bank account, his insurance, or anything. Actually I was his second mistress. He had one that he even took along with him, that I didn't know about, of course, and he allowed me one hundred dollars a month. He made ten thousand dollars a year and had an expense account. In 1945 that was quite a bit of money. And out of the hundred dollars a month, when we didn't travel, this was money to run the house. I was supposed to account for every cent that I spent, which I wouldn't do because this is not my disposition, and so we fought back and forth because I wanted to be his wife. I think the wife should share in the husband's finances and insurance.

PIERRE: Were you able to confide in your son about this situation? Was he aware of it?

MRS. OSWALD: No, no. Lee was just five and six years old at the time. Then, finally, I did know about the woman, and I naturally wouldn't live with him and expected to divorce him. But in the meantime he filed charges against me, and he got the divorce from me, which was most unfair, because I had caught him in the woman's apartment with witnesses, and I thought: "Well, now surely he can't get a divorce from me." The reason why I didn't divorce him immediately was that the other two boys were in a military school at my expense; I had sold my last piece of property, and it meant disrupting their lives. So I wanted to wait to divorce this man until the school term; but in the meantime he filed charges against me, and he did divorce me.

PIERRE: This breakup of your marriage would have occurred approximately at the time, then, that Lee began his first school year, wouldn't it?

MRS. OSWALD: Yes, yes, that's right, just about that time.

PIERRE: And as I understand it he was in Grade 1 three different times in three different schools. How did that come about?

MRS. OSWALD: Well, in all states your school system is different.

PIERRE: You were moving around at the time?

MRS. OSWALD: Well, I had left this husband, as I told you. Then I went back to him. So I left Texas and went to Louisiana, and they thought he had never been to school when he was in first grade; so they demoted him to kindergarten. Then, when I came back to my husband, we went back to Texas. Then they put him in the second grade. It's just the difference in the school systems.

PIERRE: Well, did they demote him from the second grade again?

MRS. OSWALD: No, no. Just that twice.

PIERRE: How was he in school? Was he bright?

MRS. OSWALD: Yes. I have testified before the Commission and in 1959 I made this statement: Lee was the type of child that needed special schooling because he was overly bright for schooling. There's some children that you can't teach anything to. They have wisdom. I would feel very self-conscious saying this now if I hadn't said it in 1959, but it's in print in 1959 when he was supposed to have defected to Russia. This was a boy who had wisdom.

PIERRE: How were his grades, Mrs. Oswald?

MRS. OSWALD: They were satisfactory. Just passing, which—

PIERRE: Just passing?

MRS. OSWALD: —which means satisfactory.

PIERRE: If they were just passing, that certainly doesn't indicate on the face of it that he was as bright as you say.

MRS. OSWALD: Well, because you have book learning and you have wisdom. There's your difference, you see. He was further advanced than what they wanted to teach him. So that type child doesn't have a straight A. Your straight A, I think, comes from the children whom the teachers can teach. They can study and they make their straight As, and they have book learning. I might say this: the man we were speaking of, that I was married to, was an electrical engineer and a Harvard graduate, but he had book learning and that's all. He didn't know how to apply himself, and this is what I'm trying to say. Lee didn't have a formal education, but he had the know-how. There's quite a difference.

PIERRE: Would you describe your son as a loner in these formative years?

MRS. OSWALD: No, no, I wouldn't describe him as a loner. Many, many people since the assassination have remarked about the lonely look about the boy, and *Time* magazine has a picture of Lee when he was arrested, and it catches this lonely look; but he was not a loner.

PIERRE: But was he able to make close friends moving around as he was—as you were?

MRS. OSWALD: Well, actually, we didn't move around that much. The only places we were, were from New Orleans to Fort Worth and from Fort Worth to Tovington for a short time, and Tovington back to Fort Worth and to New York.

PIERRE: Well then, did he have any close buddies?

MRS. OSWALD: Yes, when we lived in Fort Worth, Texas. He went to school there up until the eighth grade, which is junior high; all the children came to my house because this was a brand-new neighbourhood. I was not financially able to have the lawn sodded, and everyone else was having their grass growing, and the children were not allowed to play on the grass, so they all played in my yard and my grass and in my home.

PIERRE: In this period, when your son really didn't have very much money, did this have any effect on him?

MRS. OSWALD: You mean as he grew older? No, because Lee and I are very much alike, and we don't require money and don't think of money as a necessity. Now this might sound ridiculous, because we don't. I do know that money is a necessity, but I can live very, very cheaply. I do now. I live in a modest little home. I just pay thirty-five dollars a month rent. Yet every newsman and everybody who has been in the home has remarked what a lovely little place it is. Maybe three or four days before payday, if I was short of funds, which I was all the time, I knew how to manage: I would probably cook a big pot of soup, and we'd have substantial food, where maybe someone else would go out and spend that dollar and a half for a few hamburgers.

PIERRE: It didn't bother him, then, that he had a bicycle at school when the other kids had cars?

MRS. OSWALD: Well, no, no. He asked me to buy him a bicycle; he was sixteen and a half years old when we had come back to New Orleans, and he was still at school and all the children had cars, as you said.

PIERRE: He was the only one with a bicycle?

MRS. OSWALD: That is correct.

PIERRE: I'm told that he was interested in many hobbies, such as astronomy and things like that.

MRS. OSWALD: Yes. From a little, bitty boy, he'd often climb the pillar of the porch and go up on the roof with his brother's binoculars and look at the stars, and I'd have to get his brothers to get him down off the roof. He loved animals; he knew everything there was about animals.

PIERRE: What did the other kids think about his stargazing?

MRS. OSWALD: Oh well, this was the point that I tried to bring out before about his grades. Lee was quite advanced than his older schoolmates, even though he *did* have friends. He played chess and Monopoly, and these are things that require thinking. This is the type child I'm trying to picture.

PIERRE: Did the others tend to kid him because of the astronomy and the chess and things like that at school?

MRS. OSWALD: Yes. Because, see, their interest was different. The other children might want to run and play. Lee wanted to run and play and he did, and he liked comic books and he liked the radio programs. But most of all he was interested in news and history, from a small child. I mean, he did the other things. But what he liked was animals and news. In other words, if he was watching on television a Western story, and on another program news came on, he would turn that Western off and listen to the news. This was more interesting to him than ordinary, everyday things.

PIERRE: Was it a problem for him at the graduation ceremonies at the end of public school, because of his lack of clothes to wear?

MRS. OSWALD: No, but this was a problem for me as a mother because I felt very badly about it. Lee graduated from junior high in June, and in New Orleans, Louisiana, it is very humid and hot. All he had to wear at the graduation was a winter suit, which was very, very heavy, and he was the only boy in all of the class that had on a winter suit. The other children had on summer suits. But I want you to know he didn't complain, and he went to his graduation exercises and the pictures were taken. Now I know many, many children would have balked at that and would have refused to have gone through with the exercises, but this didn't bother Lee.

PIERRE: I wonder how he felt *inside* at this time, Mrs. Oswald? Inside of himself.

MRS. OSWALD: Well, I think Lee was noticing things, and he wasn't saying anything. Because in Moscow he said, "I have always seen my mother as a worker, with always less than what we needed." So he was probably noticing these things, but he never complained.

PIERRE: He never let on outwardly, at least.

MRS. OSWALD: No, no.

PIERRE: Now you moved to New York and he entered high school there. Correct?

MRS. OSWALD: Yes.

PIERRE: And he had trouble in high school?

MRS. OSWALD: Yes.

PIERRE: What happened?

MRS. OSWALD: Well, New York is New York, and that's a big city to everybody. So here is a thirteen-year-old boy going to New York with his mother, and the reason why we went? His second brother, Robert, joined the Marines, leaving Lee and me alone, and his older brother, whose career is service, was living in New York, married. I thought it would be better for Lee to be near family, so I moved to New York with him. After we were there a few days he played hooky from school, and I call that quite normal. I don't say it's the right thing to do, but he's in a big city and he was in the Bronx Zoo, and they picked him up in the Bronx Zoo watching the animals. He was cautioned, and I was cautioned about him playing hooky, and of course I thought Lee was going to school and he wasn't. He was riding the subway all day long and going to the Zoo and the Planetarium. This was something new. He had never played hooky before.

PIERRE: Well, they must have taken that fairly seriously at the high school, because he was remanded for psychiatric treatment, wasn't he?

MRS. OSWALD: Yes, they did. In New York they don't tolerate attendance away from school. In Texas the children can stay home months at a time, and they don't take this action. But in New York they immediately took action, and because he was a child of one parent, they thought that he might be better off in a home than with the one parent who had to work.

PIERRE: But surely just playing hooky wouldn't lead them to give him psychiatric treatment, would it?

MRS. OSWALD: Yes, because it's this type of a home, surely. This would be a normal procedure, and this home was a home for criminals also. They took this boy, who was a truant, and he was placed in this home where they had children who had knifed people and killed people and dope addicts. When I went to visit my son at the home I was searched. I had brought candy bars and chewing gum and the usual things for a child, and the wrappers were taken off all the candy bars, and my pocketbook was searched. I asked why, and they said because many, many parents smuggle dope and cigarettes in to their children. This was the type of home that a truant boy was put into, which I wished I had the money or the education or whatever you want to say to correct these things that exist.

PIERRE: And then he was released on probation?

MRS. OSWALD: He was released to me by the judge, and the judge asked him if he would go to school, and he said yes, and he promised he would go to school. Then we were brought into a probation office, and the probation officer talked to him, and he said, "Yes, sir, I'll go back to school." He'd learned his lesson, and the probation officer said, "Well now, Lee, you're to report to me once a week." I said, "No, he will *not* report to you once a week. He has promised you that he will go back to school; let's give him that chance. If he doesn't go back to school, then I will allow my child to report to you once a week. He is not a criminal." So I made bitter friends with the probation officer, naturally.

PIERRE: Don't you think the probation officer may have been trying to help him?

MRS. OSWALD: Well, this isn't the point, though, the way I took it. Because if a child is going to report—we're talking about a thirteen-year-old child—if he's going to report weekly to a probation officer, that certainly is the rest of his life is against him. He was a psychiatrist—I mean this was a probation officer. I believe to this day that I did right because I said, "The boy has promised to go back to school to you and to the judge and to me, and let's give him this chance. If he doesn't go back to school, I will be the first to see that he reports to you." And Lee went back to school. He never had any truancy before or after this incident.

PIERRE: How long did he stay in high school?

MRS. OSWALD: He stayed in high school until his seventeenth birthday, and then he joined the Marines. That's the tenth grade in our home town.

PIERRE: He had a little less than two years of high school, then?

MRS. OSWALD: Yes.

PIERRE: How were his grades in high school?

MRS. OSWALD: Satisfactory, which means a passing mark.

PIERRE: He didn't distinguish himself as a scholar or student there, then?

MRS. OSWALD: No, no.

PIERRE: Again, this would be what you were talking about before?

MRS. OSWALD: Well, there are very few that get straight As. I mean, satisfactory is the normal passing grade in the United States.

PIERRE: There's been a lot of discussion, as you know, in the public prints about the fact that he didn't date girls at that time. Did he have a girlfriend or not?

MRS. OSWALD: Yes. He had girlfriends in school, and he used to be on the phone talking to girlfriends; but there again, you see, you must understand things. We were poor people; we're living from hand to mouth, payday to payday. This is a young boy, and I don't have the money to give him to date.

PIERRE: Did he go to dances at all—high school dances?

MRS. OSWALD: Yes, if there was any school dances, he went to the dances, but I mean to date, well, none of my children did for the same reason. The other two boys didn't date until quite later in years. It's because of your environment, let's say. Suppose I was a wealthy woman, had a lovely home where I could have the children for parties, and my child would have the proper clothes and the money to spend on a date, he would have dated. But I was not in a position to give them money to date, and of course they depended upon me for that money. I had no money but what I earned. I had no Social Security or anything, and this is the part that the people must understand. You see, you have a difference in environment here. We have millions and millions of people in my circumstances.

PIERRE: Was he able to have a room of his own when he was a boy?

MRS. OSWALD: Yes, he had a room of his own. And now his older brother—and I haven't been able to contact him, and I felt very bad about this—in the Warren Commission Report states that Lee had always slept with his mother, because when he joined the service, which was age seventeen, Lee was ten and sleeping with me.

PIERRE: At the age of ten?

MRS. OSWALD: You see, I told you I was married, and Lee had his own bed, of course, all the while. After I divorced this man, all I got from that divorce was fifteen hundred dollars, and I paid a thousand dollars down on a home. Well, I had to buy furniture. I bought used furniture, and one of the boys slept on an army cot, and the other in a twin bed and, because of circumstances, Lee slept with me—which was a short time because Lee took his bed. But it just implies that all through his life he slept with his mother, which isn't the case, you see. It's quite a difference.

PIERRE: Now, when he joined the Marines, he also had some trouble with them. I believe there were two courts-martial there. Would you like to talk about that?

MRS. OSWALD: Oh, that's perfectly all right. I have talked to many, many men about this, and thank goodness the Warren Commission even gives him credit for this. He was supposed to have sassed a commissioned officer, which we know thousands of men do all the time. We don't say it's the thing to do, but this wouldn't make him an assassin.

PIERRE: He was supposed to have had illegal possession of a pistol, too.

MRS. OSWALD: Of a pistol. These two things. Otherwise he had an honourable discharge and a good-conduct medal.

PIERRE: Mrs. Oswald, the Warren Commission has portrayed your son as a lonely boy who did not have a normal home environment for his formative years. Would you like to comment on that?

MRS. OSWALD: Yes. It's a very sad thing. I have released sixteen letters that Lee wrote to me from Russia: "Dear Mother" and "Love and kisses" and a normal boy asking about his mother and writing about his family [she shows a card]. This is a Mother's Day card sent to me in May of 1959, when Lee Harvey joined the service, rather went to Russia in October of 1959, a Mother's Day card; and this was sent to the Warren Commission and has Exhibit Number 266 on it, "To my mother on Mother's Day," and it's a beautiful card. So this refutes the Warren Commission's theory about the boy not loving his mother.

When Drink Was Cheap and Sinful

From *Pierre and Janet Berton's Canadian Food Guide*, 1966

"HOW WELCOME IT IS," wrote Annie Macpherson, an English charity worker, in 1870, "to see at every Canadian's table the wholesome cup of tea at dinner as well as supper and not the ever-ensnaring glass of wine as at home!"

Perhaps. Yet, if our ancestors had drunk more good wine with their meals and less raw whisky before and after, our culinary heritage would certainly have been richer. To this day wine is an exception on Canadian tables, and we have our pioneer background to blame for it.

At the time of Confederation, beer and wine were all but unknown, though, ironically, one Canadian vintage from Cooksville, Ontario, won a gold medal at the Paris Exposition of 1867. This must have been a fluke. The Baroness Brassey, dining at Montreal's St. Lawrence Hall, reported that "the wine was infamous, which is always the case here: most of the inhabitants seem to drink iced water with their meals and then go into the bar 'to have a drink.'" They do so to this very day.

Bad, cheap whisky was the curse of our pioneer days. It caused so much misery, so much poverty, so much rowdyism and drunkenness that it swiftly gave rise to the fierce backlash of the temperance movement, which was eventually to render Canadian cuisine spiritless. Even as late as the 1950s a Toronto immigrant restaurateur, who knew no better, was fined two hundred dollars for slipping a drop or two of kirsch into his fruit salad.

Today we tend to sneer at the temperance societies with their naïve carols about "the strength cold water brings," but we forget the conditions that brought them into being. Heavy drinking was an accepted pioneer custom, and every bee, wedding, election, funeral and political rally was washed down with gallons of whisky. A few years before Confederation you could buy a glass of raw rye for a penny. When Canada was formed it cost about a nickel—for as much as you could gulp without taking breath. Often enough it was free: many a store had an open barrel at the back with a dipper hanging beside it. Canadians were perhaps the hardest drinkers in the world. In 1840 a visiting temperance lecturer declared that Toronto was worse than any other town of its size on the continent. It did not improve. By 1876, one visitor remarked on "the startling frequency of drinking shops. . . . Every other little store is licensed to sell Ale, Wine and Spirituous Liquors. Very often there are two together; sometimes there are actually four." On the road from Toronto to Barrie, Edwin Guillet tells us, there was a tavern every mile of the way. A farmer bringing pigs to market could treat the entire crowd for a quarter, and since treating was encouraged by the saloon keepers, a man might be obliged to down a dozen drinks before he staggered out to the wagon where his shivering wife awaited him.

Saloon keepers had a habit of standing on the sidewalks urging passersby to enter and "almost forcibly propelling them," in the memory of J.V. McAree, the Toronto columnist. Since drink was cheap it was in the saloon keepers' interests to urge the customers to consume more than was good for them. The spectacle of drunkenness on the streets was a common one, accounting for the majority of arrests. "There was hardly an arrest that was not a disgusting and shocking spectacle," McAree remembered. "Today people would consider it horrifying. . . . The prisoner would usually be pretty helpless and would have to be half dragged, half carried by the police. It was the same with women. Perhaps most of the prisoners would do their best to stagger along beside the policeman, followed by a crowd of youngsters. With others it was a point of honour to put up the strongest resistance."

Tales of rowdyism on holidays and at fair time are numberless. The *Brant Review* of October 10, 1885, describing the scenes following the fall fair at Paris, Ontario, reported the main street "was almost blocked by a drunken, cursing, howling mob." This was typical, for whisky was the universal panacea, stimulant, painkiller, boredom reliever and psychological reinforcement of those days. It was everything, in short, save an appetizer.

Many a farmer and workman drank himself into bankruptcy, and it is not surprising that by Confederation, the strong and enthusiastic temperance movement was already well established. The "old pledge" societies, whose members believed in real temperance and allowed for an occasional glass of wine and beer, had been replaced by the inflexible "new pledge" groups, which believed in total abstinence. By the 1860s women were being admitted, and their presence helped turn "the damned cold water drinking societies" into social organizations. Temperance hotels sprang up for those travellers who could not stomach the presence of a bar. Suddenly it became more respectable to be a temperance man than a tippler.

"The reader will notice that I make no mention of anything like strong drink," wrote Edward Roper, describing a camping trip up the north arm of Burrard Inlet, near Vancouver, in 1887. "It is the very last thing anyone thinks about on such an expedition—anyone who considers himself respectable, I mean. I don't suppose any of us were teetotalers, but temperance is clearly the rule in that country; and I believe none of us thought of anything stronger than tea, which we drank in large quantities, hot and cold but always potent."

Two other travellers, J.A. Lees and W.J. Clutterbuck, a year later described an experience in the Queen's Hotel, a small log building in New Westminster: "We found on the table in the sitting room a sedately bound volume of considerable bulk, entitled *Reveries of a Bachelor*, new edition. This implied a neatly veiled compliment to married men, for the book was nothing but an ingenuous dodge for evading the N.W. drink regulations. A secret spring was revealed to us by the landlord disclosing the neck of a whisky bottle most artfully concealed within the leaves."

Such subterfuge became increasingly necessary as the temperance movement gained power and the laws were changed to accommodate it. As Douglas Sladen reported in 1895, even the *idea* of serving so much as a glass of wine with food was considered *de trop*. At every social gathering, he wrote, "the blight of the Prohibition Act hung over all the festivities which generally consisted of tea and fruit and confectionery and ice cream and introductions." No host "was unregenerate enough to offer us a 'square drink' even though weather made it as easy to raise a thirst as if one had been east of Suez." And so, for the next generation, most of the country was as dry as the Sahara and much of the food as pallid as straw.

Van Horne Moves the Troops West

From *Historic Headlines*, 1967

I N THE DARKLING MIDNIGHT of Easter Monday, 1885, a scene of unparalleled misery and fortitude unrolled like a Japanese scroll in the most desolate and forlorn corner of the new Canada.

A column of soldiers—a long, wriggling snake of a column it was—inched its way across the knee-deep slush of Lake Superior's frozen surface. It cannot be said that they were marching. "Plunging" is a better participle. Drenched to the skin by a pelting and pitiless rain, their toes, ankles and calves numbed by the encasing rubble of snow, water and ice, their bodies racked by uncontrollable coughing and wheezing, the men of the 10th Regiment, Royal Grenadiers, Toronto, stumbled forward through the shrieking storm.

The trail—two sleigh ruts in the slushy ice, filled with water—was a labyrinth of hidden pitfalls. Every few minutes a luckless grenadier would sink to his thighs in a slush hole caused by a passing mule train. Others would simply break through the supporting crust and plunge to their knees in a freezing gruel of melt. As the storm grew worse and the snow softened, each step meant a new immersion. Men began to drop out of the ranks, flinging their exhausted forms onto the snow until they were picked up by the baggage sleighs that followed.

This terrible trail across the frozen lake, which led from the end of completed track at Nipigon to the head of track at Red Rock, was only seven miles long. But it took the Toronto troops five and a half dreadful hours to breach the gap.

All across the gnarled armour of Lake Superior's north shore in those brave April days, with the temperature hovering between 10° and 30° below zero, raw volunteers by the thousands were being shuttled, trundled, sledded and marched along the uncompleted route of the virtually bankrupt Canadian Pacific Railway. They came from Halifax, Quebec, Montreal, Toronto and half a dozen smaller communities, and they were off to fight the Indians and the half-breeds whom Louis Riel had rallied on the northwest prairie. They left with the music of brass bands and the cheers of massed multitudes ringing in their ears, with adventure in their hearts and patriotic phrases on their tongues; but by the time the grey stick forests of the brooding Precambrian land were reached and the snows fell thick upon them and the comfortable passenger coaches of the new rail line were exchanged for open sleighs or flatcars, the echoes had long since been dimmed, and adventure gave way to misery.

It was an ordeal of epic proportions, unique in military annals. Colonel George T. Denison of the Governor-General's Body Guard summed it up in his memoirs, when he wrote that "a great deal has been said about the passage of the Alps in 1800 . . . but as far as the hardships and difficulties and exposure to the men were concerned I am satisfied that our trip was much the worst." And Riel's American biographer, Joseph Kinsey Howard, declared that "it is inconceivable that troops anywhere, with the exception of Russia or Siberia, have undergone a worse ordeal."

The north shore of Lake Superior put more men out of action than Louis Riel, Gabriel Dumont or the great chiefs, Poundmaker and Big Bear, were to do in the prairie skirmishes that followed. Some men went insane and some, like the Midland private who leaped from a train window, tried suicide. Many more suffered the tortures of snow-blindness, and this unhappy company included the Toronto brigade commander himself, Lieutenant-Colonel W.D. Otter, who had to be led, sightless, by his staff across the frozen lake. Scores suffered attacks of pneumonia, rheumatism, bronchitis, pleurisy and tonsillitis. On one day twenty-two men of the Halifax Battalion reported sick with sore throats—and the Halifax Battalion had the easiest time of all. By the time it reached Winnipeg a third of the strength of the Governor-General's Body Guard, a crack cavalry regiment, was reported "broken down" with rheumatism and diarrhea.

Most of the men recovered in an astonishingly short time. And when the job was done the nation and its leaders awoke to the real significance of the railway. Fifteen years before, when Riel had first set the West aflame, it had taken General Garnet Wolseley ninety-six days to move a volunteer army from Toronto to Fort Garry. Wolseley's successor managed the feat in as little as seven; and *he* wasn't even a general—he was a railway man.

William Cornelius Van Horne, general manager of the CPR, born a Yankee, buried an Imperial knight, is perhaps the most engaging figure to bestride the nation's first century. The list of his talents, abilities, enthusiasms and idiosyncrasies seems endless: poker player, conjurer, caricaturist, geologist, gourmet, art collector, practical joker, gardener, telegrapher, engineer, executive and financier. His luck, his daring, his fearlessness and his ability to make swift, resolute decisions have inspired a thousand anecdotes. Of him, a CPR engineer once wrote, "He was the kind who would go out to the side of a mountain and say: 'Blow that down!' He wouldn't ask if it could be done; he would just say: 'Do it!'" The Winnipeg *Sun* described him as "calm and harmless looking" but quickly added, "So is a she-mule; so is a buzz-saw."

"If you want anything done," said Van Horne, "name the day when it must be finished. If I order a thing done in a specified time and the man to whom I give that order says it is impossible to carry it out—then he must go."

When Van Horne arrived in Winnipeg in the opening days of 1882, to almost universal antagonism, he promised to build five hundred miles of track in a single season. His opponents scoffed, but when he put ten thousand men to work on the Prairies and made good his pledge, the scoffing ceased and the antagonism ended. Under different circumstances Van Horne might have been a great general, for he had the ability to appreciate a situation swiftly and exploit it to the limit. When opportunity knocked for this railway in March of 1885, Van Horne was the first to recognize it.

At this juncture, the financial position of the Canadian Pacific was desperate. Van Horne was driving track at breakneck speed, flinging trestles across the gloomy crevasses of the Selkirks, levelling the prairie roadbed with monstrous scrapers, and blasting his way through the Canadian Shield north of Superior with mountains of dynamite manufactured on the spot. There were fifteen thousand men at work on the Superior section alone, and it took three hundred dogteams just to supply them with food. A single mile of track could cost $300,000, which explains why the company had a floating debt of seven million by the end of 1884 and why, in the first three months of 1885, its expenses exceeded its revenues by $342,000. The treasury was empty; the Lake Superior section was being finished on faith and pledges.

Nor did it seem possible to raise further funds. The company's directors were in pawn for every cent they owned, and CPR stock was dropping at an alarming rate on the London exchange. To the public, goaded by an alert Liberal opposition, the CPR coffers looked like bottomless pits into which government money was endlessly shovelled. Further grants or guarantees were politically impossible, and Sir John A. Macdonald said as much to George Stephen, the CPR's harried president, on March 26.

But even then a strange angel had appeared on the western horizon to save the situation. Louis Riel, the most enigmatic figure of Canada's first century, chose this moment to raise a revolt among the native peoples of the Northwest and handed Van Horne his opportunity.

Van Horne's communications were as good as anybody's (he could read a telegraph message directly off the key), and he certainly heard the first faint cries of trouble as swiftly as the government did. It happened that he was in Ottawa in late March, discussing with his colleagues the ruin that faced them all. It was Collingwood Schreiber, the railway's chief engineer, who remarked that Sir John seemed more concerned about trouble in the Northwest than he did about the CPR.

There are moments in history when light bulbs seemed to appear over the heads of the leading protagonists, as they do in comic strips. This was one of them. At once the thought flashed through Van Horne's mind: *How could the government refuse to aid a railway that sped troops out to the West, took the Métis by surprise, and crushed a rebellion?*

He acted immediately, promising an astonished and unbelieving defence ministry that on forty-eight hours' notice he would guarantee to move troops from Ottawa to Qu'Appelle in twelve days. He made only one stipulation: he and not the army was to be in complete control of food and transport. His experience in moving troops during the American Civil War had taught Van Horne to avoid a divided authority and red-tape interference.

The first intimations of the Saskatchewan Rebellion, as it came to be called, appeared in fragmentary reports in Ontario newspapers on March 23, jammed in between the inevitable ads for such patented cure-alls as Dr. Radway's Sarsaparillian Resolvent, which promised cheap and instant remedies for every known disease from cancer to salt-rheum.

It was not, however, until the Duck Lake massacre on March 26—when Riel's brilliant general, Gabriel Dumont, attacked and decimated a Mounted Police detachment—that the seriousness of the situation became clear. The Minister of Defence, A.P. Caron, placed troops throughout Canada on a twenty-four-hour mobilization call and appealed to Van Horne for help.

Van Horne was en route to Toronto in his private railway car when the message came. True to his word, he had cars waiting at the Ottawa station within forty-eight hours. Nine days later—three short of the promised twelve days—the first troops disembarked at Qu'Appelle.

It is all but impossible to recreate fully the mood of enthusiasm, excitement, jubilation, romance, high adventure, dedication and unabashed patriotism that swept through central Canada after the first headlines told of an expeditionary force heading west. To a considerable extent in these cities and towns, life revolved around the militia. Young officers were in demand at the highly social winter sports that marked the era: the snowshoeing and bobsledding parties, the great skating fêtes, the ice-boating excursions and the outings of the toboggan clubs. *The* great social event of the year in every city was the militia ball. One saw uniforms everywhere: at the opera house (and every town had an opera house), at the garrison theatricals and at those strange social rites known as *conversaziones*. Tailors' advertisements featured military fashions over civilian, and the most popular weekend entertainment for the general public was watching the local militia parade through the streets or listening to a military band concert in the park.

Now, suddenly, the militia was parading through the streets in earnest, roused in some cases by Mr. Bell's new telephone (there were only four hundred telephones in Toronto in 1885) but more frequently by the ghostly sounds of a midnight bugle echoing through the streets or the pre-dawn knock of their officers who dashed from house to house in hired hacks routing out the volunteers.

The immense crowds who thronged the main streets of Canada in those April days—jamming Yonge Street in Toronto so tightly that it was impossible to move a foot in any direction . . . pressing so hard against one window in Montreal's Anne Street that it fell three storeys to the street . . . cheering "The Queen," "Imperial Interests" and "This Canada of Ours" (in that order) on the Kingston station platform—these multitudes could not know that the year 1885 was a historic turning point for their country and that the railway was the key to it all.

The signs of fundamental change were there, and Mr. Bell's invention was one of them. The new phonograph, still a plaything for the wealthy, was beginning to compete with the popular Saturday newspaper features: the full-page sermon by a leading ecclesiastic and the romantic serial starring a lovesick heroine wronged by a dastardly villain. The first Eaton's catalogue had just been published and the first electric streetcar had just been tested, though in most of Canada horse-drawn cars continued to clatter over cobbled streets. In 1885 the *Globe* commented, in some awe, that "the thought of a motor run by an invisible force and drawing a car with fifty people aboard seems almost an impossibility. . . ."

The *Globe* also thought that an open Sunday was an impossibility, but some of its rivals seized the opportunity provided by the rebellion to publish special editions on the Lord's Day. Various invisible forces besides electricity were making themselves felt. Discussion of religion might be taboo in the militia messes, but, like politics, it was a prime topic everywhere else. On the one hand, devotees of Mr. Darwin's new evolutionary theories were appearing on the lecture circuit to sow new doubts; on the other, new evangelical organizations, such as the Salvation Army, were rising to prominence. For thirty-five years the various sects, like the various British North American colonies, had been consolidating for practical reasons. The year 1885 saw the end of that as the new frontier beckoned.

In short, the settled and stable community of Canada was giving way to a new period of instability. The "closed frontier" society of 1850–1885 was being replaced by the "open frontier" society of 1885–1914. The Canadian Shield, long a barrier to westward development, had been pierced by Van Horne's dynamite. The railway was to lead directly to new movements of population and a variety of social phenomena, from the Prairie land boom to the Klondike stampede, that would destroy the established social order.

But in April 1885, the West, or the "Northwest" as it was universally called, was almost as remote and as mysterious as the Gobi. Beyond the thousand-mile desert of Precambrian rock lay an ocean of empty grassland peopled by Indians, railroad navvies and plainsmen. Boom towns—Crystal City, Rapid City, Mountain City, Dominion City—sprang up like exotic plants at the end of track and wilted just as swiftly when the railway passed them by. To a large extent they ran on illicit booze. An astonished Toronto reporter, travelling west with the troops, described the free and easy life he found in one such frontier camp and contrasted it with the sedate East:

When one arrives at the 'end of line,' he finds at the Station House a motley assembly. Here is where the man who has a turn that way can study the human face divine and the human dress astonishing. Men well dressed, fully dressed, commonly dressed, awfully dressed, shabbily dressed, partly dressed; men sober, nearly sober, half drunk, nearly drunk, quite drunk, frightfully drunk, howling drunk, dead drunk; men from Canada, the States, the United Kingdom and from almost every state in Europe; men enormously rich and frightfully poor, but all having a free and easy manner which is highly refreshing to the man fresh from the east who is accustomed to the anxious expressions of men on our silent streets at home.

Far to the east, on the Atlantic coast, another separate world existed. In 1885, when the nation talked of separatism it meant the Nova Scotian variety, not the French Canadian (the English had not yet hanged Louis Riel). The previous year a Liberal government had been swept into power in Nova Scotia on a platform that included secession from Confederation. And when the troops began to rally in central Canada, the various Halifax battalions had difficulty in getting up to strength. The Halifax *Chronicle* of April 3 reported an "extra-ordinary refusal of men to go to the front," adding that two-thirds of the troops had declined to parade. Halifax businessmen were threatening to dismiss any man who volunteered and petitioning Ottawa to keep the forces at home. The defence of the land was obviously a novel idea to Nova Scotians, whose eyes were trained seaward and whose outlook had been shaped by the necessity of defending the coast of British North America. The columns of the Halifax newspapers were sprinkled with letters attesting to this: "Why should our volunteers, especially our garrison artillery, be sent out of the province to put down trouble in the Northwest? Nova Scotia has not a thing to do with their affairs; let Canada West look after their own matters. . . . In case of war being declared with Russia we should have no defence. . . ."

Finally the federal government bowed to pressure and allowed the various Halifax battalions to form a composite unit for service against Riel. And when the troops departed, singing "Far Away," and "We're Off on the Morning Train" and, most popular of all,

"The Girl I Left Behind Me," the send-off was as tumultuous as any in Canada. "One of the most remarkable scenes ever witnessed in this city . . . an event without parallel in provincial annals," the *Chronicle* called it; and so, indeed, it was—not only in Halifax but also in every city in the land. The troops were off to defend their homeland (or thought they were), not in some far-off nook of Empire but on Canadian soil. In the first century of Confederation this was the first and only time it was to happen.

They set off, most of them, badly equipped and in considerable disarray. The Seventh Fusiliers of London found they didn't have enough fur hats to go round and had to make do with some very unfamiliar tobogganing outfits. The Riverside Rangers lacked underclothing until a subscription was taken up on the spot by civilian well-wishers at the drill hall. When the York Rangers entrained it was found that much of the issue clothing was old and rotten and that the knapsacks were so badly fitted and packed that "a day's marching with them would be sufficient to break down a Hercules." The Governor-General's Body Guard found that all the waterbottles were leaky and useless and that the government had neglected to supply satchels for the horses, so that the men were forced to wrap their kits in their blankets. Members of the Midland Battalion, lacking knapsacks, wrapped their kits in brown paper. There was scarcely a fully equipped man in Montreal's 65th: some lacked tunics, others trousers, others rifles. Many of the volunteers hadn't fired so much as a blank cartridge, and the regiment was desperately short of ammunition. The Toronto Grenadiers were using equipment that had seen service in the Crimean War, thirty years before. Many of the ancient Slater-Enfields were unworkable or unreliable because of age and wear, and the smart soldiers purchased their own weapons privately. The troops that arrived in the Northwest were armed with a weird conglomeration of weapons—Winchesters, Sniders, Martini-Henrys—with a resultant confusion of ammunition supplies.

Some deficiencies in kit were made up by the enthusiastic civilian populace. A Montreal clothing firm supplied twenty-five pairs of warm mittens to the men of the 65th. The Belleville town council voted a shirt and two pairs of socks to every volunteer it sent to the Midland battalion, and the ladies of Lindsay donated a suit of under-clothing to all *their* volunteers. The London board of aldermen donated socks and underwear to the men of the Seventh Fusiliers and pledged themselves to support the men's families until their return. Subscriptions to support the volunteers' dependants were fairly common. In Montreal the donations list was headed by gifts of $5,000 each from George Stephen and Donald Smith of the CPR.

And so, with bands blaring, flags rippling and the crowds soar-ing, the men boarded the trains, clutching their New Testaments (donated), with the usual admonitions to avoid strong drink ring-ing in their ears. Off they went, from Peterborough and London, from Kingston and Quebec, and from all the other towns, day after day from March 28 to April 13, heading for that Sahara of naked rock that rims Superior's marge.

Van Horne believed in food the way some men believe in the Holy Ghost. He was the kind of man who, when travelling the track, wired ahead for two chicken dinners and, on arrival, ate them both. He kept up the morale of his navvies with Lucullan fare, and he now determined that the troops should eat well, when-ever possible, since he knew what lay in store for them. At Dog Lake, which is near the site of the present White River, reputedly the coldest spot in Canada, the Queen's Own Rifles were treated to a late-night supper that included beef, salmon, lobster, mackerel, potatoes, tomatoes, peas, beans, corn, peaches, currants, raisins, cranberries, prunes, fresh bread, cakes and pies and all the tea and coffee they needed to wash it down. The Dog Lake camp squatted at the end of track. Between this point and Red Rock, some 245 miles to the west, lay four gaps in the line totalling 86 miles. At Dog Lake the ordeal began.

For the first forty-two-mile gap, between Dog and Birch lakes, Van Horne had commandeered three hundred teams and sleighs. The troops on arrival tumbled into these, eight to twelve men per sleigh, sitting on cross seats with their kits tucked beneath them. Out into the black snow-flecked night the teams plunged, with the teamsters—Métis, French, Scots, Swedes, Finns, Irish—cursing in half a dozen tongues as the horses lurched along the graded railway bed. "The roughest bush ride it was ever my misfortune to travel," one Torontonian called it in a letter home.

As long as the sleighs travelled the roadbed the trip was endurable, but when an unbridged ravine was reached, the track followed a tortuous tote road that took the sleighs on a roller-coaster course over boulders, stumps and windfalls, flinging men and equipment into six feet of snow. Some soldiers, slumped in their seats, tried to sleep only to awaken beneath a blanket of snow, emerging like corpses in the 10° degree below zero weather and leaping from the sleighs to run beside the horses to keep from freezing.

There was a brief respite at Magpie, the halfway point, where the horses were changed. Here the men, jostling each other around a fire and beating their mittened hands against their chests, were refuelled with pork, molasses, hardtack and tea. Back in the sleighs again they found that their kits were alternately soaking and freezing and that the road was rougher than before. The sleighs grazed the trees as the horses, forced off the roadbed at the unbridged gaps, stumbled down the narrow forest trails, often locking their harnesses against a stump or tree trunk and dumping their passengers into the snow. Men were rammed against the animals' flanks or flung over the sides of steep banks to be buried completely in the drifts. Caps, mitts, mufflers and sidearms were lost and never recovered. One man was literally buried under a mountain of luggage; another found himself lying in the snow underneath a horse. When sleep became impossible, the irrepressible Canadians began to sing until finally the teams pulled into the construction camp at Birch Lake where, if they were lucky, flatcars were awaiting them.

The troops nicknamed Birch Lake "Desolation Camp" and it deserved its name. A fire had swept through the scrub timber, leaving the trees naked of bark and bleached a spectral white. A chill wind, rattling through the skeletal branches, added to the feeling of despair. The only shelter here was a single tattered tent, not large enough to hold the scores who sought refuge in it. The temperature dropped as low as 35° below, but some battalions had to remain here—their drenched clothing freezing to their skins—for seventeen hours until the flatcars, pulled by a single tender, were shuttled back across the ninety-two miles of track.

When the men of Toronto's 10th Royal Grenadiers, crouched around the campfires, stumbled forward into the snow in a stupor of sleep, the regimental surgeon forced them to their feet again: sleep, under those conditions, could easily mean death. Then, in the morning, when the sun came out and the temperature grew more tolerable, an unexpected problem arose: the glare from the snow burned the men's faces until the skin peeled away. There was no respite. When the shadows fell and the cold came down, some of the troops became hysterical in their suffering.

The flatcars were not much better, but the men were grateful to be on the move. These were fitted with upright stakes placed in sockets along the sides. Rough boards had been nailed onto the stakes to prevent men and baggage from tumbling off. The men were packed onto benches arranged lengthwise along the cars, squeezed together like sheep as much for warmth as for efficiency. Even at that, eight members of the Queen's Own became delirious with the cold on what one member of the regiment described as "the longest night any of us ever put in."

The track along this ninety-two-mile stretch was washboard rough. The ties had been hastily laid on top of the snow, much of which melted beneath them in the heat of the noon sun. Derailment was commonplace, and the train crept along in the biting wind at about six miles an hour. The flatcars presented a particular problem to the cavalry, for there were no ramps down which to lead the horses. The troopers were obliged to build makeshift ramps from old ties, overlaid for safety with their personal blankets. All the horses' hind shoes were removed for safety's sake.

The track ended again at Port Munro, a construction station and supply depot on the shore of Lake Superior—a deep, natural harbour dominated by a sheer thousand-foot crag. The troops, on arrival, were quartered in the hold of the Toronto motor launch *Breck* (whose owner later sued the government for $848.93 damages but received only $245.50). Here many of them enjoyed the first real sleep they had had since departing civilization.

There were only enough teams and sleighs at Port Munro to carry the baggage and so the volunteers were forced to march for twenty miles across the treacherous glare ice of the lake. Most battalions had come equipped with goggles to prevent snow-blindness, but not all had been as farsighted. In some cases, the troops were forced to construct their own eye-shields out of birch bark, Indian fashion. Groping their way along a narrow nine-inch track gouged in the ice, their eyes swollen, their feet often cut and their knees and shins bruised from continued falls, some men did indeed go blind. Others went temporarily mad. And those who missed the glare of the sun suffered through a night of driving rain. Yet still the men could sing as they stumbled along, strung out for seven miles across the ice, and the sounds of "Hold the Fort" echoed against the dark Precambrian scarps that brood over this section of the lake.

Next stop: McKellar's Harbour; sandwiches, salt pork and more of Van Horne's strong coffee. . . Another twenty miles in open flatcars crawling at a snail's pace over tracks hastily laid on the snow. . . At Jackfish Bay, potatoes, fat pork, tea, hardtack and blackstrap, and then, for the lucky ones, sleighs through the wet sleet for seven miles to Winston's Dock; for the rest, another forced march in the heaped snow.

At Winston's Dock the bone weary troops were again piled into flatcars for a fifty-six-mile run; and here, gazing between the slats, they began to gain some understanding of Van Horne's tremendous feat. For miles on end the roadbed had been blasted from the billion-year-old schists and granites. Van Horne had constructed three dynamite factories along this section, and he needed them; he had chipped the roadbed into the sheer surface of the cliffs themselves; he had cut giant Vs directly through the barrier; and when cuttings didn't suffice he had punched long tunnels through the Precambrian precipices. As the trains rattled along between the black escarpments, the men produced Moody and YMCA songbooks from their kitbags and began to sing again.

The final trial—and the worst—lay ahead at the end of track: the brief but terrible seven-mile trail through the slush from Nipigon to Red Rock, which took as long as five and a half hours to negotiate. All contemporary reports agree that this was the worst of all. A member of the Halifax Battalion, which arrived some ten days behind most of the troops when the weather was milder, still called it "the worst ice that ever mortal man was tempted to travel on." A private in the York Rangers, writing home, told of one incident that occurred around 10 p.m. when no man could see more than three feet ahead of him so that it was almost impossible to find the water-filled gutter, made by the runners of transport sleighs, that the troops used as a guide. "On the way across, one of the boys of the 35th was so fagged out that he laid down on the sleigh and would not move an inch. Captain Thompson asked him to move to one side but not an inch would he stir, so he caught hold of him like bag and baggage and tossed him to one side to let us pass."

At Red Rock a welcome sight awaited the exhausted marchers: comfortable, well-heated railway coaches and, for those who could stay awake, bully beef and hot tea. Scores preferred sleep. The men of Toronto's 10th Royal Grenadiers dropped into the seats, contorted into every conceivable position, and, refusing food or drink, slept like dead men while the train rattled west toward Port Arthur, Winnipeg, Qu'Appelle, Swift Current and Calgary. This, in effect, was the end of the epic trek. Everything that followed, even the rattle of gunfire in the prairie coulees, was anticlimax.

Van Horne, true to his promise, had steam up in Ottawa on March 28 when the first troops from Quebec City arrived. (The Defence Minister, alive to the political ramifications of a Métis uprising, had wanted French-speaking troops on their way first.) These men arrived in Winnipeg, where Mr. George Tuckett himself presented them all with gifts of Tuckett's tobacco, on April 4, just seven days later. They were in Qu'Appelle on April 6. By mid-April, the entire Field Force, save for the Halifax Battalion, was in the Northwest. The swiftest time for a unit to travel from Ottawa to Winnipeg was seven days. It never took more than nine.

It is clear from the rapid fire of telegrams between Van Horne in his private car and the Defence Ministry in Ottawa, that the CPR was running the show. March 28: *Can Van Horne move horses? Yes, he can move fifty.* March 29: *Van Horne has had steam up in Toronto for a day. Get the troops moving or soft weather will add to the delay.* April 2: *Van Horne is holding back the Midlands; too many troops moving out.* And so on.

Yet, at the very same time telegrams of a different kind were being exchanged between CPR executives and government leaders. The railway was bankrupt. George Stephen, the grave, spade-bearded Scot who had risen from draper's clerk to bank and railway president, had been hinting for more funds since the previous July. On December 10, in a private letter to the Prime Minister he had declared "the credit of the company both at home and abroad is at the moment gone and the ability of Smith and myself to sustain it is about exhausted. . . ."

The requests grew more desperate, the trips to Ottawa's gilded Russell House from the Montreal head office more frantic; Stephen himself, facing personal and professional ruin, was close to break-down. In those early April days, while the troops of the Northwest Field Force stumbled through the sleet-etched night, Stephen in Ottawa was enduring his own private hell. "It is as clear as noonday, Sir John," he wrote on April 11, "that unless you yourself will say what is to be done, nothing but disaster will result. . . ." But "Old Tomorrow" would not say.

Then on April 16, when every battalion but one had reached the West (the Nova Scotians, at that moment, were being sledded from Magpie to Birch Lake), Stephen learned from Van Horne that since he could no longer pay wages the work must stop. "Please inform the premier and the finance minister," Stephen wired Sir John's secretary. "Do not be surprised or blame me if an immediate and most serious catastrophe happens."

It took another two weeks for Sir John to sway the caucus, but sway it he did. On April 30, with the Field Force now in action against Riel's Indians and Métis (the battle of Fish Creek had taken place April 24, and Colonel Otter, no longer snow-blind, had lifted the siege of Battleford the following day), Parliament finished first reading of a bill authorizing a temporary loan of $5 million to the Canadian Pacific. The newspapers had been crammed with reports of the great trek and so the opposition was weak. As Van Horne wrote to a friend in Scotland: "There is no more talk about the construction of the Lake Superior line having been a useless expenditure of money, nor about the road having been built too quickly. Most people are inclined just now to think that it would have been better had it been built three or four weeks quicker." The actual money would not be in the company's hands until a third reading of the bill, but it served to secure enough credit from the Bank of Montreal to enable Van Horne to carry on.

Events now began to move swiftly on parallel lines: the revolution grinding to a halt, the railway speeding to completion. On May 15, Louis Riel surrendered at Batoche. On May 26, Chief Poundmaker surrendered at Battleford. On May 28, Van Horne reported the last rail laid on the Lake Superior section of the line. On July 2, the last of the Indian rebel leaders, Big Bear, gave himself up. By this time most of the volunteers were travelling home in relative comfort, to the grateful plaudits of a waiting populace.

Van Horne made sure the officers got sleepers, even though these weren't in the contract, "as it is most important that the report of officers as to the treatment of troops on our line should be most favourable." In addition, he made sure that all gifts to the troops from friends and relatives were carried free. Already the new railway was well on its way to becoming a Canadian institution.

The country itself would never be the same again. Three thousand men from the cloistered East had seen the unsettled West, and the static Canadian society became a mobile one. Since 1885, Canadians, by and large, have been a semi-nomadic people. Children born in the East have, often enough, moved west to raise their children. Young men raised in the West have, often enough, travelled east again to seek their fortunes. Just ten years after the railway was completed a son was born to a Dutch schoolmaster in Grey County, Ontario, but when this boy grew up and became famous nobody thought of him as an easterner. His family moved out to the country of the Saskatchewan Rebellion, and John Diefenbaker became a westerner to the core.

There is a coda to Van Horne's great trek that makes the financial epic of the Canadian Pacific as breathless as *The Perils of Pauline*. The government did not get around to a third reading of the new bill until July, about the time Big Bear surrendered to an astonished Mountie sergeant at Carleton. At this point the railway's short-term funds were running out like sand in an hourglass. The haggard Stephen and the peppery Smith both faced simple, stark ruin. (They had put their signatures on loans totalling $100 million because, as Stephen said, "when they come for us they mustn't find us with a dollar.")

The loan was finally passed at the last cliff-hanging moment, and the irony was not lost on O.D. Skelton, the Canadian historian, who wrote years later that "in one fateful day in July, when the final passing of the bill was being tensely awaited, the Canadian Pacific, which now borrows fifty million any day before breakfast, was within three hours of bankruptcy for lack of a few hundred thousand dollars."

In addition to the loan, the railway submitted a bill for $852,331.32 for carrying the troops west. In July 1886, after the inevitable war claims commission had duly deliberated, the government paid $759,361.69.

But by then, the Canadian Pacific was well into the black. On November 7, 1885, Van Horne, with hands plunged deep into pockets, had posed laconically for the most famous of all Canadian textbook photographs as the white-bearded Donald Smith hammered in the last spike in the Rockies. Five hundred miles to the east, the man who had unwittingly helped to make it possible sat in a Regina death cell, praying and penning a final testament. Louis Riel had just eight days left to live.

And far away in Berlin, certain members of the German General Staff, who had been both astonished and impressed by Van Horne's feat, continued to study in their methodical way the detailed report on the movement of the troops that the Kaiser's consul in Winnipeg had prepared at their specific request.

The Dirtiest Job in the World

From *The Smug Minority*, 1968

O N MY SEVENTEENTH BIRTHDAY, which fell on July 12, 1937, one of the worst years of the Depression, I went to work for pay, and there was jubilation among my friends and relatives. In an era when jobs were scarce I had a job; and having a job was the goal of everyone in those days. Having a job in the thirties was a bit like having a swimming pool in the sixties; it conferred status. It didn't really matter what the job was. It could be unrewarding, mindless, foolish, unproductive, even degrading. No matter: it set you apart as a paying member of a society whose creed was that everyone must work at something, and the harder the better, too.

My job was in a mining camp in the Yukon, some 1,500 miles from my home in Victoria, B.C. I worked ten hours a day, seven days a week, and I was paid $4.50 a day plus my board. Almost everybody who learned about my job had the same thing to say about it: "It will make a man out of you!" And when the job came to an end at the start of my university term, almost every adult I knew examined my hands to note with satisfaction the heavy calluses. Back-breaking work was considered to be a high form of human endeavour. A man who worked hard couldn't be all bad, whether he was a convict breaking rocks in a prison yard or an executive neglecting his family by toiling weekends at the office.

I worked for three summer seasons at that same job, and it was commonly held that I was "working my way through college," another laudable endeavour in a society that believed, and still believes, that every individual must pay his own way regardless of position, health, mental ability, or physical condition.

The first year I worked on a construction gang; the following years I worked on the thawing crew, engaged in preparing the ground for the actual gold mining that was to follow. Thawing

239

permafrost with cold water is a fascinating process to almost everyone except those actually employed in it. As far as I know, it is the world's muddiest job, involving as it does the pumping of millions of gallons of cold water into the bowels of the earth.

In earlier days steam had been used to thaw the permanently frozen ground so that the dredges could reach the gold; but the lovely, verdant valleys had long since been denuded of their timber, and no fuel was left to operate the old-time boilers. So now a new process had been devised to tear the valley apart and convert it into a heaving sea of mud.

On Dominion Creek in the Klondike watershed, where I toiled those three Depression summers, the gold lay hidden in crevices of bedrock some twenty or thirty feet beneath the surface. The valley was perhaps a mile wide at this point, and it was being ripped to pieces so that man might reach this gold. First, every shred of plant life was sheared off by a bush-cutting crew. Then all the black topsoil, most of it frozen hard as granite, was sluiced away by giant nozzles flinging water against the banks at a pressure so high it could cut a man in half. By the time the thawing crew arrived, the sinuous valley, misty green each spring, flaming orange each fall, had been reduced to a black, glistening scar.

It was our task to dam the creek anew to build up water pressure and then introduce a spider web of pipes across the newly ravaged valley floor. From these pipes at sixteen-foot intervals there protruded an octopus-like tangle of hoses. Onto each hose was fastened a ten-foot length of pipe, known as a "point" because of the chisel-bit at the end. This point was driven into the frozen soil by means of a slide hammer. When it was down the full ten feet, an extension pipe was screwed onto the end and this was driven down, too, inch by painful inch. If necessary, further extensions were added. And all the time, without cessation, ice-cold water was being pumped through every pipe at high pressure. In this way an underground lake was created beneath the valley floor and, though its waters were only a few degrees above freezing, that small change in temperature was enough to thaw the permafrost.

And so we toiled away, up to our ankles, our knees, and sometimes even our hips in a pulsating gruel of mud and ice-water. The men who drove those points into the rock-like soil were soaking wet most of the time, for it was difficult to add extensions or withdraw a point without water spurting in all directions. All day long they laboured, with their fingers curled around the handles of their slide hammers, their torsos rising and falling as they drove each pipe inch by inch into the earth. When a point became plugged it had to be hauled up and unplugged while the ice-water squirted in their faces. Each man was logged on the amount of footage he had driven in a day, and if that footage was seen to be too low he could expect to draw his time slip that evening. There was a story current in my day that the general manager had come out from Dawson on a tour of inspection and seen a man standing immobile in the distance. "Fire that man!" he cried. "I've been watching him and he hasn't moved for half an hour." Later it was discovered that he *couldn't* move; he was up to his hips in mud.

As the water continued to flow into the ground, the floor of the valley began to go to pieces. Immense craters ten or twenty feet deep began to appear. Whole sections fell away, sometimes taking men with them. The mud grew thicker. The pipeline supports toppled as the soil crumbled, and the pipes themselves—mainlines and feeder lines—began to buckle and break and to shoot icy fountains in every direction. When this occurred it was the job of the pipeline crew, of which I was a member, to replace the pilings, drive new pipes and repair leaks. Sometimes the sun was out and we stripped to our shorts; sometimes a bone-chilling wind swept down the valley accompanied by a sleety rain. It did not matter. We worked our ten hours (later it was reduced to a merciful nine) day in and day out, without a holiday of any kind.

When you work for ten hours at hard labour, whether you are seventeen or fifty-seven, there is precious little time or energy left for anything else. We rose at six, performed our swift ablutions, wolfed an enormous breakfast, and headed off for the job, which had to begin at seven. At noon we started back up the valley slopes through the mud to the mess hall, wolfed another vast meal, and finished just in time to head back once more. At six we were finished, in more ways than one. I have seen men so tired they could not eat the final meal of the day, which was always consumed in silence and at top speed. (It was said that any man who stumbled on the mess hall steps on the way in found himself trampled by the rush coming out.) When this was over, large numbers of men of varying ages simply lay down on their bunks, utterly fagged out, and slept. There was nothing else to do, anyway—no library, no recreation hall, no lounge, no radio or films, nothing but a roadhouse five miles distant where you could buy bootleg rum. Civilization was represented by Dawson, forty miles away; we never visited it. We were like men in a prison camp, except that we worked much harder.

Under such conditions any kind of creative act or thought is difficult. I remember one man, a German immigrant, who was trying to learn to draw by correspondence. He had some talent, but in the end he had to give it up. He was too tired to draw. I had brought along a pile of books required in my university course for summer reading, but most of the time I found I was too tired to read. Those who did not immediately go to sleep after supper spent their spare time washing their work clothes or lying in their bunks indulging in verbal sexual fantasies. I often wondered if this was what the adults meant when they said that mining camp life would make a man of me. Certainly I learned a great deal more from these sexual bull sessions than I had at my mother's knee. It was not until many years later that I discovered most of it was wrong.

It is difficult to describe the absolute dreariness and hopelessness of this kind of job. The worst thing about it was that there was no respite, since—in a seven-day-a-week job—there was no break of any kind to look forward to until the coming of winter rendered further toil impossible. There was one wit among us who used to leap from his bunk once a week, when the bull cook banged the triangle at 6 a.m., crying jubilantly, "Thank God, it's Sunday!" This always provoked a bitter laugh. Without any change of pace, time moves sluggishly; without any break in the routine, a kind of lethargy steals over the mind. The blessed winter seemed eons away to all of us.

Yet for me, in my late teens, life in this mining camp was immeasurably easier than it was for the others. There were men here in their sixties who had lived this way all their lives. There were men in their prime with wives and children to support—families they did not see for half of every year. There were all kinds of men here and few who were really stupid. I worked with immigrants from Austria, Germany, Switzerland, Italy, Sweden, Norway and Denmark, as well as with Canadians. Most were intelligent and a great many were extremely sharp and able. All were industrious. Each had displayed enough courage and independence to somehow make his way several thousand miles to the one corner of North America where a job of sorts was comparatively easy to get. But all had one thing in common: according to my observation, none had been educated up to his ability.

There were many men in that mining camp easily capable of obtaining a university degree, and there were many more who might have completed high school and then gone on to technical school. I saw them each evening, lying on their bunks and trying to force their hands open—hands that had been curled into almost permanent positions around cold pipes; I saw them each morning, shambling down to that grotesque mudpie of a valley; during the day I saw them—scores of ant-like figures, bent double over their slide hammers, struggling in the gumbo, striving and groaning; and the thought that came to my mind was ever the same: "What a waste of human resources!"

For this "job," which everybody had congratulated me upon getting, which was supposed to be so ennobling, which was to make a man of me, was actually degrading, destructive, and above all useless. It was degrading because it reduced men to the status of beasts. There was one wag who went around with his zipper purposely undone and his genitals exposed. "If I'm working like a horse, I might as well look like one," he'd say. It was destructive because it reduced a glorious setting to a black obscenity. And it was useless because the gold, which was mined at such expense and human cost, was melted into bars and shipped to Fort Knox in the United States, where it was once again confined below ground. Every man jack of us knew this; it was the subject of much bitter banter and wisecracking; each of us, I think, was disturbed by the fact that we were engaged in an operation that was essentially unproductive. If we'd been growing wheat, we would at least have had the satisfaction of knowing our labours were useful. The whole vast, complicated operation seemed to me to be pointless. Even the stockholders failed to profit by it greatly; for years the company was forced to pass its dividends. Would we or the nation have been worse off if we had stayed drunk all summer?

For myself, as a teenager, there were certain minor advantages that did not apply to those older men who worked out of necessity and desperation. Certainly I was healthy enough. Certainly I got to know a bit more about my fellowmen. It occurs to me now, however, that both these goals could have been achieved in a pleasanter and more productive fashion. As for the financial gain, much of that was illusory. After I paid for my equipment and my return fare home, there was precious little left. The first year I scarcely broke even. In succeeding seasons I was able to pay my university tuition but not much more. Like my fellow students, I could say that I was working my way through college, but like most of them I could not have continued a university career had I not been able to board at home and take money for clothing and extras from my parents. During four years at university, I met only a handful of students who were able to support themselves wholly through summer employment.

The one valuable asset that I recovered from my mining camp experience was status. It allows me to use a line in my official biography that I notice is seized upon joyfully by those who have to introduce me when I make after-dinner speeches: "During the thirties, he worked in Yukon mining camps to help put himself through university." When that line is uttered the audience is prepared to forgive me almost anything: outlandishly radical opinions, dangerous views on matters sexual, alarming attitudes toward religion. I am pronounced worthy because in that one sentence is summed up the great Canadian myth: that work—*any* work—is the most important thing in life, and that anybody who is willing to work hard enough can by his own initiative get as far as he wants.

The Life of Union Station

From *The Open Gate*, an anthology, 1972

RAILWAY STATION, especially a large one, is something like a home: it acquires a certain aura after it has been used. I do not believe in ghosts or haunted mansions, but I am always conscious when I enter any old building of the unseen presence of those who came before. It does not matter if the furniture and bric-à-brac have been stripped away; a sense of presence remains—a feeling, an echo perhaps, that tells you lives were lived here, tragedies enacted, triumphs rewarded, loves consummated and that this building knew the cycle of birth, life and death, of hope and despair, of sadness and joy. You cannot experience any of this when you enter a brand-new structure. Freshly complete edifices lack a soul. It is the older ones, the ones that have served their purpose over the years, that rejoice in this kind of psychic patina. The sense of history, the feeling of nostalgia, the echoes of the past can never be worked into an architect's blueprint.

Union Station is such a building. For forty-five years it has been the soul and heartbeat of Toronto. There was a time when almost everybody who arrived in the city and almost everybody who left it passed between those familiar columns of Bedford limestone. Tears, not so idle, have washed those marble floors, and cries of joy and despair have echoed up to that vaulted ceiling of Italian tile. How many kisses have been exchanged in that vast concourse? Ten million? Twenty million? More than we know, for there was a time when impecunious young Torontonians, lacking a front parlour or a secluded doorstep, mingled with the swirling crowds of well-wishers and, quite unremarked, smooched shamelessly in public, moving from platform to platform to make their spurious goodbyes.

It is no accident that the great station resembles a temple, for there was a time when we worshipped railways as ardently as the ancients worshipped Zeus or Apollo. At the start of World War II,

when men in uniform began to crowd through in almost unbeliev-
able numbers, a Toronto newspaper called Union Station a "cathe-
dral of travel and traffic." The comparison is apt, for the building's
basic plan was conceived twenty years before it opened—in 1907,
when the railway era was at its zenith. Two more transcontinental
lines were being planned, and every new town that was promised a
spur line was enjoying a real-estate boom. No wonder, then, that
the façade was conceived as monumental and that each of the
twenty-two pillars, forty feet in height, should weight seventy-five
tons and be rooted in solid rock. The building was made to last;
some years ago the concealed wiring in one of the offices was laid
bare, and it was discovered that every wire was in a conduit, a clear
example of the thoroughness of the construction policy.

The care that went into the planning of the station is reminiscent
of the love lavished on medieval churches. Examine, for instance,
the hall that was originally referred to as the "ticket lobby." (Ticket
lobby! That pedestrian phrase scarcely does justice to a 260-foot
concourse whose ceiling soars 85 feet above the customers.) The
Missouri Zumbro stone in the walls was selected for its natural fos-
silized structure and for its high reflective qualities, so that the effect
is at once mellow and light. The floors and stairways that lead to the
exits are of Tennessee marble, chosen both for its beauty and for its
hard-wearing qualities. The arched ceiling (again the temple analogy comes to mind) is faced with Vitrified Guastavino Tile, whose
colour harmonizes with that of the walls. Long shafts of light flood
in through the arched windows, each four storeys high, at both ends
of the hall; here, too, the ecclesiastical motif is undeniable. And if
you look up to the cornice above you will see engraved in the
stone, not the names of blessed saints, but those of all the cities and
towns of Canada served by the two railways whose home this
station has been since 1927.

Cathedrals usually took centuries to complete, but Union Station was built over a period of about thirteen years and would have
been finished sooner had the tragedy of the Great War not inter-
vened. The young Prince of Wales, dapper and elegant then (it

would be another decade before that Tyrone Power smile was replaced by the sad-hound look of an exiled duke), presided at the official opening on August 6, 1927. The happenstance of a royal tour had brought him through Toronto at a point when the station was close enough to being completed to allow it to open. The opportunity was too good to pass up. The ceremony took exactly thirteen minutes—as one reporter dryly noted, a minute of pomp for each year of construction. There is no record that His Royal Highness, who had by that time seen almost everything in his endless world tours, was visibly awed by the magnificence of the structure, but a lesser ministerial member of his entourage exclaimed that "you build stations like palaces out here." After the grimy, barn-like atmosphere of Waterloo and Victoria in London, the marble temple on Front Street must have seemed palatial indeed.

The palace, alas, was not quite in working order. "New Union Station hums with life to-day," the *Star's* headline read on August 11 when the building was thrown open to the public. The glow quickly wore off when the passengers and well-wishers discovered that the changeover from the old station to the new was by no means complete. The former, which had served the city since 1873, was some distance away, and that was where most of the tracks seemed to end. Passengers were dropped at the Old but were required to walk to the exits of the New, sometimes dodging between shunting locomotives and stumbling over a labyrinth of rails. An energetic newspaperman actually paced off the distance: 103 paces from Bay and Front to the ticket lobby, another 61 to the ticket booth, 110 from the booth to the gate, 149 from the gate to the platform and another 192 to the train itself, still in the original sheds. The distance, he reported, was about a quarter of a mile. That was an extreme calculation—not everybody had to walk that far—but it was not until the end of January 1930, when the New Year's rush was done, that the completion of the viaduct allowed trains to enter the new station and the inconvenience was ended.

By that time the new station was in the process of spawning a whole series of structures and pulling the business centre of Toronto south toward the lake. The Royal York Hotel, a legitimate child of the station, had been completed and tied to its mother by the umbilical cord of a tunnel below Front Street. The largest central heating plant in Canada had been built to heat not only the station and the hotel but everything on the south side of the street between Yonge and Simcoe. The Post Office occupied the east wing of the station, and the complementary Dominion Public Building completed the graceful curve, reminiscent of Regent Street in London.

But the Depression had already struck, and train travel was sharply reduced in the decade that followed. The Traveller's Aid Society, whose bright beacon had hung over the corner near the passenger exit ever since the station opened, was forced to cut its staff in half. Hungry families boarded trains headed for the West and what they hoped was a new life. One mother with four children, including a baby in arms, left Toronto for Alberta with just three loaves of bread, a few apples, and very little else. Fortunately the Traveller's Aid spotted her, as they spotted thousands, and alerted their branches along the way to help the family at each stop.

The saga of these dedicated women, who met every train that steamed into the depot and who had an uncanny knack for finding passengers in need of succour, parallels the story of Union Station itself. Indeed, the varied work of the Traveller's Aid mirrors the change in Canadian mores from 1927 to the present. One is struck, when reading the old feature stories in the newspaper supplements, by the change of attitudes since the station first opened. In its early days, for instance, the good ladies seemed to spend a great deal of time protecting single women from the attentions of middle-aged mashers.

This concern for moral safety reflects both the make-up of the organization, which sprang out of the YWCA and the Women's Christian Temperance Union, and also conditions in Union Station at the time it opened. Runners from local bordellos haunted those marble halls, hiding in washrooms until the trains arrived and then dancing attendance on runaway farm girls, mental defectives, and bewildered newcomers. Conductors were trained to spot strangers who introduced themselves to unattached women and when these men followed their new-found friends into the station, the Traveller's Aid pounced and so did the police. Those days are indeed gone forever.

When the war struck in 1939, the role of the Traveller's Aid changed and so did that of the station. For six years it was in a very real sense the hub of the city. Some of the small incidents reported in the minutes of the society underline the spirit of those times. There was a woman whose nerves gave way after she bade goodbye to her sailor son. There were the two boys from northern Ontario who arrived destitute in the city where rooms were at a premium and who were put up at the Fred Victor Mission. There was the soldier's wife who turned up en route to Stratford to show her husband the seven-week-old baby he had never seen. And there were the two newlyweds, still covered in confetti, who found the hotels were jammed but who were finally put up on a chesterfield in a house on Huron Street.

In 1941, the women's auxiliary of the Canadian Legion, one thousand strong, dedicated a suite of reception rooms and an information bureau for the use of thousands of soldiers, sailors and airmen who haunted the station between trains. No veteran of that war who passed through Toronto—I was one—will ever forget that bright oasis in the middle of an overcrowded and often callous city.

Nor will the war brides who began to pour in through the station in the mid-forties, awed, baffled, often frightened by the raw land their husbands had tried to tell them about. "Often they're lonely and some of them cry a little when they talk to me," Mrs. L.M. Curtis, a Traveller's Aid worker, remarked at the time, "but they're very sweet . . . although they may dress and speak a little differently."

But the great emotional moments were reserved for the uniformed men who clambered aboard the trains puffing eastward, many of them never to return. It is no accident that the most poignant of the home-front news photographs were invariably made in railway stations. Mingling with the departing troops were stranger transients: child evacuees from London sent across the water to new foster parents; German prisoners of war, well guarded, heading for the camps of northern Ontario; and later, men on crutches, in wheelchairs and on stretchers being helped off the ambulance trains.

Dr. Peter Bryce, a well-known Toronto clergyman, described the scene at Union Station in October of 1943, when Canadian reinforcements were streaming across the Atlantic and the railways' passenger load had increased by more than 250 percent:

Vast crowds assemble there day after day, embarking and disembarking from the trains that pass in and out of Toronto. In the throngs are men and women representing every branch of the armed services, with their mothers and fathers, their wives and sweethearts and sisters and brothers and friends. Babies are there, and children of all ages. When the time comes for the movement of trains on one of the main lines, it seems as if a wave of emotion surges through the rotunda.

I saw a mother bravely kissing her boy goodbye as he left for overseas. Not long ago another of her boys was reported killed in action. I heard a young airman in his boyish way telling his wife "to keep her chin up; the job will soon be done." Their baby will be born before very long. A young mother, not more than twenty-two or twenty-three years of age, pushed through the crowd, carrying a baby, and trying to keep track of two other little children. She looked tired and troubled. A group of Wrens, in their natty uniforms, were receiving final instructions from an officer, and trying to keep their eyes from a tall, fine-looking air officer, with beaming countenance, who carried a lovely baby in a little basket lined with blue. Near him was a proud granddad, holding a sturdy boy of two months, who, with his mother, in a day or two, would be welcomed by a soldier at a railway station near an eastern camp.

By this time all eyes were turned toward the station. Torontonians treated it in the same way that Muscovites treated their subway stations, and for similar reasons. A gallery of mural art—"four nation-inspiring paintings"—was planned on a grand scale. Organ recitals on a giant Hammond were instituted from three to four every afternoon and from seven to ten each evening with the church's Dr. Charles Peaker and the entertainment world's Quentin Maclean alternating at the console. The organ was still playing when the troops began to arrive home and the crowds, gay to the point of hysteria, surged back to the station to weep new tears of joy.

Then, for the best part of a generation, Union Station became the focal point for the greatest immigration boom the country had known since the palmy days before World War 1 when Clifford Sifton's "men in sheepskin coats" helped to fill up the empty plains. The difference was that most of these immigrants were settling in eastern Canada—half of them in Ontario. In the days before the big jets, the greater part swarmed through Union Station—in such numbers that the CNR's lunch-counter menu was rendered in nine languages. How many came through? Nobody really knows, but there must have been at least half a million. By 1960 the CNR's colonization department was finding farm jobs for some of them at the rate of 150 a month.

The Times of London took note of the scene in 1961:

A particularly moving sight in this country is the arrival, generally late at night or early in the morning, of European immigrants at the Toronto railway station after a tiring journey from the ports of Halifax, Quebec City or Montreal.

Laden with bulging suitcases and holding small fretful children, they wait bewildered and apprehensive as a large crowd of friends and relatives on the other side of the barrier in the station concourse scan the faces of the new arrivals for someone they may not have seen for many years.

Of all the cities, it is now to Toronto, rather than to Winnipeg, that the immigrant goes in large numbers, be he German, Italian, Dutch, English, Polish, Ukrainian or Hungarian. It is here that work is to be found. . . . It is here that "streets are paved with gold". . . .

This was, perhaps, the station's greatest hour. Within a few years the traffic declined, and again the Traveller's Aid figures tell the story. In 1945 the society assisted 100,000 travellers. By 1957 that figure had dropped to 10,500. By 1971 it was down to 4,610. Again the station was reflecting the changing lifestyles of the nation: a large proportion of those who tumble off the trains into the echoing vastness of the great hall are transient youths. Much of the work the earnest ladies performed so well has been taken over by new organizations oriented to a different generation—one that scarcely requires its morals policed.

As these words are written, the fate of Union Station remains in doubt. It seems insane that a building constructed so solidly—designed to last for generations—should be demolished after less than half a century. Europe preserved its medieval cathedrals (those that were not destroyed by war), and European cities have profited in a variety of ways from this good fortune. In Canada, alas, we refuse to allow our cities to retain the texture of the past; that may be one reason why they seem so dull to seasoned travellers. It is quite clear that there will never again be a railway station like Toronto's, built on a palatial scale as a kind of monument to a time when the world ran on steel rails. Union Station, after all, is more than a piece of architecture; it is part of our history as a transcontinental nation.

Just as St. Peter's seems to echo with the footsteps of those who went before—peasant, pope, artisan and genius—so the great station has its own echoes. There is the runaway girl of seventeen from the Quebec farm, searching for a friend among the pillars of limestone; there is the lost four-year-old who answers only to the name of "Dearie" and says his parents are named "Dearie" also; there are the mail robbers trundling a bundle of $25,000 in cash across the tracks and losing it all in a wild scramble for escape; and there is a young man snoring away on a stone bench early on a Sunday morning, waiting for a train to come in as so many waited before him, and so many waited after. The young man was wearing a Stetson, for he was not long out of the West and so knew a great

But there was more to it than that. I lived in a house under a wooded hill, and I knew that from my back door, through that hill, all the way north across the Arctic Circle to the cold ocean, there was nothing but trees, rivers and rocks—scarcely a human being and probably no white men at all. I lived with the wilderness; it was all around me, and I have no doubt, looking back at it, that this had a great effect on me.

We lived in a area where the caribou came through by the thousands twice each year; where you could pull fish, big fat greyling, out of the Klondike River; where the salmon moved upstream by the thousands at spawning time; where you could take any island you wanted in the river, if you had a boat, and camp on it all summer long without asking anybody.

I took that kind of background for granted, and it was not really until I began writing about that country that I realized that it has had a great deal of effect on the kind of person I am—for good or for bad. But then I wonder if that is not true of all of us? We are all shaped by our environment, and it is a theory of mine that one of the things that makes us a distinctive people, and I am certain that we are different from any other people in the world, is the presence of this great northern wilderness bearing down on us. Ninety percent of us live within two hundred miles of the American border, but there is not one of us who is not aware of the presence of the North. Every foreign observer who has come here has made that point. André Siegfried, years ago, called it "a window out onto infinity."

This great, sombre backdrop, I think, has affected our personalities and our temperament. It has made us different from the people to the south. I don't think you can live with the flat, metallic lakes, the brooding firs and pines, and the great expanses of grey rock that stretch all the way from Yellowknife to Labrador, with the naked birches and the rattling aspens, with the ghostly call of the loon and the haunting cry of the wolf, without being a very special kind of person. It is no accident that one of our best-known paintings by one of the Group of Seven is called *The Solemn Land*.

I think the North and the presence of the wilderness have helped to make us a more private people than some others. I think it has made us reticent and thoughtful. I think it has made us careful, sometimes too careful. These are qualities that you see in the North, and you see these qualities transmitted right through this country.

Someone wrote, I think it was William Henry Chamberlain, that the presence of the North has bestowed upon us "a sensation of tranquillity." If it has, I am all for it.

We are just beginning, I think, to realize that this is one of the assets that we have in this country, a much greater asset than we thought. We have begun to think of the North in broader terms than we did in the past. I must tell you that this was brought home to me forcibly on the trip my family and I took down the Yukon in 1972. We were like dots on the broad expanse of this great wild river, which rolls on for 2,200 miles. We could go for an entire day without seeing any other form of human life, white or native—only the eagles wheeling in the sky, and the animals: the moose feeding in the swamps, the odd grizzly on the hillside and an occasional lynx. (We saw one sitting on the edge of the water, and he stared at us uncomprehending. We realized that the lynx had never seen a human being before.) And the ghosts of the past in the form of little ghost towns all the way down.

As we were drifting down the Yukon, I remembered some years ago writing a piece about a hydro development that had been planned for the North. They were going to take this part of this beautiful river, dam it up, and make a big lake covering most of the country I have described—trees, little ghost towns and all—and run it backwards through channels bored in the coastal mountains into penstocks on the American side to provide power for electromechanical or metallurgical industries.

I must say that in my naïveté fifteen years ago, I did not particularly question that in any kind of critical fashion. That was before I had seen what was done to Tweedsmuir Park by the Kitimat operation, where they drowned half of a national park, making it impossible to get to the shoreline whether you are a human being or an animal,

257

where the trees form a rotted mass of garbage for hundreds of feet out from the shore because they have raised the water levels there.

As I thought of that hydro development and its twelve million horsepower, I told myself, "It's not worth it! No amount of hydroelectric power is worth the savage destruction of this beautiful country." But then, you see, until very recently—and I am afraid to a large extent it is an official attitude today, and certainly an industry attitude—we have thought of our North in terms of plunder. It has always been a country of boom and bust, and I know this very well because I was raised in a mining town. Once the plunder is gone, once the gold is torn up from the ground, there is nothing left for people except one thing: the call of the land itself.

I think the future of the North lies in something much more permanent than plunder. I think it lies in the presence of the land, largely untouched, and its history.

The Canadian Arctic Resources Committee, a small group in Ottawa that as far as I know is the only independent committee holding a watching brief on behalf of the public as far as the North is concerned, has recently commissioned a study of the North. It has not been published nor made public, but they have given me permission to quote briefly from it. This study makes clear what I think most Northerners have known for some time: that northern Canada, up until this time, has been treated as a colony of southern Canada and is viewed largely as a resource hinterland for the great metropolitan centres of southern Canada (as indeed the prairie country was viewed, at the time of the building of the railway, as a colony of Montreal and Toronto).

To a very large extent this vast country, the territorial parts of it, is run mostly by civil servants under the territorial system of government. Ottawa owns and controls most of the land and its resources because most of the land is Crown land. It cedes some of the surface rights to the territories, but it holds the subsurface rights in the palm of its hand.

The Yukon and the Northwest Territories are governed by regulations that do not have to be examined by Parliament and are not examined by Parliament, and the evidence of the past certainly has been that the regulatory bodies have considered any public discussion or critique of this system both meddlesome and officious.

Last February, the Chairman of the Canadian Arctic Resources Committee, Douglas Pimlott, wrote to the Prime Minister of this country asking that the public, especially the Northerners (and that includes the native population), be involved in the development plans that are going on in northern Canada with special reference to oil exploration and the construction of oil pipelines. I will quote you a paragraph from that letter. He said:

Neither the petroleum industry nor the government has sought the considered views of the public and there is no intimation they intend to do so. We suggest this is a serious misjudgment of the mood of the country.

He asked for a meeting to go into it more deeply. That was eight months ago, and the letter has yet to be acknowledged.

You see, what concerns most of us who care about the North is that the rights of the Northerners and the problem of the environment—twin concerns—have until now been made subservient to the demands and the pressures of industry.

We in this country still tend to operate on an ancient assumption that goes back to the days of Columbus: those who can make the most economic productive use of the land and the resources have a superior right to them. We always move the native people when we think it is economically necessary (not for them but for us). There is so much evidence of this from all the past that I don't think I need to repeat it to you here.

The authors of the report I have just referred to quote a talk by an Assistant Deputy Minister of Indian Affairs and National Development—a speech in which he refers to the rights of peoples, or lack of rights of peoples. He said this: "Here are 200 people who wanted a ranch of 40,000 square miles and under that ranch we felt there might be some valuable resources that could benefit the same people."

259

In this case he felt that tearing up the ground to get at the minerals was more important than leaving these people on the ranch.

The authors pointed out that there are very large cattle ranches in the province of British Columbia, owned by white men, from which the natives were driven years ago. They are cattle ranches today because that is the highest order of use that could be conceived of for them. You see, every time we move in on the natives we say we do so because we believe in the greatest good for the greatest number. We say these resources belong to all the people, but in doing this we come very close to operating with what has been called the tyranny of the majority. There is not much difference between these past examples and what happens in the Soviet Union, where huge hydroelectric developments are taking place in Siberia, or in the State of Brazil, where to the detriment of the native peoples highways are being pushed right through lands that up until now have been, I would say, the moral property of other races.

But it is not just the native rights we have to be concerned about; it is the land itself. I think the next few years are going to be absolutely crucial to the future not only of the North but also of Canada. I think that northern issues have to be given much wider discussion. You see we are very, very lucky because up until now about eight-tenths of our country is relatively unspoiled. I must say I winced when, floating down the Yukon out of Whitehorse, I saw that great mountain of garbage toppling from the high bank into the Yukon River and polluting it for a hundred miles; but rivers can clean themselves up very quickly if we take steps to let them do that.

If you travel the North you will see that we have not yet loused it up. That is nothing but an accident of history—it has been too far away and too expensive to get there. But we haven't yet done to the North what we have done to the South. So there are no costly rollbacks involved in preserving this last great wilderness. Thus we can profit by the mistakes of other people, by the mistakes we ourselves have made and the mistakes that have been made in other countries.

We have to remember that the North in many areas is very fragile. Let me give you a couple of examples of what I mean. Things grow very slowly in the North. Up in the tundra around Coppermine I saw little vines about as thick as my little finger. They were actually birches and willows. If you cut through these vines and put them under a microscope you will see as many as fifty to one hundred rings. That is how old they are, and that is how long it takes them to grow. There is an even more dramatic example from history that I like to quote. When Leopold McClintock in 1853 was searching for the lost Franklin Expedition, travelling across the tundra with its lichens and mosses, he came upon a set of cart tracks so fresh-looking they seemed to have been made the previous day. But he knew that those tracks had been made by Sir Edward Parry, another Arctic explorer, thirty-three years before. Hardly a speck of moss had grown over them.

Refuse, garbage, human excrement take a long time to rot in a cold climate. The problem of pollution in many areas of the North is far more fearful than it is here.

We are now faced with the whole question of the giant pipeline coming down the Mackenzie Valley, and we have in this country a chance with that pipeline to build a model for the development of the rest of Canada. I am not suggesting that we do not build the pipeline, but I am suggesting that we look before we leap and that when we do, or if we do, we learn something from the past and from the present because we have some horrible examples.

One is the James Bay project. It's a mess. It's in dispute in the courts, and it's quite clearly an example not only of poor planning but probably even lack of planning. It is also an example of something else, and this, I think, is my key point today. It is the ability of regulatory bodies and agencies of provincial governments to effectively close all avenues of public participation and to keep all information tightly sealed. The idea that the public should have any rights is a novel one to government. It has always been a novel one to bureaucracies, and I suggest that we have to get out of this secrecy syndrome or we will stumble on from one débâcle to another in the hinterland.

Nobody is suggesting, and I am certainly not, that all resource development be stopped in the north of this country. I am simply suggesting we start looking first and leaping second.

The Canadian Arctic Resources Committee is very strong in the belief that there ought to be a forum for discussion independent of government and independent of industry (there is not one at the moment) that could add its voice to future planning.

I have seen a great deal of this north country myself, not just the Yukon, which is my home country and which I return to from time to time, but the whole of the North.

I have seen one of the most beautiful lakes in the North, Kluane Lake, where there are measurably nine different shades of green and purple from the margin to its centre.

I have seen the St. Elias Mountains, the highest on this continent, and the great Nahanni Valley, with its mile-deep gorges and its waterfall twice as high as Niagara, which is now, thank God, a national park—saved at the last moment from the oil interests.

I have seen the great Mackenzie Valley and the fantastic sight of the Mackenzie Delta, one hundred and fifty miles of wriggling channels and little ponds. I have seen it from the air at sunset. Somebody once described it as a giant mirror splintered into ten thousand pieces shining up at you.

I have seen the Arctic islands with their caribou and reindeer. I have seen those geological and alluvial oddities with the elfin names: pingoes and polygons and eskers and drumlins.

I have seen the herds of musk oxen moving across the Barren Lands.

I have seen the remnants of the Ice Age, which are still to be seen there and nowhere else in this country. We have covered them over or chopped them down.

I have seen the Yukon freeze up in the fall, and I have seen Hudson Bay break up in the spring. I have seen Baffin Island and the Torngat Mountains of Labrador and the reindeer herd on Banks Island.

I don't want to see this beautiful country trampled over or exploited or wrecked haphazardly. As you know, we regret that we made so many mistakes in the South. Well, we now have the chance to profit by those mistakes in the North.

We have the one thing that people all over the world are crying for: we have open space, wilderness space, wild rivers. Gold, base metals, copper, oil are all depleting resources, but a river goes on forever and so does the tundra if we don't stamp all over it. There is so much we need to know about this country before we plunge into it blindly.

We haven't really taken a wildlife inventory; we haven't done the forest regeneration studies that are needed, or the soil studies, or the land use studies. We don't really know what to save, or what to exploit, or where we should do these things. We have a priceless asset, but it is a perishable one. Undoubtedly a good deal of it has to be made available for exploration, for mining, for forest development, for agriculture, for hydro power and for tourists, too (something we sometimes forget), but not all of it. I think a lot of it should be left alone, certainly for the present, or kept for the people who had it first.

It has always seemed to me, and I was raised with them, that the native peoples realized long before we did what the true value of this country is. I always like to tell the story of the Dog Rib Indian and the Oblate Priest. The Dog Rib Indian said to the Priest, "Tell me, Father, what is the white man's Heaven?" And the Priest replied, "It is the most beautiful place in the world." Here is what the Indian said. He said, "Tell me, Father, is it like the land of the little trees when the ice has left the lakes? Are there great musk oxen there? Are the hills covered with flowers? There will I see a caribou everywhere I look? Are the lakes blue with the sky of summer? Is every net filled with great, fat whitefish? Is there room for me in this land, like our land, the Barrens? Can I camp anywhere and not find that someone else has camped? Can I feel the wind and be like the wind? Father, if your Heaven is not like all these, then leave me alone in my land, the land of little sticks."

And if you set that to music it might make a pretty good National Anthem.

The Gospel According to De Mille

From *Hollywood's Canada*, 1975

OMMISSIONER Samuel Taylor Wood, who succeeded General MacBrien as the top Mounted Policeman in Canada, had been born into the Force. His father, Zachary Taylor Wood, one of the great heroes of the Klondike stampede, had risen to assistant commissioner, a post he held until his death. The younger Wood, who was a great-great-grandson of Zachary Taylor, twelfth president of the United States, had a quarter-century of service in the force and was all policeman. When he took over in 1938 he had no intention of buckling under to the kind of Hollywood pressure that had embarrassed the Mounted Police for some two decades.

At that point, however, Wood had not yet encountered Hollywood power in the person of Cecil B. De Mille, who was planning his sixty-sixth motion picture and his first in Technicolour. It was logical that De Mille should choose Canada to provide a background for what was still a relatively novel process. If we believe his press agents, De Mille even *day-dreamed* in colour, seeing in his mind a moving procession of red-coated riders, brilliant against the stark white of the Canadian snows. No doubt he also saw those snows stained with Technicolour blood, but the press releases do not go into gory detail.

De Mille had made one previous movie about Canada, in 1914—the Hudson's Bay Company story titled *The Call of the North*. His publicized specialty then, as later, was absolute historical accuracy. Press kits for De Mille's historical pictures were always loaded with stories about the master's scrupulous fidelity to the smallest detail.

The Mounted Police might have been more suspicious of De Mille's protestations about accuracy at the outset if they had read one of the several trade descriptions of *The Call of the North* or seen

264

the film, a print of which reposes at George Eastman House in Rochester, New York. This was the first of the movies to deal with La Longue Traverse, or Journey of Death. We have already seen that the movie-going public accepted this legend, aided by De Mille's own assurances that "no stone was left unturned to make the picture absolutely true to the life it portrayed." Much was made of the fact that, to add a touch of authenticity, De Mille imported "fifteen big Tiger Indians with authentic canoes from Ahitiba, Canada, far north of Winnipeg." A search of the most detailed gazetteer fails to turn up any community called Ahitiba, while the definitive list of Indian bands in Canada makes no mention of any Indians who called themselves or were called Tiger.

De Mille's knowledge of historical and contemporary Canada can be gauged from a conversation he had with Clifford Wilson of the Hudson's Bay Company. His original plan, he told Wilson, was to make a picture about the great fur company, choosing the period of strife with the rival North West Company before 1821. "He explained to me, however, that he would have to take sides and show the North West Company as the villain of the piece. And certainly he didn't want to offend the North West Company!" At that juncture, the North West Company had been defunct for more than a century.

De Mille wanted something more than mere Mounted Police co-operation in making his picture. He wanted to make it look like an officially sanctioned film, stamped with the Force's seal of approval. His desires were made clear in a wire that Paramount sent to its Toronto office manager, M.A. Milligan, in May of 1939:

WHILE WE WISH TO MAKE NO PRESENT PUBLIC ANNOUNCE-
MENT CECIL DE MILLE PLANS AS HIS NEXT BIG EPIC PICTURE A
STORY OF RCMP FOR WHICH IS NOW STARTING PREPARATIONS
STOP NATURALLY THIS PICTURE WILL BE A TREMENDOUS INTER-
NATIONAL SUBJECT ESPECIALLY FOR CANADA AND BRITISH
EMPIRE IN GENERAL, ALSO MARVELOUS PUBLICITY FOR RCMP
STOP DE MILLE IS ANXIOUS TO SECURE FULL COOPERATION

CANADIAN GOVERNMENT AND RCMP AUTHORITIES STOP HE
SPECIFICALLY NEEDS WHOLEHEARTED ASSISTANCE OF MEN IN
CHARGE OF THIS ORGANIZATION FROM WHOM HE WANTS NOT
ONLY DATA BUT COOPERATION IN PHOTOGRAPHING MOUNTED
POLICE THEIR HEADQUARTERS EQUIPMENT ETC AND SCENERY
ALL THROUGH WESTERN CANADA AND CANADIAN ROCKIES
STOP CAN YOU ARRANGE ABOVE IMMEDIATELY. . . .

The studio's assumption that the Mounted Police were hungry for publicity and would jump at the chance to see themselves on the screen was a widely held notion in Hollywood, where everybody thrived on publicity, good or bad. One director put the attitude succinctly to Bruce Carruthers, a former Mountie corporal who operated as a free-lance technical director in Hollywood. "Bruce, where would the Mounted Police be if it wasn't for motion pictures?" As Carruthers later remarked, "I naturally cleared up this point for him rather quickly." The RCMP's attitude, of course, was the antithesis of Hollywood's. The Force didn't want publicity, and when Milligan passed the Paramount request on to Commissioner Wood in Ottawa, Wood's reply was guarded.

He didn't object to helping in a minor way, but only if the Force had total script control. The studio must also promise that no attempt would be made to suggest that the movie was made with RCMP co-operation. Finally, no Mounted Policeman could turn up at any première to add colour to the proceedings or suggest official recognition.

De Mille now decided to come to Canada himself, to Ottawa, a visit Wood attempted to discourage. Paramount announced that the picture would be called *Royal Canadian Mounted Police* and that it would be filmed on location at Banff. De Mille's associate producer, William Pine, was already in Canada during that July of 1939—the year of the Royal Visit—along with Frank Calvin, Paramount's research chief. Calvin's stay in Regina produced a flutter of exclamatory news features all stressing De Mille's much-publicized passion for accuracy.

"In preparing an historical picture, such as the proposed picture dealing factually with the story of the Mounted Police, everything possible is done to assure accuracy of the material," the Regina *Leader Post* reported in a lengthy interview with Calvin. "The language, the costumes, the customs are the subject of painstaking study."

"As a rule, in a De Mille production, people in the audience are usually wrong if they question something, because he goes so thoroughly into everything," Calvin told the interviewer.

At this point, De Mille had no story and no cast. He had a vague notion in his mind that he might somehow tie the Mounted Police in with the Bengal Lancers. This idea was sketched briefly to Commissioner Wood, whom Pine visited in Ottawa. Wood did not like that idea at all, nor did he like De Mille's proposed title. It would, he wrote to Pine, "be inaccurate and inappropriate as a picture such as you described to me could not possibly portray an outline of the work of the Force, and frankly I cannot see the parallel you draw between the Royal Canadian Mounted Police, which has multifarious duties, and the Bengal Lancers, which is a fighting unit of the British Indian Army." Pine and De Mille had hit the commissioner in his most sensitive spot by voicing the firmly held Hollywood misconception that his men were soldiers rather than policemen. Wood then went on:

I trust you will forgive my frankness if I explain further that the type of picture you have in mind appears to be one more attempt of the melodramatic type, and I cannot refrain from feeling some disappointment as I had imagined you had an opportunity of making a better picture, showing the spirit and history of the Force, than has heretofore been produced, but this does not seem to be what is intended.

Pine responded with hasty assurances that the "few words of description I gave you . . . was no more than a mere thought of possible action."

"I can assure you, however, of one fact," he continued. "Any motion picture Cecil B. De Mille produces will be true in detail and based on fact. *He never garbles facts or distorts history.*" (The italics are mine.) Pine then added that De Mille hoped "to evolve a story out of some historic occurrence that will portray the spirit that has made the Force the outstanding organization of its kind in the world."

In Regina Frank Calvin had been keeping a file on the two Riel rebellions, and by the end of July it began to appear that one of these would form the historical basis for the script. That intelligence dismayed the Mounted Police hierarchy. "The last thing I should like to see is to have your picture placed in the North West Rebellion period," the departmental secretary, G.T. Hann, wrote to Pine. "The old-time stories of the pill-box period have been told so often that I feel certain that I did not advise that. . . ."

Hann suggested something more modern that would show a case of Mounted Police detective work. "To be quite frank with you, I feel your opportunity is not in something of the old days, but in something much more modern."

These suggestions were politely ignored. De Mille himself was already on the site of Duck Lake, Saskatchewan, the scene of the so-called Duck Lake Massacre that touched off the rebellion of 1885. The picture, he told the press, would star Clark Gable.

By September, when the war in Europe broke out, De Mille had four writers working on the script. "As far as his next picture is concerned, Cecil B. De Mille is just going to pretend there isn't any war," a press release announced. The title of the film had by now been changed to *North West Mounted Police*, and the press was reporting that "full co-operation in the making of the picture had been promised De Mille by officials of Canada's famous Mounted Police." De Mille announced that he planned to shoot a good portion of the picture on location in Canada.

The report about full co-operation obviously bothered Wood, who had not even seen a script. Until he did, he wrote Pine, the Force would not consider any kind of co-operation. But the script wasn't in any shape to be seen. Carruthers, whom De Mille refused to use in spite of Wood's recommendation, reported to the commissioner on November 27 that "he now has five writers working, none of whom know what they are doing and they are in constant trouble." Carruthers also reported Hollywood gossip that Wood *himself* would be technical director on the picture— a rumour Wood hastened to deny. "We have lost considerable interest now that we know it is only to be 'another picture' of the Force," he told Carruthers.

De Mille, however, hadn't lost interest in the Mounted Police. He wanted to tie the RCMP as closely as possible to the picture in the public's mind. When the script was finally in shape a few days before Christmas, he did not mail it to Wood; he sent Pine by air to Ottawa to deliver it personally. This gesture produced the expected results. The *Ottawa Citizen*, in a story picked up nationally by the Canadian Press, reported:

> . . . *Wm. H. Pine, Mr. De Mille's associate producer, arrived by plane from Hollywood this morning, script in bag, ready to submit it to Commissioner S.T. Wood of the* RCMP *for his approval. Scriptwriters and workers have been engaged on the story since last June, receiving the collaboration of "the silent force" in their task. . . .*

This was too much for Wood. He flatly refused to have anything further to do with the production unless Paramount agreed to stop publicizing the fact that the script was being vetted by the RCMP or capitalizing on the fact in any way. Paramount agreed, and the commissioner, mollified, made a series of suggestions, most of them dealing with the removal of American military terms. The larger implications went unremarked or unnoticed.

In February Wood went so far as to lend the production a training instructor from Regina, Sergeant-Major G.F. Griffin, to put the actors through their paces. By this time De Mille had been forced by Paramount's budget control to abandon any location shooting in Canada; the movie would be shot on the studio's back lot. Clark Gable wasn't available for the leading role and neither was Joel McCrea, whom De Mille had hoped would play a Texas

Ranger in the movie. Gary Cooper was cast for that part; Preston Foster would play the Mounted Policeman.

The publicity mills began to grind as soon as the cameras did. Carruthers, still ignored by De Mille, was approached on the quiet by two Paramount publicity men to get his reaction to a series of ideas they were working on to sell the picture. What, for example, did he think of their plan to hold the world première in Canada, with the RCMP and possibly the Prime Minister in attendance? Carruthers, who was embittered by De Mille's rebuffs, replied that he couldn't see anybody from the Canadian government enthusing over a picture "which portrayed the police as deserters and nincompoops." Carruthers had managed to sneak a copy of the script out of the Paramount lot—not an easy thing to do because, as he said, "Scripts are guarded in the studios like state secrets." He did not like what he read. He was certain that the script was a more recent one than the copy that had been shown to the commissioner and that it contained sequences that Wood hadn't seen.

The publicity men had some other ideas. They wanted to set up Junior Mounted Police Clubs across the United States with Carruthers's help. (Carruthers said De Mille didn't have enough money to buy his services.) They wanted to set up a monument to the Mounted Police in Canada. (But, said Carruthers, the Force isn't dead.) They suggested that De Mille present a set of colours to the Force, but the idea bogged down because they had no idea exactly *which* colours to proffer. And perhaps, they suggested, the RCMP band might tour the United States to help exploit the picture.

Carruthers reported all of this to Wood in a confidential letter. "As it is customary to figure on 12% of the production costs for exploitation, De Mille will move Heaven and Earth with $240,000.00 to get publicity in any and every way possible," he warned.

Hann, the departmental secretary, in a memorandum to Wood also advised that "it is obvious that the original script has been changed and that Mr. Cecil B. De Mille is likely to make very strenuous efforts to make unusual requests for publicity."

In Hollywood that spring Sergeant-Major Griffin was drilling his Mountie actors. That fact did not escape the notice of the Paramount publicity department who lost no time in sending out a release that again suggested an official tie-up between De Mille and the RCMP:

De Mille, a demon for authenticity, wants his troops to do credit to the real Mounted Police, who are co-operating in the production. . . .

To understand exactly what it was that Cecil B. De Mille was doing to Canadian history, it's necessary to recall briefly the events surrounding the Northwest Rebellion of 1885.

Louis Riel, whose earlier uprising in 1869–1870 had earned him the title of the Father of Manitoba, was teaching school in Montana when a group of Métis rode across the border in the summer of 1884 and asked him to return to Canada to help them present their grievances to the Canadian government. The grievances of these French-speaking mixed bloods, who lived around St. Laurent on the South Saskatchewan River, were real ones, no less impassioned than those of the English-speaking Protestant half-breeds, the Indians and the whites, all of whom were in ferment. Ottawa, however, ignored all petitions and protests, and the Métis' intention (which was also Riel's) to proceed peacefully and legally was eroded.

At last, Riel set up a provisional government of his own at Batoche. Bloodshed was inevitable and it came at Duck Lake, largely as the result of a Mounted Police blunder. Inspector Leif Crozier, blocked from getting supplies and ammunition from the Duck Lake store, impetuously ordered a detachment of Mounted Police and white volunteers to proceed to the scene by sleigh, rather than waiting for a column of reinforcements to arrive. A parley took place near the Duck Lake store between the NWMP and the Métis. It is unclear who fired the first shot—it was, apparently, the result of a misunderstanding—but in the fracas that followed the Métis were better deployed and the police, although they had superior weapons including a cannon, were defeated. Three Mounted Policemen and nine volunteers were killed in addition to eleven wounded. The Métis suffered five casualties.

This incident touched off a widespread prairie revolt. The Canadian government dispatched some 7,000 militiamen on the still-unfinished Canadian Pacific Railway to do battle with Riel's forces, who were joined by Cree Indians under two great chiefs, Poundmaker and Big Bear. Outnumbered and outgunned, the natives fought skilfully, but the issue was never in doubt. The troops had not only modern rifles and cannon on their side but also three Gatling guns—the first successful machine gun ever devised—being tested in battle for the first time by an American cavalryman and Indian-fighter, Lieutenant Arthur Howard. The hostilities lasted from March until July, by which time all the leaders had surrendered including Big Bear, who was the last to give in.

De Mille did more than twist these historical facts to suit his purpose. He turned them inside out. From the very opening of the film, with its introduction voiced by De Mille himself against a background of snow-capped Rockies, everything was wrong:

> *The Canadian Northwest! Here the first traders from the Old World intermarried with the Indians of the plains and the forests and founded a new race, the Métis of Canada. Here for two centuries these half-breed hunters and traders multiplied and prospered, a law unto themselves. Then surveyors and homebuilders pushed westward, bringing laws of land and property, which threatened to end forever the free ways of the wild. . . . Resentful and confused, the half-breeds under the leadership of Louis Riel revolted against the advance of unwelcome law. At that hour a handful of hard-riding men in scarlet coats, the North West Mounted Police, stood between Canada's destiny and the rebellion that was being kindled across the border in a little Montana schoolhouse.*

De Mille's opening suggested that the Métis were opposed to the idea of Canadian law as represented by the police. Nothing could be further from the truth. The mixed-bloods welcomed the extension of Canadian law to the plains and, if anything, wanted more (to prevent undisciplined buffalo hunters from destroying the herds, for example). Their quarrel wasn't with the NWMP but with an unbending and distant government that refused to give them title to lands that they had farmed for years. The impression that a handful of red-coated police managed to contain the rebellion, and not an overpowering military force, was continued throughout the picture. But there was worse to come.

Louis Riel, who was nothing if not dynamic, was presented by De Mille as a weak, indecisive puppet, controlled by the villainous Jacques Corbeau. In the movie it is Corbeau who masterminds the entire rebellion, over Riel's weak protests, in order that he may be free to sell whisky to the Indians. "I'll let you lead my people," he tells Riel, "all I want is the whisky business." Riel goes along with him. But in real life it was Riel who restrained the more impetuous Métis from shedding unnecessary blood.

The Gatling gun was introduced in the picture's opening sequence, but in De Mille's version of Canadian history it was Corbeau and his Métis who had the weapon and who used it. "I got a gun that shoots a thousand slugs a minute," Corbeau tells Riel. And Duroc, his sidekick, played by Akim Tamiroff, remarks gleefully, "Trust Corbeau to know the newest way of killing."

Throughout the picture the Métis were portrayed either as blood-thirsty killers or comic buffoons. One of the buffoons was Shorty, played by Lon Chaney, Jr., who appeared to be frozen into his earlier performance as Lenny, the half-wit in *Of Mice and Men*. When Shorty's wife presents him with a baby boy early in the movie, he dances about in the street in childish delight and then looks puzzled when shown the infant: "She not very beeg. How you make sure she boy?" Everybody has a good chuckle over that one.

Corbeau is shown as the mastermind and leader of the revolution that follows. In Riel's presence, he shoots down two Mounties who get nosy over the hiding place of the Gatling gun. Then he seeks out Big Bear and, demonstrating the gun, attempts to get the

Cree chieftain to join him in the forthcoming bloodshed. The chief is impressed. "Redcoats no longer our friend," he says. "This is our friend who fights with a thousand teeth of fire." Sergeant Jim Bret of the Mounted is present, but makes no attempt to arrest Corbeau, a failure that would have lost him his stripes in real life.

The Duck Lake affair, which followed these scenes, was presented as a treacherous and unprovoked ambush in which hundreds of Métis, armed with the Gatling gun, mowed down and killed some fifty redcoats, including the inspector in charge.

It is unnecessary to follow the rest of picture in detail. Its polished production and big names only partially obscured the fact that Hollywood's most publicized director had employed the same clichés that had been standard in Mountie movies since the early days: the wicked half-breed who sells booze to the misguided natives; the passionate half-breed girl who loves not wisely but too well; and the grim-faced policeman who is forced to bring his sweetheart's brother to justice, even at the risk of losing the woman he loves. ("When this is over I'm going to get him . . . if I have to follow him over the ice-caps!") Suffice it to say that the Mounted Police single-handedly put down the revolution in a matter of days, partly because Dusty Rivers, the Texas Ranger, destroys the Gatling gun, and partly because Sergeant Bret, in a face-to-face confrontation with Corbeau, persuades Big Bear *not* to join Riel— another historical right-about-face.

The Métis see the error of their ways and are shown, in a comic scene, straggling back to their homes. "You come home. I'll give you all the fight you want," says big Shorty's tiny wife as they march down the trail, defeated. And so the picture moves to its romantic conclusion with the Mountie and not the Ranger getting the girl.

Even while the picture was still before the cameras De Mille's press agents were describing scenes from the script to reporters, inviting columnists onto the set to watch the shooting, and assuring everyone that the movie was a totally authentic account of the Canadian rebellion.

One seasoned columnist who swallowed it all was Virginia Wright, the drama editor of the Los Angeles *News*. Miss Wright, one of a dozen key journalists who were invited to the set early in May, wrote an enthusiastic description of the six-acre forest that De Mille had created on the Paramount backlot—a pine forest, of course. She was present when the big scene with Big Bear was filmed—a scene in which the Indians are about to join Corbeau, only to realize that he has lied to them. Wrote Miss Wright: "Because he lied the Indians refuse to be a party to any half-breed revolt. If this episode sounds like phony dramatics, De Mille has the facts to prove that it happened during the Real [*sic*] rebellion in Saskatchewan."

The publicity men fed another anecdote to the press party, which Miss Wright also reported as fact:

> *Indicative of the sort of thing to expect from this latest De Mille opus is the producer's insistence that the Indian chief change his name. History has him down as Little Bear. De Mille, as you might expect, christened him Big Bear.*

That story kept turning up in newspapers all over the continent, even including the scrupulous *New York Times*, whose Hollywood man also accepted De Mille's version of the Duck Lake Massacre without a raised eyebrow.

With the picture nearing completion Paramount stepped up its publicity campaign. It badly wanted to hold the première in Ottawa and to turn it into "an international celebration sponsored by the Canadian government." The plan was to get Canadian National Railways to place an entire train at the studio's disposal, to be called the North West Mounted Special. The train was to transport some sixty stars and studio officials across the United States and Canada, with celebrations at every whistle stop.

The CNR apparently was partially convinced by R.C. Moriarty of Paramount, who told the railway publicity director, W.S. Thompson, that the film was "the first serious attempt to present on the screen the authentic history of the North West Mounted

Police and we have produced it in close co-operation and with the approval of Commissioner Wood and officials directly connected with the Royal Canadian Mounted."

Thompson checked with Wood who replied that "the picture does not portray any such history but is simply another melodramatic romance woven around the name of the North West Mounted Police." Wood saw no reason for helping at all, nor did G.H. Lash, the government director of information, who replied that "there is much more important work for us to do." There was, after all, a war on.

With Ottawa out of the picture, Paramount opted for Plan B. For some months the Regina Board of Trade had been lobbying to have the première held in the Queen City, long the headquarters of the Mounted Police. The vice-president of the board, J. Alex MacKenzie, had been dispatched to Hollywood for that purpose and had returned with glowing accounts of De Mille's "devotion to accuracy" in making the picture. Now, with Wood cold to any official help, the studio seized on the Regina offer and with good reason: if the board of trade was pulling the strings, it would be impossible for the Mounted Police not to be front and centre.

Wood had already warned the commanding officer at Regina that "the claims for the picture are extravagant" and that he mustn't provide escorts "or anything of that nature" without permission from headquarters. But then he was forced to add: "Of course if the Board of Trade at Regina are very anxious to have the première showing in Regina we cannot very well refuse to attend if we are invited. . . ." And that, of course, was exactly what the studio wanted.

The board now mounted a massive campaign around the première. Festivities were to last for several days. Storefronts were to be covered with log slabs to suggest the pioneer era, with prizes for the best display. Life-sized replicas of Mounted Policemen were provided to all merchants. The local daily, the *Leader Post*, published a special thirty-two-page souvenir edition of Mounted Police history. Paramount announced that four of the picture's stars, and possibly De Mille himself, would be present for the opening.

The results probably surpassed what the studio publicity department had expected. Regina went wild in a three-day celebration, climaxed by one of the biggest parades in its history as well as the première of the movie. De Mille did not appear, but William Pine and the four stars all turned up. Madeleine Carroll, whose British connections in this time of overseas crisis were not overlooked (her sister had just been killed in the London blitz), presented a cheque to the RCMP on behalf of Famous Players Canadian Corporation, the picture's distributor. The cheque was actually for the Red Cross, but by making the presentation to the RCMP, the movie company managed to get two assistant commissioners of the Force on the theatre's stage and in the press photographs.

By this time the Mounted Police, for all their reluctance, had become thoroughly involved in the affair, sucked in in spite of themselves. They could hardly refuse the Board of Trade's invitation to lead the parade on horseback. They were needed at the première to help hold back the crowds who jammed the streets outside the theatre. And they couldn't very well turn down the Board's invitation to aid in a worthy cause. The press photographs of the event give the distinct impression that the Mounted Police are not only committed to the film but are also actually running the celebration. As the *Leader Post* put it: "Scarlet-coated Mounties, stern-faced and straight-backed, were the guiding light of the entire procession. The renowned Redcoats led the parade on their dancing horses, and the riders carried lances and flags that stood out in the line as a sunset in an artist's picture."

Thus Cecil B. De Mille managed to achieve all his objectives and get what he demanded when he first set out to make a movie about the Mounted Police, especially the undeniable visual evidence that convinced the average moviegoer that this was an official motion picture, blessed by the top officers of the Force.

The question of historical accuracy was not seriously debated. Frank Morriss, the *Leader Post*'s critic, neatly sidestepped the issue: "The matter . . . will have to rest with Hollywood and the Mounted Police experts who were on hand when the cameras ground in the movie capital," he wrote, again suggesting official RCMP approval. Roly Young, in an enthusiastic review in the *Globe and Mail*, Toronto, did not even mention the problem. "There have been plenty of movie yarns about the Mounties in the past," he wrote, "but they fade into insignificance when compared to De Mille's production." It was, he added, "a film that will make Canadians want to stand up and cheer." Jack Karr, in the *Toronto Star*, pushed aside any petty problems regarding accuracy: "Out of the pages of Canadian history comes this tale of Saskatchewan in the days of the Riel rebellion. And while those pages may have become a trifle blurred through the sights of a motion picture camera, sufficient authority has been observed to persuade even the most devout scholars of Canadiana to put any stray lapses in the field of fact on the entertainment side of the ledger and let it go at that." The picture, he wrote, was "like no other film ever built around this vast and colourful country of ours. . . . The ball has now been set rolling. Canada has finally been recognized by Hollywood as worthy of something better than routine treatment. . . ."

In the United States the picture was widely praised as De Mille's best effort in years and accepted, with demur, as historically accurate, "predicated on actual historical events," as *Variety* put it. The *Hollywood Reporter* called it "the true saga . . . of Canada's amazing organization . . . when there were a scant 500 of the Mounted all told and barely more than a handful of these by sheer, intelligent bravery crushed the uprising of thousands of Indians and half-breeds under white leadership which threatened to slice half the Dominion from the British Empire." And the *Motion Picture Herald* wrote that "the picture is a dramatization of the Riel Rebellion of 1885 which threatened to destroy Canada and was put down by fifty North West Mounted Police in a manner celebrated by Canadians in song and story."

De Mille's version of Canadian history even reached some of the classrooms of the United States. Photoplay Studios, a weekly group-discussion guide published in New York and recommended by the Motion Picture Committee of the Department of Secondary

Teachers of the National Education Association, devoted an entire issue to the picture, with photographs of the stars, a detailed synopsis of the story, a list of historical questions based on the movie, and some other features in which the long arm of the Paramount publicity department was apparent.

Only Charles Jefferys, the Canadian historian and artist, seemed to have realized the lengths to which De Mille had gone to change history. "Only a genius could have evolved from historic facts such a masterpiece of misinformation," he wrote in the *Canadian Historical Review.*

That kind of comment, of course, didn't bother the great director. When somebody asked him why he had switched sides and given the Gatling gun to the Métis, he brushed the question aside. He had to do it, he explained, in order to increase the odds against the North West Mounted Police and make them look like greater heroes.

My Love Affair with the Crystal Garden

From *The Crystal Garden, West Coast Pleasure Palace*, Victoria, 1977

TO ME, THE CRYSTAL GARDEN has always been fairyland. I knew her during the best years of my life, which were, I think, the best years of *her* life. I spent my teens in her embrace, from the age of twelve—in 1932—until, at nineteen, I went off to university in Vancouver. Vancouver had something called a Crystal Pool, sterile and gardenless; it held no attraction for me. After Victoria, all swimming pools were anticlimax.

I learned to swim in the Crystal Garden and I learned to dance there, too. I swam and danced my way through the thirties, and when I think back on those Depression years, the glumness fades into the background to be replaced by the music and the scents and the sounds and the emotions of those days at the Crystal: the faint smell of chlorine and the taste of salt . . . the orchestra playing "These Foolish Things" and "The Touch of Your Lips" . . . crumpets dripping with butter . . . dancing the Continental, cheek to cheek, heart beating wildly . . . corsages of pink carnations tied with silver ribbon . . . rented bathing suits that didn't quite fit . . . water polo and total exhaustion . . . and then the wonder of those enormous hand-dipped cones that sold for a nickel at Terry's down the street . . . or the three-glass milkshakes—so thick a spoon could stand upright in them—that cost a dime at the Dairy on View Street . . . or the nickel hamburgers at Wimpy's on Yates: *nickel hamburgers!* After a morning at the Crystal, one needed sustenance. And Victoria in the thirties *was* the Crystal Garden. At least it was for my generation.

When my family left the Yukon in the late summer of 1932— my father suddenly jobless—we chose to come to Victoria because it was cheap and handy. We bought a house in Oak Bay for three thousand dollars, and that exhausted our savings. We owned no car, could not even afford a radio. But I had a bicycle, and the Crystal Garden was less than half an hour away.

Up St. David Street to Oak Bay Avenue. A group of us, all pedalling furiously on a Saturday morning—*every* Saturday morning in the winter months, towels round our necks or in wire baskets. Down Oak Bay Avenue to Fort Street, pushed along by gravity to Douglas, and then left toward the noble glass vault of the Garden. Dashing through the doors to the changing room . . . flinging off clothes . . . rushing for the pool. Last one in is a bum, rotten egg, stoopnagle, dumbbell, old woman! We hurl ourselves into the saline waters, our shouts bouncing off the tiles and the glass, arms flailing in something we like to think is the Australian crawl— Johnny Weismullers, all of us, beneath a jungle of potted palms.

I could not swim that first year at the Garden. In the Yukon I had been taught to shun the water. The sombre river, sliding and hissing past the town of Dawson on its long curl up and over the Circle toward the Bering Sea, had claimed too many lives. If you tumbled in, your chances of emerging alive were small. A stick tossed into that frigid water was instantly sucked under; a human body suffered the same fate.

The waters of the Crystal were warm and buoyant. Little by little I overcame my conditioning, standing at first in the shallow end under the miniature waterfall that fed the pool—a skinny twelve-year-old, advancing step by hesitant step into the depths: clutching the sides and kicking, trying to remember to keep the legs straight; practising the dead-man's float, face down in the water; trying out the overhand at four feet while all around me aquatic children, much younger, wriggled about like otters; gulping gallons of salt water, struggling, kicking, gasping, spluttering until the moment came when I could do it, could actually advance a stroke or two and then three or four and was finally swimming *over my head*. Oh, the triumph of it, there under the bright Crystal dome! Soon, with the callousness of the young, I found myself performing Weismuller-like feats and sneering at others who, like myself only a few months before, lingered timidly at the three-foot end.

Unlike my Victoria-born friends, I had not grown up with the Crystal Garden and so did not take it for granted as they did. I had never seen a swimming pool before. To a boy from a northern village of frame and log this glistening palace was something out of a storybook. Its size astounded me. The pool, at fifty yards length, was the largest in the world (or at least in the British Empire, which in those days was as good as the world). Yet the pool was only part of an intriguing whole. Above, through that jungle of tropical fronds, we could see the elderly Victorians—some of them a decrepit thirty years old—sipping their tea and spreading jam on their crumpets. The time would come when I, still in my teens, would join them.

Some time around 1936, with the aid of Mrs. Violet Wilson, the dancing mistress, I was able to take advantage of the Garden's other major attraction. I cannot remember when I first danced there or when I last danced there. All I can remember is the music, never loud or raucous, but always romantic: "Smoke Gets in Your Eyes," "Cling to Me (and Whisper That You Care)," "Meet Me Tonight in Dreamland," "When Did You Leave Heaven?" We carried programs and filled in our partners' names for the Home and Supper Waltzes, the Foxtrots and the Medleys. The girls wore their hair in page-boy cuts or in snoods, and they wore long shiny dresses, all very much alike, which could be purchased at the Bay for five dollars. Those were the days when young men phoned the night before to ask about the colour of the dress so they might order a matching corsage. Gardenias cost fifty cents, and there were certain nights when their sweet perfume turned the Garden into a tropical paradise.

Those days are long gone. There are no more nickel cones today, the way they made them at Terry's. You can't get a thick milkshake, no matter how much you pay. Nickel hamburgers have vanished with "Roccabella," the *recherché* boarding-house (my mother's phrase) where our family first stayed. And the beautiful crystal palace of my youth is no longer fairyland.

To return now and see her, empty and shuttered, is a dismaying experience. She was one of the city's greatest assets, a glittering complement to the ivied Empress across the way. On all the West

Coast there was nothing remotely resembling her. Most communities today have some sort of swimming complex, but there has been one Crystal Garden only, a pleasure dome for all seasons, a focal point for a community, a magnet for visitors.

No mere swimming pool can replace her, for she is quite simply irreplaceable. Irreplaceable, but, thankfully not irreparable. She can be renewed and she must be. The cost may seem heavy today, but is there anyone present who will dare to say that future generations will count it an extravagance rather than an investment? I see that nobody has raised a hand.

The Car as a Cultural Driving Force

From *Canadian Geographic*, December 1989/January 1990

THE ASTONISHING THING about the automobile is that there are people still living who can remember a time when there weren't any. I am not one, but I can remember a place where at one time there were scarcely any. The northern community in which I was raised boasted three livery stables and a blacksmith shop, but in the winter only one motor car was to be seen on the roads. It was the milkman's Model-T Ford, and I can remember him having to hand-crank it at every stop.

In the summer a few more cars took to the gravel streets. As befitted his station, Judge Macaulay had the poshest automobile in town, a black Studebaker with fabric top, known then as a "touring car." That was a great word in the 1920s. Few of us owned a car, but we all played the popular Parker Bros. card game, *Touring*.

Of course, we lived in a backwater. For in 1926—that was the first year I can remember squatting in Billy Bigg's blacksmith shop, watching him hammer horseshoes into shape—the world beyond the Yukon had gone car crazy. We did not know it, but the greatest social transformation in history was under way.

We realize now that, more than any other invention, the automobile has changed our lives. It has affected the way we think, the way we act, the way we talk. It has upended the class system, sounded the death knell of Main Street, and played hell with the Lord's Day. As a precursor of the sexual revolution, it has been as important as the Pill. It has telescoped time and squeezed geography. It is both our slave and our master. For even as it has liberated us, it has made us its prisoner.

There was a time when transportation was the prerogative of the rich. Before the automobile arrived, the carriage, the coach-and-four, the private railway car and the hansom cab were accepted modes of travel, but only for the well-to-do. We are reminded of that era today when the Governor General rides to Parliament in an open landau.

The motor car has changed all that. It has been the great leveller in terms of social distance as well as physical space. The factory worker, sensing the surge of power under the gas pedal of his truck, feels himself the equal of the businessman in his Dodge convertible. As Marshall McLuhan points out, it is the pedestrian who has become a second-class citizen.

The car gave the masses geographic mobility; and that meant social mobility, for the ability to choose is a concomitant of class. With the invention of the automobile, the poor could escape the confines of city tenements and narrow villages. In fact, the development of new mass-production techniques—the legacy of Henry Ford—blurred caste distinctions, creating in North America a vast middle class, most of whom owned cars.

The car brought to a settled world a glorious spontaneity that was not possible in the age of the horse and the railway. Horses required long rest periods; they could not manage steep inclines without assistance. Railways ran on schedule to predetermined destinations. But with the coming of the automobile, car owners could leap into their vehicles on impulse and take off in any direction. This ability to control the time and the direction of travel marked for millions the beginning of a new freedom. It is also the reason why most wage earners today get a paid vacation.

With this independence came privacy. Alone in their cars people can sing, shout, talk to themselves or quietly plan their day, free from importuning associates or carping relatives. This human desire to be alone is, I believe, the chief reason why the idea of the car pool has never really taken hold in Canada. The highways are crowded with five- and six-passenger automobiles, most carrying only a driver.

As examples of the way the motor car has affected our lives, one need look only at such basics as health care, religion and education. The ambulance has brought swift medical aid to everyone; the bus has done away with the little red schoolhouse;

and rural Canada is littered with boarded-up churches because the car, which made it possible to travel longer distances to worship, also may have made it too attractive to skip worship in favour of a Sunday drive.

Since the early days of the Tin Lizzie we have talked the language of cars. Just as words and phrases such as *free wheeling, green light, fast lane, going like sixty* and *step on it* indicate the swifter pace of the automobile era, so words like *car hop, motel, passion pit* and *drive-in* suggest a totally different lifestyle.

Urban sprawl, urban rot and urban renewal all spring out of the motor-car era and hint at the problems created by the suburban explosion, perhaps the single most important demographic change wrought by the automobile. The car made possible the escape from Shelley's "populous and smoky city," and from the very outset this was seen as its greatest liberating force.

As a 1908 advertisement for the Sears motor car put it: "The Sears is the car for the businessman who has tired of home life in a congested neighbourhood and yearns for a cottage in the suburb for his family." Such blandishments were remarkably prescient, even though reality does not quite mesh with the fantasy. The countryside of 1989 is no facsimile of that of the century's first decade. One problem was that the people who escaped from the city insisted on bringing the city with them.

It has been determined that apart from vacations, the trip to work is the longest regular journey most car owners are prepared to make. With the growth of superhighways and faster cars, that trip lengthened in distance but not in time. Business followed the commuters with such amenities as shops, theatres and department stores. The result was the suburban shopping centre.

It was the shopping centre that helped squeeze out that great Canadian institution, Eaton's catalogue. It sucked the lifeblood from the main streets of thousands of small towns. It turned the cores of such cities as Edmonton into virtual population deserts after work hours. It changed shopping habits and shopping hours. It encouraged the growth of retail chains, dooming individual merchant enterprise and contributing to the depersonalization and the conformity of the nation.

None of this, of course, could have been envisaged in 1900 when the automotive age can be said to have begun. That was the year when the early self-propelled vehicles began to look less like motorized buggies and more like motor cars, with a proper steering wheel instead of a tiller, a hood and a side door, and a speed that could reach a terrifying forty miles an hour.

The universal phrase "Get a horse!" suggests the derision in which early automobiles were held. In 1900, the horse was the pivot around which a vast industry revolved, an industry doomed to oblivion within twenty years. There were at least sixteen million horses in the United States, perhaps two million in Canada. Harness shops and carriage factories ran full blast. Thousands of wheel-wrights and blacksmiths depended on the horse for their livelihood. An entire industry thrived on nails manufactured for horseshoes. Hay was one of the biggest cash crops. Every town had its livery stable, hitching post and horse trough.

Today we think of pollution in terms of automobile exhaust. We forget that in the city of Toronto in 1890, tons of manure had to be swept off the streets every day. The stench of urine and the clouds of flies rising from the roadway plagued pedestrians and drivers alike. Women crossing the stinking wooden cobbles at Yonge and College streets were forced to raise their skirts and expose their ankles to prevent lumps of dung from sticking to their hems.

Nor is the traffic jam unique to our era. Photographs of Manhattan in the last century show traffic brought to a standstill by trams, carts, drays, carriages and buggies.

As was the carriage, the early motor car was a toy for the wealthy, nothing more. After the turn of the century, John Craig Eaton of the Toronto department store family acquired a Wilton. Billy Cochrane, the famous Alberta rancher, bought a Locomobile. R.B. Bennett, then a rising Calgary lawyer, had an Oldsmobile. Automobile owners were considered eccentric and their cars examples of what many considered "conspicuous waste" (Thorstein

Veblen had just coined the phrase). In 1906, Woodrow Wilson, then president of Princeton University, termed the motor car "a picture of arrogant wealth" and announced that "nothing has spread a socialistic feeling more than the use of the automobile." Only a minority saw the automobile as a boon. Generally, it was reviled.

Like many later twentieth-century institutions—movies, radio, television—the motor car was seen initially as a symbol of the sickness of contemporary society. In his book *The Condition of England*, published in 1909, C.P.C. Masterman wrote that "wandering machines, travelling at an incredible rate of speed, scramble and smash along all the rural ways. You can see the evidence of their activity in the dust-laden hedges of the south country road, a grey, mud colour, with no evidence of green; in the ruined cottage gardens of the south country villages." The motor car, in short, was destroying the very countryside it also made available to the urbanites.

To the Canadian farmer, the car was also an anathema. It scared livestock and killed poultry. "Is it not time something was done to stop the automobile business?" the Newcastle, Ontario, *Independent* asked in 1904. "They are becoming such a curse to the country that we cannot stand it. . . ."

If some saw the auto as the wrecker of rural life, others saw it as a means of bringing the joys of the countryside to city dwellers. But it was one thing to extol those joys and quite another to enjoy them in the early automobile. The roads were almost impassable—a tangle of ruts and mudholes that sucked cars down to the axles. Signposts did not exist. Even towns could not be identified: the villagers knew where *they* lived. Local post offices often bore the sign Post Office with no other identification. The treadless tires blew easily and often (they were rarely good for more than 3,000 miles), while changing one was a nightmare. A rear end projecting from beneath a hood on a country lane was a typical spectacle in pre-World War 1 days. Engines failed so often that one popular song of the era was "Get Out and Get Under."

The early motor car was also a repair shop on wheels. One store sold an automobile repair kit weighing eighteen pounds. Driving was an experience akin to mountain climbing. The Damascus Hatchet, a patented device, was advertised, with enormous optimism, as follows: "When the wheel drops out of sight in the mud, get out the Damascus, cut a pole for a lever, right things up, and then on your way again."

Touring even required special clothing—linen duster, cap and goggles for men, and for women, long skirts, sleeves fastened at the wrist with elastic bands, motor coats and turbans or wide-brimmed hats tied under the chin.

Of course women were expected to be mere passengers. It was believed that they could never act with speed in an emergency or muster the strength to push in a clutch or struggle with a gear shift. These myths were shattered in 1909 when Alice Huyler Ramsay drove across the continent in a green Maxwell, without male help.

Such ocean-to-ocean trips marked the beginning of the end of the era of the motor car as a toy. Soon it was to become as essential as the telephone. Its change in stature was rapid and complete by the early 1920s, thanks to a succession of ingenious devices that transformed what was essentially a motor-driven buggy into the family car of the mid-century. In 1911, the Dunlop company developed the anti-skid tire; within three years it was outselling its treadless counterpart. In the same year, the electric self-starter was an option, signalling the ultimate demise of the hand crank. The all-steel body also arrived in 1911, a forerunner to the closed car of the early 1920s, "a power-driven room on wheels—storm proof, lockable . . . its windows [closed] against dust or rain." And in 1914, the introduction of the spare wheel eliminated the ghastly business of tire repairing.

But the greatest revolution was Henry Ford's introduction, in 1908, of the cheap car—the famous Model-T—followed by the company's development in 1914 of the assembly line. The affordable car had arrived. In 1908, a Model-T runabout cost $825. By 1916, the Ford assembly line was turning out the same vehicle for $345.

The assembly line dealt a lethal blow to the old concept of craftsmanship based on long apprenticeship. Young, unskilled men with no previous training could master the simple techniques in a few weeks. To quote a pair of contemporary social observers: "As to machinists, old-time, all-round men, perish the thought. The Ford Motor Company has no use for experience, in the working ranks, anyway. It desires and prefers machine-tool operators who have nothing to unlearn, who have no theories of perfect surface speeds for metal finishing, and who will simply do what they are told, over and over again, from bell-time to bell-time."

Individuality gave way to conformity with results that none could have foreseen. Since experience was not a precondition, immigrants and other unemployables soon found work on the assembly line—and that changed the demographic make-up of the continent. But the deadly monotony of the line (more easily endured by some than others) also required a much better wage rate and a shorter working day. Ford's five-dollar, eight-hour day brought about the dominance of the middle class.

Again, because work was now seen to be boring and unfulfilling, mass production techniques—lampooned in Chaplin's movie *Modern Times*—brought the Protestant work ethic into disrepute. Since work was no longer satisfying, leisure took on a new importance, aided and abetted by the shorter work week. People began to live for their off-hours.

Mass production was also responsible for the youth cult that has been a feature of North American life in our era. Unskilled nineteen-year-olds were quicker on the assembly line than their fathers and therefore more valued. As the craftsmen of one generation lost status to the blue-collar workers of the next, respect for age and parental authority began to decline. As the sociologist James J. Fink has pointed out, "maleness" was also to suffer with the slow realization that women could fill any job on the line as easily as a man. Mere strength was no longer a criterion.

As the 1920s dawned, it became clear that the horse had become the toy and the automobile the necessity. Robert and Helen Lynd, the two sociologists who wrote a study on an American community they called Middletown, came up with some interesting revelations about the motor car. Families, they found, were mortgaging their homes to buy one—and most were buying on time payments. The automobile industry had helped launch the revolution in credit that marks this century.

"We'd rather do without clothes than give up the car," a mother of nine told the Lynds. "I'll go without food before I'll give up the car," said another. Pursuing their research, the Lynds asked people in rundown homes, "Do you have a bathtub? Do you own a car?" Of twenty-six persons questioned who had no bathtubs, twenty-one owned a car. As one woman is said to have remarked, "You can't go to town in a bathtub."

The car, the Lynds concluded, had revolutionized the concept of leisure. The Sunday stroll, once a feature of the Lord's Day, was abandoned, replaced by the Sunday drive. And the car was the main device holding the family together. One mother declared, "I never feel as close to my family as when we are all together in the car."

The idea of a summer vacation was beginning to take hold because of the automobile. In the 1890s people worked the year round, "never took a holiday," as some boasted. But, by the 1920s, a two-week vacation had become standard among the business class. The blue-collar workers had yet to achieve that status, but the rise of unionism in the automobile plants made it simply a matter of time.

The car was the perfect symbol for a restless decade, the quintessential artifact of the Roaring Twenties whose hallmarks were speed, sleekness and glamour. The music was fast and the girls, it was claimed, were faster. So were the cars. The Tin Lizzie had become a joke—a chariot for rubes. The Stutz Bearcat in flaming red and yellow symbolized the era. The Canadian Good Roads Association, founded in 1919 in Montreal to lobby for better highways, was by 1927 also lobbying to cure the "speed mania."

No woman dressed in the cumbersome styles of 1919 could feel comfortable in one of the new, closed automobiles. Overnight, to the horror of their elders, the bright young flappers chopped off their tresses, flung away their stays, hiked their skirts above the knee and piled into the rumble seat. "The auto," one American judge groaned, "has become a house of prostitution on wheels."

It had also become a symbol of sudden success. Each new model was awaited with national anticipation. No celebrity had arrived until he or she was pictured beside a custom-built car or at the wheel of a straight twelve: Clara Bow, wheeling down Sunset Boulevard in an open Kissel; Gary Cooper, dominated by his gigantic red and yellow Duesenberg. The gangsters, too, were motorized and glamorized: Capone with his bullet-proof Cadillac; Dillinger in his Ford (the Number One Public Enemy even wrote a personal testimonial to Henry). The car chase became a cinema staple; "taken for a ride" was the catch-phrase of the era.

But for most of the continent, the motor car was something more than a glamorous status symbol. It could now be used to drive to work, to go shopping, to visit friends, to drive the kids to school or the dentist, to take the family picnicking. "I do not know of any other invention," Thomas Edison declared, "that has added to the happiness of people more than the automobile."

When the new million-dollar Automotive Building opened at the Canadian National Exhibition in Toronto in the fall of 1929, it set the seal on a car-oriented decade. This was the largest and finest structure anywhere devoted exclusively to the display of automobiles and accessories. Here one could glimpse the tip of an industrial iceberg being created by the invention of the motor car. For behind the shiny new models, with their running boards and big headlamps, stood dozens of other industries, businesses and services: oil refining, rubber manufacturing, retail sales, used-car lots, gas stations, auto supply stores, car washes, metal and paint and glass industries, taxi companies—and, in the future, car radios, drive-in theatres, motels, driving schools, car rental firms and a vast array of roadside fast-food franchises that would turn the entrance to almost every city and town on the map into a true "Gasoline Alley."

Within a matter of weeks, Wall Street crashed and the Depression had arrived. Ironically, its greatest symbol of both hope and despair was a car—in the United States, the decrepit Hudson in which the Joad family in the movie *The Grapes of Wrath* moved from the dust bowl of Oklahoma to the fruit orchards of California; in Canada, the "Bennett buggy" (after Prime Minister R.B. Bennett) of the drought era, a car without an engine, drawn by a horse. For, as the Lynds found when they returned to their Middletown in the midst of the Depression, people refused to give up their cars.

The Joads' western pilgrimage symbolized the gypsy aspects of North American society, a restlessness that goes back to the days of the immigrant ships, the covered wagon, and the Red River cart. The automobile arrived just after the frontier had been tamed. It fulfilled the ancestral urge to move on. And its symbol became the motel, the lineal descendant of the wayside inn.

The "auto tourist camp" of the early 1920s—not much more than a park with washroom facilities, and handy to a garage—became, in 1925, the tourist cabin and the auto court. The tiny, spartan cabins grew more luxurious as the years went by, but the lure was always the same: you could park your car at the front door of the motel room. Today, the small-town railway hotel, with its gloomy beer parlour, is all but obsolete, and in the cities, the major hostelries have had to change their entrances to accommodate the car. Who uses the front door of the Hotel Vancouver or Toronto's Royal York nowadays?

The auto court also flourished in the 1930s because people could not afford hotels, any more than they could afford a biennial model change. For fifteen years of depression and war, the auto industry was stalled. Cars were sleeker, certainly. "Streamlining" was a word on everyone's lips. The traffic light arrived. People talked of "knee action" and "freewheeling." The roadster, the runabout and the rumble seat became obsolete. But when war came and people could again afford new models, they found there were none. Then, with the introduction of the flamboyant new Studebaker after 1945, the dam burst. The car became more than a workhorse. To quote a Buick ad in the mid-1950s: "It makes you feel like the man you are."

People went car crazy. They cared not a hoot for performance, efficiency or safety. What they wanted was power, glamour and status. The car was seen by psychologists as an extension of the owner's personality. Cadillac drivers were proud, flashy salesmen. DeSoto drivers were conservative, responsible members of the upper middle class. Studebaker owners were neat, sophisticated young intellectuals.

"One of the most costly blunders in the history of merchandising," Vance Packard wrote in *The Hidden Persuaders*, "was the Chrysler Corporation's assumption that people buy automobiles on a rational basis." The company decided, in the early 1950s, that the public wanted a car in tune with the times: sturdy, easy to park, no frills—a compact with a shorter wheelbase. That decision almost wrecked Chrysler, but in hindsight we can see that the company was twenty years ahead of its time. The car it thought the public of the 1950s wanted became the status symbol of the late 1970s. The idea of the car as a reverse status symbol—compact, gas-efficient, devoid of tail fins or chrome and not obviously expensive—derives from a massive about-face of attitudes toward the automobile and what it signifies. The change was spurred, of course, by government decree after the oil shortage, by traffic snarls, by a rising toll of highway deaths, by inner city rot and untrammelled suburban growth and by a consumer attitude that, for the want of a better word, we could call Naderism.

As the chairman of General Motors, James Roche, said in 1971, "the American love affair with the car is over." After half a century, the car was seen again as a villain, polluting the air, destroying the countryside, causing death and mutilation, wasting money, time and gasoline and fomenting a casual attitude to planned obsolescence.

Critics pointed to the car as the least-efficient means of transportation. In 1965, Elinor Guggenheimer, a New York City planning commissioner, pointed out that in 1911 a horse-drawn lorry could travel across Manhattan at an average speed of eleven miles per hour while a modern taxi then could only achieve six.

Streets and parking lots, it was discovered, gobbled up between 35 and 50 percent of the available space in a large city. Nine miles of freeway could destroy twenty-four acres of farmland; the average interchange took up eighty acres. Radio stations began to report daily on the pollution index in major cities, with the car as a leading culprit. And car manufacturers ceased boasting about "big car comfort." Foreign compacts became chic. Businessmen and housewives began to boast about how many miles their new car got to the gallon. North America's "Big Three" reeled under these blows and retooled. A new era had begun.

The new era has seen a return to the cities. People want to live downtown. Toronto has virtually no apartment space left in the inner city, but there are For Sale signs blossoming in the suburbs. There is even talk of closing the city centres to all cars except taxis, an experiment that has been tried in some European communities. Does this mean that Marshall McLuhan was right when he predicted that the car is finished? The guru of the 1960s insisted that the home computer would so diversify the work force that commuting would be unnecessary, that the car culture would die.

What he failed to realize, as all critics of the car have failed to realize, is that the automobile's greatest attraction is not as a commuter vehicle or as an aid to shopping. The former suburbanites who got rid of their cars when they moved to the inner city still line up on weekends to rent them. For when all is said and done, the major appeal of the motor car, with all its faults and weaknesses, is still what it was at the turn of the century: a liberating force. People want the freedom to move off at will without waiting for the horse to recover or a taxi to arrive, without standing in line for a streetcar or looking up rail or air schedules. In that sense the car remains the genie in the bottle. Release it carelessly and it becomes our master. Guard it vigilantly and it remains what it was always intended to be, a slave ready to serve us at our whim.

River of Ghosts

From *The PEN Canada Travel Anthology*, 1994

T HE RIVER OF MY CHILDHOOD is a devious river. It rises in peaks of the coast mountains range, just fifteen miles from the Pacific Ocean, and then, like a prospector desperately seeking paydirt, embarks on a long search for that same Pacific water, coiling in a vast 2,200-mile arc over Yukon Territory and Alaska before spending itself in the Bering Sea.

Every river has a personality, but the Yukon has more than most because its character changes as it grows, broadening and maturing on its long journey to the ocean. The Mackenzie is a bore. It flows directly into the Arctic almost in a straight line, with scarcely a curve and rarely a twist, moving resolutely on beside a long line of mountains. It is much the same with the St. Lawrence and the Saskatchewan, which define the horizontal nature of our country. But the Yukon is more human. It has moments of uncertainty and frivolity, as it changes from baby blue near its source to a sullen grey at its delta. It skitters back and forth, hesitates, changes its mind, charges forward, then retreats. There are few dull moments on the Yukon. New vistas open up at every bend.

It is not practical to travel the Yukon River in a single season. My own advice for cheechakos is to settle for the first four hundred miles—the stretch from Whitehorse to Dawson—and to drift with the current, watching the forest unfold. The trip need not take longer than ten days or two weeks. Outfitters in Whitehorse can supply rubber Zodiacs, which are the safest and most comfortable method of travel. On this stretch the river moves through history, for this is the water highway of the gold-seekers of 1898, and the marks of their passage are everywhere.

The river of my childhood is also a river of ghosts. You can travel for twenty-four hours and never encounter a single human being. Moose raise their snouts from the marshes at the mouths of tributary creeks; black bears scuttle up the hillsides; lynx peer out from the willows at the river's edge like big tawny cats. But the signs of human passage all belong to the past—to the days when the river was the only highway to the city of gold. Ghost towns are dotted along the entire length of the Yukon—ghost cabins, ghost steamboats rotting in the willows, ghostly cemeteries and, of course, the artefacts left by those who came before.

I can remember sitting on the bank one evening, looking out on the empty river and on the endless hills drifting off to the north, ridge upon ridge, all the way to the sullen Arctic. There was no hint of man—no boat upon those swift waters, golden now in the rays of the late evening sun, no smudge of smoke staining the far horizon where the spiky spruces met the pale sky—not even a clearing in the forest or an old blaze on a tree. But there, hidden in the mosses, I spotted a little aluminum pot complete with handle, and recalled that the previous day we had come upon a wooden rocking-horse in the woods.

On a deserted bank near the ghost settlement of Lower Laberge, I spotted a little white table sitting all by itself as if waiting for guests to arrive. Furniture in the wilderness! One finds it all along the Yukon.

For fifty years, before the Alaska Highway changed the pattern, this was steamboat country. The ghosts of those brave days still haunt the Yukon Valley. Near Lower Laberge, the hull of the old *Casca*, like a vast, wooden whale, looms out of the willows. It is hard to connect this rotting hull with the proud stern-wheeler, pennants flying, whistle sounding, paddle-wheel whirling, that rounded the Dawson bluffs in my childhood. On an island near the mouth of the Teslin River the remains of another steamer, the *Evelyn*, can still be seen. She has been sitting there, slowly rotting away, since 1922. And five miles downriver from the ghost community of Big Salmon, the original *Klondike* lies in a watery grave, nothing more than a hull-shaped ripple in the whispering river. (A newer *Klondike* is now a monument in Whitehorse.)

At Little Salmon—an Indian village wiped out by the influenza epidemic of 1919—the rotting cabins rise out of a blaze of fireweed.

Here, the graves are as numerous as the cabins. They are, in fact, like small dwellings, a village of spirit-houses with sloping roofs, glass windows and curtains, containing dried flowers, teapots and plates for the use of the dead.

Some communities have vanished without a trace. Only the presence of tall blue delphiniums and bright Arctic poppies spattering the grass tells us that there was a time when families lived here, and men and women tended flourishing gardens.

The one live community left on the river is Carmacks, now nothing more than a truck stop at the point where the Alaska Highway touches the Yukon. This, too, is historic ground, named for George Carmack, who ran a trading post here and mined soft coal before he found the nugget that touched off the great stampede. The seams of coal can still be seen on the riverbank, just before the famous Five Fingers Rapids. Here the river, caught between two cliffs, seems to be blocked by a wall of broken rock. Through that barrier the water has torn five narrow channels or "fingers." The rock itself is conglomerate, composed of various small shales forced together like bricks by the pressure of time. These four pinnacles, jagged and misshapen, are rendered more grotesque by the trees and shrubs that grow out from them. Between and around these flower-pot islands the river races savagely. In the old days, the steamboats on the downstream used to slip through the right-hand channel and over the ledge of rock in a matter of minutes, but the struggle upriver, especially in low water, was a different matter. It took hours to winch the boat through, so slowly that it seemed to make no headway at all in its struggle with the ten-mile current.

Five Fingers Rapids is the only real impediment on the Yukon for all of its 2,200 miles. The easiest way through is by the steamboat passage on the right. On the high bank above, you can see a white smear about a foot beneath the topsoil, uncovered by erosion. This is a layer of volcanic ash, about a foot deep, known locally as Sam McGee's Ashes. It runs for many miles through the great valley of the Yukon. Centuries ago this entire region was smothered in ash from what must have been an awesome volcanic explosion.

Geologically, the Yukon Valley is very ancient. The interior plateau was too dry to support much rainfall, most of which fell on the other side of the coastal mountains. Thus the Ice Age, which covered so much of the country, did not intrude upon the Yukon. The original drainage pattern is still to be seen in the series of terraces that rise like gigantic steps from the river to the hilltops. Ages ago, when the Yukon was young and these great valleys did not yet exist, this was unstable land, forever tilting, heaving and rumbling. These various upheavals produced the wonder of the present broad valley, where the benchland drops off in successive steps. Looking up at the hills through half-closed eyes, one seems to be gazing on a gigantic staircase.

On the old steamboat charts, every bend in the river has a name—Vanmeter Bend, Keno Bend, Fourth of July Bend, Steamboat Bend. This last bend coils around a long peninsula, and here, in the old days, the steamboat would stop to let off those passengers who wanted to cross the neck of the peninsula, pick flowers and enjoy the fresh air. An hour or so later they would join the steamboat on the far side.

There is something new to see around every bend, for the river itself changes and shifts from year to year. Islands vanish, reappear, change shape, diminish or join on to others, depending on the vagaries of the weather, the current or the season. At Fourth of July Bend there is an immense escarpment—Dutch Bluff—and at the mouth of the Pelly a spectacular wall of rock, a sheer cliff of columnar basalt that rises 450 feet to a poplar-topped plateau. It runs for eighteen miles downriver to Twin Falls, looking as if it were fashioned by some monstrous hand.

The oldest community on the river is found at the point where the tawny Pelly pours into the Yukon. Founded as a Hudson's Bay Company post in 1848 by Robert Campbell, Fort Selkirk was destroyed by the Chilkat Indians in 1852, forcing Campbell to make the longest snowshoe journey on record—three thousand miles to the railhead at Crow Wing, Minnesota. The post was never rebuilt, but in my day Selkirk was a lively community. Today, the police post, the Taylor and Drury store, two abandoned churches and a mission school are still standing. It was to this point in 1898 that the Yukon Field Force of 203 soldiers was dispatched by the Canadian government to show the flag and prevent the Yukon territory from falling into American hands. The outlines of the old parade square can still be found, and the military cemetery not far away is kept in good condition.

The Yukon, which was once light green upriver from White-horse, and the original baby blue, becomes a rich brown after the Pelly joins it. It changes colour again when the White River pours in on the left. This great stream is choked, as its name implies, with glacial silt and probably volcanic ash from the Kluane Range of mountains. The mouth of the White is blocked by islands formed from that same silt, their wet and colourless flanks encumbered by the bleached trunks and branches of dead trees swept downstream in the high water and left in heaps on the sandbars. These "snags" clog the river for miles, a menace to small boats, some of which have been caught in their clutches and swamped. The same danger can also occur at the mouth of the Stewart, which pours in from the right. What remains of Stewart City—a thriving settlement in the days when steamboats pushed barges of silver ore down from the mines at Keno Hill—can be found on an island in the main stream. I remember when Stewart had a Northern Commercial store, a post office, a telegraph station, servicing facilities and a cluster of trappers' cabins. But the river has eaten away half of the island—the buildings that have survived have been moved well back from the crumbling bank—and the population is down to four.

Dawson City lies a day's journey downriver from Stewart City. Beneath the boat one now hears a rasping, hissing sound, as if some strange river creature was whispering to itself beneath the waters. In reality, it's the sound of the silt scraping softly against the bottom of the Zodiac. It adds to the spectral quality of the river.

In Dawson, the old buildings still stand, teetering like drunken miners along the main streets. A good many, however, have been restored by the federal government, for Dawson City itself has become a heritage site. It is, in my view, the single most interesting community in Canada. But then I am biased, for it was here that I was raised, in the days when the river was a broad highway linking it to the outside world, when the familiar sound of the steamboat whistle echoed over the rounded hills, when the *chug-chug* of the paddle-wheel was as soothing as a lullaby and when no ghosts yet haunted the river of my childhood.